Large-Scale Organizational Change

Allan M. Mohrman, Jr.
Susan Albers Mohrman
Gerald E. Ledford, Jr.
Thomas G. Cummings
Edward E. Lawler III
and Associates

Large-Scale
Organizational
Change

Jossey-Bass Publishers

San Francisco • Oxford • 1990

LARGE-SCALE ORGANIZATIONAL CHANGE
by Allan M. Mohrman, Jr., Susan Albers Mohrman, Gerald E. Ledford, Jr.,
Thomas G. Cummings, Edward E. Lawler III, and Associates

Copyright © 1989 by: Jossey-Bass Inc., Publishers
350 Sansome Street
San Francisco, California 94104
&
Jossey-Bass Limited
Headington Hill Hall
Oxford OX3 0BW

Library of Congress Cataloging-in-Publication Data

Large-scale organizational change / Allan M. Mohrman, Jr. . . . [et
al.]. — 1st ed.
   p. cm. — (The Jossey-Bass management series)
   Largely based on a conference held at the University of Southern
California in 1986.
   Bibliography: p.
   Includes index.
   ISBN 1-55542-164-4 (alk. paper)
   1. Organizational change—Congresses. I. Mohrman, Allan M.
II. Series.
HD58.8.L375 1989
658.4'06—dc20   89-45602
                                               CIP

Manufactured in the United States of America

JACKET DESIGN BY WILLI BAUM

FIRST EDITION
First printing: July 1989
Second printing: May 1990

Code 8938

*The Jossey-Bass
Management Series*

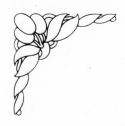

Contents

Preface

As researchers and consultants we work with organizations that are changing. Over the last ten years we have watched the scale of these changes increase from single programs in parts of organizations to transformations that encompass entire organizations and, in some cases, their environments too. More and more we are becoming involved with changes that require fundamental shifts in the nature of the entire corporation and of the people within it. We know that others are encountering this same phenomenon. We know because we work with them and talk to them and because we read the growing literature about it. But for all we know from our experience, our understanding still seems inadequate. We think others share this feeling as well. From all we read about this new phenomenon it is clear to us that our understanding is in its infancy everywhere. But it is developing.

There are two kinds of books on large-scale organizational change (LSOC): collections of readings that leave readers to pick and choose among their often disparate contents and draw their own integrative conclusions; and descriptions of particular approaches that essentially ask the reader to adopt the entire program. This book is a hybrid—the next logical step in our collective progress toward understanding large-scale organizational change. It starts with disparate views of large-scale change and integrates them in a way that enhances the separate contributions and moves a step closer to understanding the whole issue.

Large-Scale Organizational Change arose out of our own need to learn more about a phenomenon with which we are becoming increasingly involved. It started in 1984 when a group of us (Thomas Cummings, Edward Lawler, Gerald Ledford, Susan Mohrman, Allan M. Mohrman, and Ian Mitroff) from the Center for Effective Organizations at the University of Southern California (USC) began meeting regularly to discuss large-scale organizational change. After two years of developing ideas among ourselves we decided we needed to interact with others, so we hosted a small conference in late 1986. We took great care to invite people who differed in outlook but who had a strong interest in understanding how organizations can be changed. Some had primarily research backgrounds; others had mostly consulting backgrounds; but they all had much to contribute to the subject at hand. The invited participants were Robert Cole, Jay Galbraith, Ralph Kilmann, Paul Lawrence, David Nadler, Michael Maccoby, and Will McWhinney.

The conference was small. It consisted of our initial group, our invited contributors, and three students who helped us record the discussion. On the third day a public report on the sessions was presented to an audience consisting of other USC faculty and students, as well as representatives from several organizations that sponsor our center.

Each invited participant was asked to write a paper on large-scale organizational change; we distributed copies of these papers to all participants well before the conference began. Since all participants came to the conference having read the papers, we were able to structure the two days around topics that cut across all the papers, thus allowing the group to explore differences and common themes and to work toward a synthesis of ideas. This book is structured around these same topics: a definition of the phenomenon, environmental issues, actors and participants, and strategies of change. The chapters are not just the contributed papers but also statements expressing our views on major themes and issues.

Our aim is to advance the field of organizational change by focusing on large-scale change. In particular we consider whether large-scale change is qualitatively different from the examples of limited organizational change that have dominated the literature and experiences of people in the field.

We have written for others like us who have both a theoretical and a practical stake in understanding large-scale organizational change. The primary audience is researchers, consultants, and other students of the phenomenon; but in this day and age when, like it or not, organizations are being forced to change, we know there are large numbers of corporate managers and staff who have become students of change. We want this volume to be useful to them also.

Structure of the Book

Although we did not specifically ask the contributors to write for a particular part of the book, their interests and predilections ensured that each chapter would have a distinctive focus. Consequently we were able to assign each rather naturally to a particular part of the book.

The purpose of Chapter One is to define the phenomenon: large-scale organizational change, a concept that has largely gone undefined. Even though the contributed papers generally did not define the phenomenon, some of the most spirited discussion at the conference concerned definitions. In Chapter One, the authors identify three dimensions of large-scale organizational change: the depth of the change, the size of the organization, and the degree to which the change pervades the organization. These distinctions prove useful, and we refer to them throughout the book.

Part One focuses on the organization in its environment and specifically considers the environment as a source of change. Chapter Two discusses three fundamental issues involving the environment. First, has the environment changed so much that a new organizational paradigm is emerging in response? The issue of paradigm was raised in Chapter One; here we begin to specify what such a paradigm might look like. Second, what are the processes that translate environmental changes into organizational changes? And third, have organizational boundaries become so blurred that our focus should include the environment also?

Chapter Three puts the questions of *what* and *how* to change into proper perspective by asking *why* organizations change. To answer this question, the author starts by considering the environment. The logic of his analysis leads to the conclusion that the different purposes of large-scale organizational change lead to different kinds of change. He illustrates these contingencies and implies that the whys of change dictated by the environment might also lead to different change strategies.

Chapter Four, a case study of General Electric Corporation, illustrates current environmental forces and the characteristic changes corporations are going through to deal with them. The case approach is very useful in showing how one organization is dealing with large-scale change.

In Part Two our gaze swings from the broad context of large-scale change to the fundamental issue of people. Organizations are made up of people and, in the final analysis, if organizations are to change then so must the people in them. The drama, pain, difficulty, and exhilaration of organizational change all stem from the fact that it is basically a human endeavor. Chapter Five presents an overview of the participants in change, focusing especially on leaders and consultants but also considering the very real issue of how to deal with diversity among individuals.

In Chapter Six, the authors consider the crucial issue of leadership in organizational change. They focus on the special demands on leaders in the service of strategic anticipatory change. Their treatment of the issue offers valuable guidance in the design of a change strategy that develops and fosters this kind of leadership.

Chapter Seven takes the reader on a personal odyssey describing the change events at AT&T through the author's eyes as a consultant. His well-honed typology of social character provides a useful framework for interpreting and understanding the social dynamics of the change process.

Part Three gets to the heart of large-scale organizational change by focusing on strategies and methods for achieving it. In Chapter Eight we present a range of change strategies and relate them to a variety of approaches to organizing. Our focus is on whether change strategies should reflect the organization being changed from or the organization being changed to. Three other strategic issues are also discussed: the appropriate levels of analysis, the number of change levers to use, and the appropriate sequencing of change efforts.

Chapter Nine shows that change strategies are fundamentally grounded in people's beliefs about reality. These worldviews are played out in the ways that people organize and in the ways that organizations change. The author proposes a "meta-praxis" of LSOC—that is, a framework that helps agents of change choose strategies appropriate to the beliefs of the participants and the nature of the change.

In Chapter Ten, the author sets forth a well-developed approach to LSOC that he would apply in all situations. The approach is comprehensive and well grounded—and, as suggested in Chapter Nine, is likely to be useful in most corporate settings.

In Chapter Eleven, the author takes a comparative case study approach. What he compares are not strategies of change in specific organizations but the different strategies of the quality movements in Japan and the United States. The quality movement transcends organizational boundaries. It is in fact one of the impetuses for many current examples of large-scale change in corporate America. The author shows how typical American approaches to the quality movement impede change.

Chapter Twelve on strategic choices was written after the conference and builds on many of the discussions to set forth specific choices in developing change strategies.

Chapter Thirteen was written after the conference as well. It begins by describing the emergent characteristics of the new organizational paradigm and then draws implications for a new change in methodology that helps ensure a paradigm shift by being grounded in the new paradigm itself.

The concluding chapter uses the structure of Chapter One to review the findings and major themes of the book. The authors explore points of consensus as they pertain to the various dimensions of large-scale organizational change, its depth, its pervasiveness, and the size of the organization. The chapter closes with some points of disagreement that suggest directions for further thought and activity.

Acknowledgments

First and foremost, we thank the contributors to this volume, who not only wrote the chapters but participated so constructively in the conference. Michael Crozier was an additional conference participant who contributed greatly to the discussion and thus to many of the thoughts in this book. Ian Mitroff deserves a special acknowledgment. He was not only a conference participant, but a colleague of ours throughout the discussions that led up to the conference. His influence on us has been substantial.

No conference would have occurred and no book would have been written had it not been for the wise and generous support of Jack Steele and Steven Kerr, the dean and associate dean, respectively, of the School of Business Administration at the University of Southern California. Annette Yakushi managed the bulk of the conference and publication arrangements in her usual highly effective manner, and Eric DiGiovanni was instrumental in putting the manuscript together. Finally, we thank the corporate sponsors of the Center for Effective Organizations at USC for their continued support and their willingness to participate with us in a mutual inquiry of large-scale organizational change.

Los Angeles, California   Allan M. Mohrman, Jr.
June 1989   Susan Albers Mohrman
                                Gerald E. Ledford, Jr.
                                Thomas G. Cummings
                                Edward E. Lawler III

The Authors

Allan M. Mohrman, Jr., is associate director of research and a research scientist at the Center for Effective Organizations, Graduate School of Business, University of Southern California. Prior to his present position, Mohrman was a faculty member in the College of Administrative Sciences at Ohio State University. He received his B.S. degree (1967) from Stanford University in physics, his M.Ed. degree (1971) from the University of Cincinnati, and his Ph.D. degree (1978) from the Graduate School of Management, Northwestern University, in organizational behavior. He is coauthor of *Doing Research That Is Useful for Theory and Practice* (1985) and *Designing Performance Appraisal Systems* (1989).

Susan Albers Mohrman is senior research scientist at the Center for Effective Organizations, Graduate School of Business, University of Southern California. She has also been on the faculty of organizational behavior at USC and has been a visiting lecturer at Ohio State University in the School of Administrative Sciences. She received her A.B. degree (1967) from Stanford University in psychology, her M.Ed. degree (1970) from the University of Cincinnati, and her Ph.D. degree (1978) from Northwestern University in organizational behavior. She is coauthor of *Doing Research That Is Useful for Theory and Practice* (1985) and *The Design of High-Performing Organizations* (forthcoming).

Gerald E. Ledford, Jr., is senior research scientist at the Center for Effective Organizations, Graduate School of Business, University of Southern California. He received his B.A. degree (1973) from George Washington University and his M.A. (1979) and Ph.D. (1984) degrees from the University of Michigan, all in psychology. He is coauthor of *Doing Research That Is Useful for Theory and Practice* (1985).

Thomas G. Cummings is professor of management and organization in the School of Business Administration, University of Southern California. He received both his B.S. degree (1966) in agricultural economics and his M.B.A. degree (1967) in industrial and labor relations from Cornell University and his Ph.D. degree (1970) from the University of California, Los Angeles, in sociotechnical systems. His major consulting and research interests concern designing complex organizations and systems approaches to management. He is senior coauthor of *Management of Work* (1977) and *Improving Productivity and the Quality of Work Life* (1977). He is also editor of *Systems Theory for Organization Development* (1980).

Edward E. Lawler III is professor of management and organization in the School of Business Administration, University of Southern California. He joined the faculty at USC in 1978 and in 1979 founded and became director of the university's Center for Effective Organizations. In 1982 Lawler was named research professor at USC. He received his B.A. degree (1960) from Brown University and his Ph.D. degree (1964) from the University of California, Berkeley, both in psychology. He was formerly a member of the faculty at Yale University and at the University of Michigan, and he served as program director of the Survey Research Center at the Institute for Social Research. Lawler is the author or coauthor of over 150 articles and 15 books, including *Pay and Organization Development* (1981), *Managing Creation* (1983), and *High-Involvement Management* (1986).

Robert E. Cole is professor of sociology and business administration at the University of Michigan, where he also serves as European and United States project director of the International Auto Industry Forum. He received his B.A. degree (1959) from Hobart College in economics and both his M.A. degree (1962) in industrial and labor relations and his Ph.D. degree (1968) in sociology from the University of Illinois. His primary research is on Japanese work organization and its application to American firms.

Jay R. Galbraith is professor of management and a member of the Center for Effective Organizations, Graduate School of Business, University of Southern California. He received his B.S. degree (1962) from the University of Cincinnati in chemical engineering and both his M.A. (1964) and Ph.D. (1966) degrees from Indiana University in business administration. Before joining the faculty at USC he was a professor at the University of Pennsylvania and the Wharton School and at the Sloan School of Management at the Massachusetts Institute of Technology. Galbraith has written three books: *Designing Complex Organizations* (1973), *Organization Design* (1977), and *Strategy Implementation* (1978).

Ralph H. Kilmann is professor of business administration and director of the Program in Corporate Culture, Joseph M. Katz Graduate School of Business, University of Pittsburgh. He received his B.S. and M.S. degrees (1970) from Carnegie Mellon University in industrial administration and his Ph.D. degree (1972) from the University of California, Los Angeles, in management. Kilmann has consulted for many Fortune 500 corporations and has published more than 100 articles and books on planned change.

Paul R. Lawrence is Donham Professor of Organizational Behavior at the Harvard Business School. He received his B.A. degree (1943) from Albion College in sociology/economics and his M.B.A. (1947) and D.C.S. degrees (1958) from Harvard University. His research, published in twenty-two books and numerous articles, has dealt primarily with organizational change, organizational design, and the relationship between the structural characteristics of complex organizations and the technical, market, and other conditions of their immediate environments. His 1967 book *Organizations and Environment* (co-authored with Jay Lorsch) added "contingency theory" to the vocabulary of students of organizational behavior.

Michael Maccoby is a social psychologist and consultant to businesses and government groups. He is director of the Project on Technology, Work, and Character in Washington, D.C., and of the Program on Technology, Public Policy, and Human Development at the John F. Kennedy School of Government at Harvard University. He received both his B.A. degree (1954) in social psychology and his Ph.D. degree (1960) in social relations from Harvard University. He is the author of *Social Character in a Mexican Village* (1970, with E. Fromm), *The Gamesman* (1976), *The Leader* (1981), and *Why Work: Leading the New Generation* (1988).

Will McWhinney is a founder and faculty member of the Human and Organizational Systems Program at the Fielding Institute, Santa Barbara, and is president of the Association for Humanistic Psychology. He was formerly on the faculty of the Graduate School of Management, University of California, Los Angeles. McWhinney received his A.B. degree (1947) from Union College in philosophy and his Ph.D. degree (1964) from Carnegie Mellon University in industrial administration. He consults on social design, working with corporations, family-owned enterprises, and community and political structures. His current interest is developing the creative theory that follows from the "meta-praxis" discussed in this volume.

Ian I. Mitroff is Harold Quinton Distinguished Professor of Business Policy in the Graduate School of Business, University of Southern California. He received his B.S. degree (1961) in engineering physics, his M.S. degree (1963) in structural engineering, and his Ph.D. degree (1967) in engineering psychology, with a strong minor in the philosophy of social science, all from the University of California, Berkeley. He has published over 100 articles and books in professional journals and popular magazines.

David A. Nadler is president of the Delta Consulting Group, which specializes in organizational research and consulting. Previously he was associate professor in the Graduate School of Business, Columbia University. Nadler received his B.A. degree (1970) from George Washington University in political science, his M.B.A. degree (1972) from the Harvard Business School, and his Ph.D. degree (1975) from the University of Michigan in organizational psychology. He is the author of numerous books and articles concerning organizational behavior and change.

Michael L. Tushman is professor of management at the Graduate School of Business, Columbia University, and vice-president of the Delta Consulting Group. He received his B.S. degree (1970) from Northeastern University in electrical engineering, his M.S. degree (1972) from Cornell University in organizational behavior, and his Ph.D. degree (1976) from the Massachusetts Institute of Technology in organizational studies. His current interests are in the areas of organizational innovation, research and development, and strategic organizational adaptation. Tushman is the author of numerous books and articles and has worldwide consulting experience.

1

The Phenomenon of Large-Scale Organizational Change

Gerald E. Ledford, Jr.
Susan Albers Mohrman
Allan M. Mohrman, Jr.
Edward E. Lawler III

It is easy to find examples to illustrate what we mean by large-scale organizational change. When manufacturing companies such as General Motors find themselves unable to compete effectively in world markets, they implement a broad range of strategic, technological, structural, and human resource changes over a period of many years. After repeatedly earning mediocre returns, conglomerates such as General Electric dramatically shift strategic direction and alter many aspects of their structure and functioning. Telecommunications companies such as AT&T scramble to respond to consumers' wants as deregulation and divestiture change the ground rules for corporate success. Today, examples of large-scale organizational change can be found in virtually every sector of the economy. Discovering new cases requires no more effort than browsing through the latest issues of major business periodicals.

Although large-scale organizational change is relatively common, it is a troublesome phenomenon for researchers and practitioners alike. Understanding change in systems of the size and complexity of large U.S. corporations presents major intellectual challenges for theory and research—and managing change of this magnitude presents enormous difficulties.

A Proposed Definition

This chapter explores the meaning of the term *large-scale organizational change* (LSOC). It would be easy to assume that we know what it is and to illustrate rather than to define the term. Indeed, most of the chapters in this volume have succumbed to that temptation and offer no explicit definition. As a starting point, we will define large-scale organizational change as a lasting change in the character of an organization that significantly alters its performance. This definition comprises two important constructs: change in character and change in performance. It also specifies that the alterations are not temporary; rather, the organization becomes different and remains different.

By a change in *organizational character* we have in mind a fundamental change in key aspects of the organizational system as delineated by open-system theory (for example, Katz and Kahn, 1978). These include changes in patterns by which the organization relates to its environment, especially patterns by which it imports energy and raw materials; changes in the transformation processes by which inputs are converted into such outputs as goods and services; changes in the nature of the outputs themselves; changes in patterns of differentiation, coordination, and integration by which organizational resources are channeled or structured; and changes in the human resources management practices in the organization. Each of these elements tends to change continually in organizations, but usually the changes do not alter the organization's character. Ongoing changes tend to be "quasi-stationary," as Kurt Lewin (1947) indicated—that is, they are like the relatively constant shape of a flowing river. Changes in organizational character, however, are qualitative changes—like damming a river or altering its course.

A change in the organization's character requires changes in the organization's design and its processes, or flows of energy.

Design includes organizational strategies, structures, configurations of technology, formal information and decision-making systems, and human resource systems. Process refers to behavior and energy and information flows, including communication, decision making, participation, cooperation, conflict, politics, and the flow of materials. By our definition, changes in organizational design features that do not change processes are not large-scale organizational change. For example, structural changes that shuffle departments and reporting relationships, alter performance appraisal systems, or introduce new technology constitute large-scale organizational change only if they are accompanied by changes in the nature of behavior. Likewise, changes in process that do not change the design of the organization do not constitute large-scale organizational change because these process changes are not supported by changes in the organization's design and thus cannot be expected to last. An organization might temporarily motivate people through an awareness campaign about quality or about competitive conditions, for example. Through a team-building process, cooperation might be enhanced. But unless organizational design features are altered to match the new behavior, we would not expect such changes to be permanent. Hence we would not regard them as large-scale organizational change.

The second element of our definition is *organizational performance*. Performance is a broad term that can refer to the system's effectiveness as measured on a number of dimensions or to the nature of the dimensions themselves. As an organization changes its relationship to the environment, the way it transforms inputs into outputs, the nature of its outputs, and its design and processes, its performance too must inevitably change. It may go, for example, from being a regional to a global competitor. It may become a producer of integrated systems instead of stand-alone products. It may change from selling state-of-the-art products at high margin to being a low-cost, high-quality producer. Performance in various economic measures may change. Moreover, various aspects of performance may become valued differently. Global market share may become more important than short-term profit. Employee involvement in jobs and the business may become more important than loyalty and paternalism. Long-term relationships with customers may be more important than margin. Thus we would expect large-scale organizational change to alter both the nature of the organization's performance and its effectiveness as measured on a number of performance dimensions.

By indicating that large-scale organizational change is defined by its effect on organizational character and performance, we impose an important limitation on its definition. Organizational changes are excluded from our definition if they affect only local subsystems or have but a trivial effect on system performance. This definition, we should point out, is not necessarily shared by all the contributors to this volume. In fact, the first portion of the conference was spent discussing the definition.

A Look at the Literature

The literature on organizational change is of limited help in addressing the theoretical questions and practical issues relevant to large-scale change. Here we offer a broad look at the literature in terms of three characteristics. First, what is the theoretical focus of the literature? Surprisingly few works directly address the topic of large-scale organizational change (Lundberg, 1984). Second, what is the level of analysis of the literature? Large-scale organizational change, as we are using the term, implies change throughout the system. Our interest, therefore, focuses on the organization as a unit—a level that is higher than the individual, group, department, plant, or subunit levels but lower than the societal or organizational network levels. Third, what are the practical implications of the literature? Our interest is in knowledge that advances both theory and practice—dual aims that are mutually interdependent, not incompatible (see Lawler and others, 1985). With these questions in mind, we will consider two major streams of literature on change in organizations.

Organization Development (OD). One major stream of the literature on change is the organization development or planned-change tradition (Huse and Cummings, 1985), which includes literature on the implementation and process of change (Porras and Robertson, 1987) and contemporary focuses such as quality of worklife (for example, Kolodny and van Beinum, 1983; Mohrman and Lawler, 1985), strategic human resource management (for example, Fombrum, Tichy, and Devanna, 1984; Mohrman, Ledford, Lawler, and Mohrman, 1986), and sociotechnical systems (for example, Trist, 1981). For convenience, we will ignore the distinctions embodied in the different labels and simply refer to this literature as the OD tradition.

A main focus of the OD tradition has been on the description, use, and evaluation of specific interventions such as team building, survey feedback, and process consultation. Another focus has been on describing change strategies such as transition management (Beckhard and Harris, 1977). Yet another branch focuses on the introduction and impact of new structures such as participative management groups and autonomous work groups. Although there are encouraging signs of greater emphasis on comprehensive interventions (Goodman and Kurke, 1982; Raia and Margulies, 1985; Lawler, 1986), the number of empirical studies is still small.

Research and practice in the OD tradition have generally not been targeted at system change, even though many formal definitions and much of OD theory (Huse and Cummings, 1980; French and Bell, 1978) indicate that it is directed at total systems. The usual site for scholarly research and action in the OD tradition is a low-level subunit of a much larger organization—perhaps a manufacturing plant within a big corporation. Thus work in the OD tradition has often constituted studies of trees, not the forest. It is not clear how much of what we learn in changing a small plant, a group, or a department can be generalized to more complex organizations.

Scholars and researchers in the OD tradition tend to place a high value on influencing the practice of organizational change. The OD tradition includes many normative frameworks that argue for changing organizations in certain ways in order to increase organizational effectiveness and employee well-being. Organizations have in fact adopted many concepts, perspectives, techniques, and training approaches from the OD tradition. Our main reservation concerns the relationship between theory and practice. In particular, the literature appears to offer only a partial theoretical understanding and little consensus about either implementation or process dynamics of change (Porras and Robertson, 1987). The research upon which normative prescriptions are based is frequently of suspect quality and doubtful value to practitioners who want to learn how to bring about complex, multifaceted changes (Cummings and Molloy, 1977; Cummings, Mohrman, Mohrman, and Ledford, 1985). Evaluations often employ weak research designs and change treatments are frequently ill-specified, making interpretation and practical learning difficult.

Organization Theory (OT). The second major stream is the organization theory tradition. Contemporary organization theory is fragmented into opposing perspectives, many of which have been introduced to the organizational literature only within the last ten to fifteen years. These perspectives are based on contradictory assumptions about human nature and organizational phenomena. (See, for example, Burrell and Morgan, 1979; Pfeffer, 1982). They differ along such dimensions as level of analysis, emphasis on managerial choice versus environmental determinism, focus on change versus stability, and so on. Notwithstanding recent attempts at integrating these perspectives (such as Astley and Van de Ven, 1983; Fombrun, 1986; Hrebiniak and Joyce, 1985; Singh, House, and Tucker, 1986), organization theory currently offers more a menu of choices than a unified framework for understanding organizations.

There are at least four major OT approaches to understanding organizations. First, some theories embrace environmental determinism. The population ecology perspective (Aldrich, 1979; Hannan and Freeman, 1977) applies theories of biological evolution to organizations and argues that the environment selects entire groups of organizations for survival or extinction based on their organizational form.

The second approach, concerned more with organizational structuring, emphasizes managerial choice in adapting the organization's design to environmental demands or in seeking to alter these demands. Open-system theories (Katz and Kahn, 1978) and structural contingency theories (Lawrence and Lorsch, 1967) emphasize the appropriateness of different clusters of organizational design characteristics in different environmental conditions. The resource dependence perspective (Pfeffer and Salancik, 1978) emphasizes that organizations try to manage the uncertainty created by dependence on the environment for resources. The institutionalization school (Meyer and Rowan, 1977; Meyer and Scott, 1983) argues that organizations adopt structures that are seen as legitimate by key environmental actors in order to maintain access to key resources. Transaction-cost theory (Williamson, 1975) explains organizational structure in terms of managerial attempts to realize economic efficiencies within the firm. The strategy literature encompasses many different approaches (see, for example, Pennings and Associates, 1985), but most of them emphasize managerial attempts to match the organization's resources and structures with opportunities presented by the environment.

The third set of organization theories emphasizes the ways in which behavior in organizations is lawful in its randomness, as in March and Olsen's (1976) view of organizations as "organized anarchies." The fourth set of theories—phenomenological approaches to organizations, most notably theories of organizational culture (see, for example, Frost and others, 1985)—emphasizes the process of social construction of shared meaning in organizations.

Any generalization about so diverse a set of theories and perspectives is bound to be largely false. Several generalizations about OT perspectives on large-scale system change, however, are more true than false. These generalizations lead us to conclude that OT perspectives are limited as a means for understanding large-scale system change. First, these theories are not intended to explain system change; rather, they are meant to explain a few specific dimensions of organizational structure, process, strategy, and effectiveness. The resource dependence perspective, for example, has been used to explain the distribution of power within organizations. Institutionalization theory explains why organizations adopt and maintain structures that represent institutionalized views of good management practice. Neither perspective offers a comprehensive theory of the structure and functioning of organizations or an explanation of organizational change and stability. Both frameworks may help us to understand why organizations are as they are, but neither offers much guidance regarding change. Contingency models of organizational structure may help us to understand how an organization's structure needs to change in a changed environment, but they have little to say about *how* to effect the change. Similar statements can be made for many other OT frameworks.

The organization is the unit of analysis in a large body of OT research, but current organization theory is often more concerned with explaining patterns found in groups of organizations or in the social forces affecting organizations in general than with understanding the internal dynamics of specific organizations. Partly because of a theoretical emphasis on ''macro'' issues, methodology tends to be defined in terms of sophisticated quantitative analyses of data from a large number of organizations. Since this methodology limits the number of variables that can be examined, it also limits the value of the studies for understanding the complexity of large-scale organizational change. Case studies of single organizations—once the dominant research mode in the OT tradition—have become rare, although a few can be cited for most of the schools of OT thought mentioned previously. A notable example that is relevant to our topic is Pettigrew's (1985) study of Imperial Chemical Industries.

Often, too, the implications of theories in the OT tradition are obscure. The population ecology perspective, for example, offers little hope that organizations really can change form to a degree that matters from the standpoint of survival of organizational species—indeed, it suggests that major changes are more likely to reduce rather than improve the organization's prospects for survival. (See, for example, Hannan and Freeman, 1984.) Much contemporary OT research appears narrow, abstract, even irrelevant, to practitioners who find themselves immersed in the maddening complexity of large-scale organizational change. Ultimately, the OT tradition is a literature about forests; the trees themselves often are absent or at least irrelevant.

One final concern about the relevance of OT literature has to do with the organizations under study. Much, if not most, OT research has been conducted in organizations having similar bureaucratic designs characteristic of most twentieth-century American organizations. How, then, can organizations learn alternative design principles? It is not surprising, therefore, that cross-cultural research (for example, Ouchi, 1981) has been the stimulus for some of the change that is currently being implemented, since such research has exposed us to organizations that operate on different principles.

Why Has LSOC Been Overlooked?

Our discussion indicates why the OD and OT literatures have not converged in explaining large-scale organizational change. Table 1.1 summarizes these points. Neither approach focuses on change in entire organizational systems. The OD approach tends to concern itself with specific interventions; the OT approach tends to zero in on one or two specific causes of, say, organizational survival, performance, or structure. Neither camp provides much useful information about change at the system level. Organizational development tends to be too "micro" in its orientation and organizational theory too "macro"— despite the emphasis on intrasystem structure and functioning in both bodies of literature. The two perspectives differ as well in their emphasis on action. Organizational development tends

**Table 1.1. Organization Development (OD)
versus Organization Theory (OT).**

Issue	OD Literature	OT Literature
Primary focus	Specific planned changes	Specific causes and types of change
Main levels of analysis	Individual groups and group subsystems	Organization/ environment interface and groups of organizations
Practical implications	Extensive	Limited

to be an action research literature; organization theory tends to place much less emphasis on implications for practice. Little wonder, then, that OT researchers often stereotype OD researchers as being indifferent to rigor and scholarship, while OD researchers often stereotype their OT counterparts as unconcerned with practice.

There are many reasons why there is so little research on large-scale organizational change. Certainly opportunities to investigate it have been limited, although they are becoming more numerous because of the growing interest in the subject. Not many executives regard organizational researchers as helpful allies in creating large-scale organizational changes, even if some researchers have helped to implement certain interventions. But given the opportunity, it is difficult to conduct research on large-scale organizational change. The appropriate methods for understanding and measuring change in huge organizations are not always obvious.

Given the increasing demand for large-scale change in organizations, the principal obstacle to good research is the inertia created by the lack of a critical mass of theory and research on the topic. Good theories and models of research encourage further research on a topic. But first a solid understanding of the phenomenon is needed. Thus, we turn now to the key aspects of large-scale organizational change.

Three Dimensions of Large-Scale Organizational Change

Earlier we defined large-scale organizational change as lasting change in an organization's character and performance without explicitly defining what we mean by "large scale." To us large scale is a multidimensional term—shorthand for three aspects of organizational change. Large scale can refer to the change, to the organization, or to the relationship between the change and the organization. When speaking of the change alone, large scale refers to the *depth* of the change. Shallow changes involve minor variations in an organization's structure or changes in practice that do not threaten the key subsystems and fundamental tenets of the organization. In fact, small-scale changes are often made to fine-tune organizational subsystems so they fit together better. Deep, or large-scale, changes affect the most fundamental aspects of the organization. They entail shifts in members' basic beliefs and values and in the way the organization is understood. Deep change in any subsystem or part of an organization is going to put pressure on other parts to change accordingly. Likewise, other parts of the organization will put pressure on the target not to change.

Large scale can also refer to the size of the organization. Used in this way, large scale refers to organizations that are big and therefore complex—that is, any organization that involves a lot of people performing many different roles and interacting in many different ways. The two meanings taken together refer to deep change in large, complex organizations.

The final meaning of large scale lies in the relationship between the change and the organization. In particular we mean the degree to which the deep change *pervades* the large, complex organization. Given our earlier comments, we believe that deep change will eventually affect the whole organization or else it will be squeezed out by the inertia of the organization. Nevertheless, the *pervasiveness* of the change—its organizational extensiveness or the proportion of the organization's subunits that are changed—is a dimension conceptually distinct from either the depth of the change or the size and complexity of the organization.

These three dimensions are depicted in Figure 1.1. Each dimension may be thought of as having a value from 0 to 1. The larger the value on the three dimensions, the greater the degree of large-scale system change. Thus change in the biggest organization (size)—change involving modification of every subsystem (pervasiveness) and accompanied by a widespread shift in members' fundamental beliefs and values (depth)—will be of larger scale than change in a single manufacturing plant involving only a few subsystems and not accompanied by a change in the beliefs of organizational members. A set of changes cannot be considered large scale if its value on any dimension is near zero—for example, if there is no shift in its members' beliefs and values as part of the change.

Figure 1.1. Dimensions of Large-Scale Organizational Change.

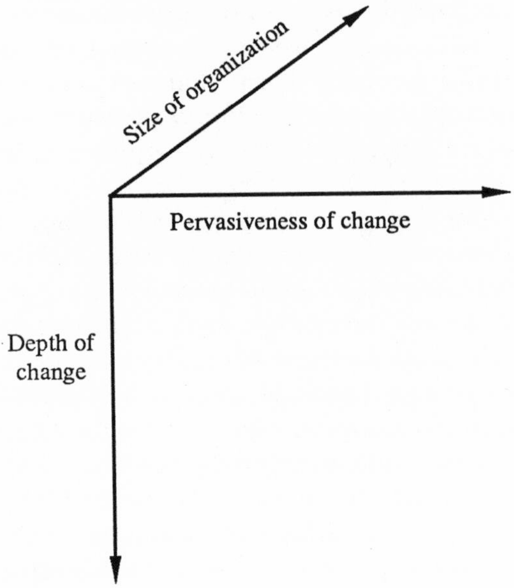

Depth of Change

The first dimension of large-scale organizational change is depth of change—the extent to which the change involves shifts in the beliefs and values of organizational members and shifts in the way the organization is understood and enacted. Often large-scale change is associated with profound shifts, as when telephone companies change from regulated deliverers of service that can pass costs on to consumers to ''communications companies'' that operate in a highly competitive environment and must make a profit through their own efforts. Such a transition cannot be accomplished without changes in the beliefs and values of organizational members and in the way they understand their organization and enact their roles.

The depth dimension encompasses a wide range of concepts that imply deep cognitive shifts. Levy (1986) reviews the usage of a great many of these related concepts, including second-order change, gamma change, transformation, double-loop learning, radical change, revolutionary change, real change, policymaking change, paradigm change, and so on. He proposes that second-order change includes four aspects arrayed in what is in effect a Guttman scale. That is, each lower point on the scale is included within the domain of all higher points. The first point in Levy's scheme is core processes—organizational structure, management, decision-making processes, rewards, and so on. The second is organizational culture, which includes beliefs, values, norms, symbolic action, and management style. Third is formally stated mission and strategy. Fourth is organizational paradigm, which includes the "meta-rules" or underlying assumptions that shape perceptions, procedures, and behavior. Levy's array makes the point that there are different degrees of depth in organizational change and that changes in beliefs, values, and assumptions are interwoven with design changes in the organization.

A key aspect of the depth dimension is the paradigm shift—a dramatic rejection of old beliefs and acceptance of new ones. The concept of paradigm and paradigm shift began with Kuhn (1962); others have since adapted it to organizational science (Pfeffer, 1982; Imershein, 1977). Paradigms have three main characteristics. First, there is a *social matrix* consisting of everyone who accepts a certain way of looking at the world and practices a way of doing things consistent with that worldview. Second, the paradigm includes a *way of looking at the world*—that is, the cognitive approaches and affective responses of the social matrix. In the case of organizational members, this would include images of the organization, beliefs about how things work in the organization, and values about organizations and how things work in them. The third aspect of a paradigm is a *way of doing things*—methods and exemplars that indicate ways of acting. These three characteristics create an inclusive construction of social reality (Mohrman and Lawler, 1985).

The paradigm concept has been used before to describe organizational change. We have noted elsewhere (Mohrman and Lawler, 1985; Mohrman, Ledford, Lawler, and Mohrman, 1986), for example, that the dominant paradigm of American organizations, which is based on assumed needs for hierarchical control and organizational stability, may be shifting toward a paradigm based on employee involvement and continuous change.

A *paradigm shift* involves self-supporting changes in the three components of the paradigm. According to Kuhn (1970), there are three stages to the shift: a period of normalcy under the present paradigm; a period in which anomalies begin to accumulate that put the paradigm at risk and create a growing state of crisis; and finally a period in which the old paradigm is replaced by a new one. A new paradigm might emerge if the organization's ways of looking at the world and ways of doing things no longer address the problems and realities that are being confronted and the social matrix that supports the status quo begins to disintegrate.

If deep organizational change entails a paradigm shift, there are implications for how the change is accomplished. We might hypothesize that deep organizational change requires a new social matrix with a new way of looking at the world and a new way of doing things. But before this can happen, members must become aware of the anomalies—cases in which the present way of doing and understanding is incapable of handling the organization's current reality. This change may involve the empowerment of individuals and groups of stakeholders who experience the organization differently from the dominant coalition and who consequently have less invested in the status quo.

Does large-scale organizational change require change in the values of organizational members in order to be effective? Clearly changes in values are often involved, but certain pervasive organizational changes apparently produce little change in values. Will McWhinney argues that no truly large-scale change occurred at General Electric despite all that has happened there in recent years; Jay Galbraith, by contrast, points out that the extensive changes certainly seem large scale to employees and managers in the company. Essentially Galbraith is arguing that GE is an example of large-scale change's pervasiveness (the dimension that we will discuss next) whereas McWhinney is defending the opposite position based on the depth dimension.

The depth dimension of large-scale organizational change casts a different light on the old issue of resistance to change. Even setting aside the question of whether the political interests of resisters actually are served by opposition to the change, the depth dimension indicates that in many cases employees will resist the change because it threatens their way of making sense of the world—and thus calls their values and rationality (and thus, in a sense, their sanity) into question. Little wonder, then, that deep changes are resisted.

Pervasiveness of Change

The second dimension along which large-scale organizational changes can vary is pervasiveness of change—the proportion of the organization's elements and subsystems that are changed. There are several ways in which change can be pervasive: It can involve all or most organizational subunits (divisions, functions, plants); it can involve all or most organizational subsystems (rewards, hiring, technology, information); it can affect all levels in the organization.

The more subunits, subsystems, and levels involved in the change, the greater the change in the system. In the extreme case, every subunit and every level in the organization is affected and both the character of the system as well as its overall performance are affected. In fact, if we agree that an organization is a complex system, it follows that large-scale organizational change must be pervasive. The stable system will have reached a quasi-equilibrium—a state in which all its elements and subsystems are congruent with one another—and thus will be self-reinforcing. A change in one or only a few subsystems will be insufficient to establish a new equilibrium with altered organizational character and performance (Katz and Kahn, 1978).

Pervasiveness is probably the most familiar of the three dimensions of large-scale organizational change. This dimension represents what is usually meant in the OD literature by such terms as multifaceted or comprehensive interventions (French and Bell, 1978), large-scale multiple systems change (Goodman and Kurke, 1982), or system-wide change (Huse and Cummings, 1985). The implications of pervasiveness for the conduct of change are substantial:

- Pervasive changes take years. Because pervasive changes are complex, the changes are long-term. It is difficult to imagine changing multiple facets of an organization the size of a Fortune 500 corporation in a brief period of time. Even revolutionary changes in such organizations take years to develop and implement.

- Pervasive changes require multidisciplinary change agents. No single individual has the full range of technical, personal, and organizational skills, contacts, and power to create change alone. Even those who focus on exemplary transformational leaders (see Chapters Six and Seven in this volume) recognize the leader's dependence on subordinates for designing and implementing change. Borrowing from an example discussed in detail in Chapter Four, we must concede that Jack Welch, CEO of General Electric, cannot single-handedly change the corporation's strategy, technology, organizational structure, reward system, career tracks, socialization process, training system, and so on. He has been able to set the wheels in motion, but he must rely on managers and specialists inside and outside the company to create the entire range of changes at GE.

- Pervasive changes require intergroup cooperation and coordination. Change must occur in units that have been treated separately in the traditional organization. Change mechanisms must cut across organizational units that have different ways of viewing the world, different performance and evaluation criteria, and different goals. The change process must involve consensus building, multidirectional dissemination of ideas and techniques, and cross-functional implementation teams.

Pervasiveness has interesting implications for research on large-scale system change. To understand the pervasive range of interventions involved in large-scale system change—much less to collect research data on such changes—obviously demands a multidisciplinary research team. This point is frequently stressed and need not be elaborated here. What is perhaps less obvious is that solitary researchers with a limited frame of reference—

or even teams of researchers with a somewhat broader perspective—may not fully appreciate the organizational context within which their work is being done. An action researcher who specializes in, for example, selection systems or job design may be a small cog in a very big machine. Researchers who are not attuned to the nature of large-scale system change may not attend to contextual variables that help explain the success or failure of their specialized interventions. The study of large-scale system change forces the researcher to become a generalist in order to understand how all the pieces of the puzzle fit together.

Organizational Size

The third dimension of large-scale organizational change is the organization's size. The rationale for this dimension is straightforward. The larger the organization, the larger the change needed to alter its character and performance. A change in the character of General Motors is a vastly greater change than a change in the character of a one-plant firm.

Although the rationale for including organizational size as a dimension of large-scale system change is apparent, its meaning is not so obvious. A variety of definitions of organizational size are possible (Kimberly, 1976)—number of employees (the most common definition), physical capacity (say, plant capacity or number of hospital beds), output volume (say, sales), assets (say, capitalization)—and each definition has its strengths and weaknesses. The specific operationalization of size may well determine what effects of size are found.

We may obtain an intuitive feel for whether there are truly differences between systems of different sizes by comparing an integrated, multinational megacorporation such as Exxon with a small corporation that sells retail gasoline in one service station. In what important ways is Exxon different from its minuscule competitors? And how might the nature of change differ between these two systems? One might expect the literature to clarify the answers to these questions. Surprisingly, however, these issues have received little attention. A keen observer might note that most statements about large-scale organizational change—

including many made in this volume—apply equally well to large and small systems. Nevertheless, there are important differences between organizational systems of different sizes that have implications for the nature of organizational change. Huge organizations pose special challenges and special opportunities for the change process. Let us see what some of these implications might be.

Organizational Complexity. Large organizations differ from small organizations qualitatively as well as in degree. In particular, they are more complex. The greater the size of the organization, the greater the organizational differentiation. That is, the organization handles growth by creating more roles and subunits. The result is greater complexity and the creation of new structures to meet increased needs for coordination and communication. Child and Kieser (1981) indicate that along with growth come more hierarchical levels, greater formalization, increased delegation of responsibilities, and possible economies of administration (offset by rising problems of administering complexity).

At least two implications for change are evident. First, the change strategy must be complex enough to handle the increased complexity of the organization. The more complex the organization, the more difficult it will be to achieve deep and pervasive change, simply because a change strategy must reach a greater number of more highly differentiated units and subsystems. Second, large organizations have certain inertial qualities. A proliferation of formal practices and procedures designed to facilitate coordination and stabilize actions eventually achieve a momentum of their own that works against change in the system. Consequently, the change strategy must not fail to address these inertial factors.

Stage of Development. If the growth in size is great enough, the organization may completely alter its structural design. Organizations tend to be designed around a simple functional form when young and small, for example, but take another form—a holding company form, a centralized functional form, a multidivisional form—depending on their growth and diversification strategy and the coordination and communication problems attendant with growth. The organization's growth and diversification strategy and its structural form have significance for the change strategy. For example, a company that has diversified into nonrelated business and has assumed a holding company form may require a decentralized change strategy because of the operating autonomy of the business units. Change in a large corporation that has increased market share in highly related businesses and has retained a centralized functional organization may be steered by a top executive group.

There are many stage-of-development models in the literature. According to Galbraith and Kazanjian (1986): "Each of the growth models presents a sequence of stages through which all organizations must pass. . . . They see the change from different organization in that each stage consists of a package of structures, processes, systems, rewards, managerial styles, and so on. A movement to a new stage then requires a repackaging of all dimensions" (p. 141). Many of these models further argue that organizations failing to proceed appropriately through the growth stages will suffer a loss in effectiveness. This raises interesting questions for organizational change efforts. Must planned change simply speed up or facilitate an inevitable developmental sequence, or can it help an organization to chart its own course? Some of the large-scale changes we are seeing today involve organizations that are no longer growing and, indeed, are getting smaller. No doubt much of what we call large-scale system change is concerned with organizations going through such a resizing.

Age. Larger organizations that are also older organizations have developed a consistent set of responses, standard operating procedures, and habits that have been reinforced by success in their environment (Hambrick and Finkelstein, 1987). Large-scale change in such a setting requires interventions powerful enough to cause organizational members to question what they think they know and to engage in learning processes that may come as a shock. These deep change efforts are made all the more difficult by the fact that the assumptions underlying organizational practices will have, over time, become almost completely eradicated from the consciousness of organizational members.

Strong Culture. Large organizations, especially those that have been successful for a long period of time, may be more likely to have developed a strong culture. Although much of the recent literature has focused on small high-technology start-ups where researchers can study the process of culture formation, many of our largest and most successful firms also have very strong cultures. (See, for example, Peters and Waterman, 1982; O'Toole, 1985.) Since strong cultures define an accepted set of norms, decision criteria, and way of doing things, they may limit innovative approaches that are not within the culture. Deep interventions designed to stimulate second-order change or a paradigm shift may be critical and especially difficult in such situations.

Degrees of Strategic Freedom. An organization's strategic freedom—that is, its ability to enter markets of its own choosing to develop new products, and to deploy organizational resources toward these ends—may be greater for larger than for smaller organizations. To be sure, strategic freedom is not complete even in huge organizations; barriers to entry, regulatory restraints, and a number of other forces limit the strategic discretion of mega-organizations. But small organizations may lack the resources to compete in more than one market whereas large organizations are able to enter a wide range of markets at the same time. We might therefore expect large organizations to respond to a changing environment first with a change in market strategy and only later with a change in the organization itself. The reverse might be true of smaller organizations with fewer resources.

The consequences of strategic choice may be quite different for large and small organizations. General Motors can diversify by acquiring multi-billion-dollar businesses like EDS and Hughes Aircraft, without showing evidence of strong ripple effects in its auto businesses. General Motors' character as a system remains stubbornly constant. In a small organization, every strategic decision may necessitate immediate changes in the system's character as it will need to align all its resources quickly in a new direction. Since it does not have the resources to allocate to the new strategic direction, it cannot afford the luxury of a gradual transition.

Power to Alter the Environment. Resource dependence theory (Pfeffer and Salancik, 1978) indicates that organizations do not just respond passively to their environment but actively try to manage and even alter it in order to improve their prospects for survival. There are several actions that organizations may take to manage the environment: acquisitions or mergers with competitors, suppliers, and customers (horizontal and vertical mergers), joint ventures with competitors, interlocking directorships with significant organizations in the environment, and movement of key employees between competitors.

Aldrich (1979) suggests that in most cases only mega-organizations are capable of adopting such strategies. Although Pfeffer (1982) notes that small organizations may band together to manage their environment—as when coalitions of small farmers obtain government intervention in the commodities markets—it is the large firm, rather than the small one, that has the resources to swallow up a competitor through acquisition. Oligopolistic economic power is possible only when there are a few large firms in an industry. The political power of the largest U.S. corporations is out of proportion to their contribution to national employment or GNP but is closely related to their ability to fund lobbying activities and contribute to the campaigns of political candidates. Thus size tends to increase an organization's ability to adapt to its environment by changing the environment itself. Size may therefore reduce its tendency to change its organizational character.

Looser Coupling. Weick (1976, 1982) argues that the degree of "coupling," or interconnectedness, of system elements has important implications for system change. As he uses the term, coupling is a broad concept. It includes not only structural linkages between parts of the organization but also "the degree to which means are tied to ends, actions are controlled by intentions, solutions are guided by imitation of one's neighbor, feedback controls search, prior acts determine subsequent acts, past experience constrains present activity, logic dominates exploration, and wisdom and intelligence affect coping behavior" (Weick, 1982, p. 378). The degree of coupling in organizations ranges from very tight to very loose. School systems are relatively loosely coupled, for example, due to such factors as the weakness of educational technology (no one can specify the best means of raising education levels) and the difficulty of controlling the teacher's behavior in the classroom.

Large organizational systems tend to be more loosely coupled than small ones. Because of their multidimensional variety, large organizations tend to have sufficient forces to create greater psychological space and looser coupling between units: geographic separation, additional hierarchical levels, additional specialized functions, differences in power, diverse markets, and different technologies. There are exceptions, though. Some large organizations, by virtue of their control systems, strong organizational culture, shared technology and markets, and similar factors, are more tightly coupled than small systems. It would not be difficult to find Silicon Valley start-up firms that are more loosely coupled than IBM. Moreover, Peters and Waterman (1982) argue that some companies have "simultaneous loose-tight properties," meaning that they maintain tight linkages of only a few variables (especially cultural values) across the entire system. Nevertheless, many large organizations, taken as a whole, are more loosely coupled than small ones.

Weick contends (1982) that change is different in loosely coupled and tightly coupled systems. Loosely coupled systems trade short-term efficiencies for adaptability—the ability to exploit future opportunities presented by the environment. Loose coupling stimulates the kind of local flexibility, experimentation, and rapid incremental adjustment that promotes adaptability. At the same time, loose coupling reduces the chances of spreading change throughout the entire system.

A number of points flow from the observation that large systems tend to be more loosely coupled than small systems. We should expect that, in general, change will be more frequent in large organizations than in small systems but will have less impact on the organization as a whole—that is, the change will be less pervasive. There will be more variation in large organizations, but adaptive variations will be difficult to exploit to the benefit of the whole. Organization-wide learning will be more difficult in large organizations, but the level of local learning will be as high as in smaller organizations.

Morever, different strategies for change are implied for large organizations. Strategies may include altering the degree of coupling; applications of cognitive therapy, as Weick (1982) suggests, help organizations think about themselves in new ways. Large systems may be treated as a collection of organizations, for which transorganizational development (Cummings, 1983) may be a more appropriate model for change than the unitary organization model.

Changing the Whole Versus Changing the Part

Our definition of large-scale organizational change has stressed that we are talking of change in entire organizations. Little attention has been paid in the literature to the similarities and differences between organizations and their subunits. Freeman (1986) notes that although corporations, divisions, departments, offices, and plants all are called organizations, research results clearly vary according to which unit is studied. Lack of clarity about the nature of systems at different levels of analysis hampers our understanding of how change varies at different levels.

We can begin to speculate, however, about the nature of the differences and their consequences for large-scale organizational change. Three differences between organizations and their subunits are particularly important: legal and financial status; operational versus strategic orientation; and the extent to which decisions are constrained. A fourth difference, size, was discussed in the previous section.

The entire organization is the legal and financial entity. Therefore, staff at the organizational level have responsibility for maintaining the legality of organizational actions at all levels and ensuring the integrity and security of the organization in equity and debt markets. From the viewpoint of the external environment, the whole organization is held legally and fiscally accountable for the activity of a subunit; consequently, subunits are constrained by "corporate" decisions made in these areas. A division, operation, or plant, for example, generally cannot decide how much of its revenues will be reinvested in research and development or capital acquisitions. It has to negotiate with the larger unit in which it is nested. The corporation itself serves as the banker, deciding where to invest its money, what rate of return to demand, and so forth. But the corporation too is constrained: It is dependent on its ability to compete in financial markets and avoid illegal strategies that would result in penalty. The difference, therefore, is that the subunit is part of a coordinated financial and legal entity and cannot be an independent participant in the financial and legal environment.

The entire organization is the most strategic and least operational level of analysis. Subunits become increasingly operational and decreasingly strategic. Divisions within multidivisional organizations are likely to maintain a great deal of strategic orientation even though their strategic freedom is limited by the need to acquire resources from the corporation at large. Departments, plants, and other subunits that are nested within numbers of larger entities are likely to be predominantly or even exclusively operational in orientation. Theoretically, these lower levels provide stability that grants the more strategic levels greater freedom in adjusting to environmental uncertainty. This means, however, that a subunit trying to adjust to changes in its own local environment may be encumbered by a great many restrictions imposed from above. Moreover, change that is initiated at the corporate level has to be implemented in an environment that has fostered stability rather than innovation.

Subunits are far more constrained than the organization as a whole. Since they exist within the overall strategic context of the larger organization, they do not have autonomy with respect to outcome preferences or resource acquisition. A division or plant, for example, may not be able to stress long-term performance and embark on a capital acquisition and training and development program at the expense of short-term performance. It may be constrained by corporate decisions regarding what kind of performance is necessary in the short term to keep stockholders happy.

Subunits often do not have autonomy over a number of aspects of the way they are designed, including human resource practices, information systems, the technology that is employed, and organizational structure. The degree of autonomy depends on how integrated the larger organization is. A holding company, for example, will generally not constrain these factors in its independent business units. It controls by specifying financial goals, not by controlling the processes in the businesses. Thus, for the purposes of large-scale organizational change, these businesses can almost be treated as stand-alone organizations. On the other hand, a corporation with integrated products may have large central staffs that determine the parameters within which organizational subunits must operate. Structure and personnel practices might be constant in all business units in order to facilitate the movement of people from one unit to another. Subunits of an integrated corporation are likely to be laterally constrained by one another. To the extent that they are required to coordinate their presence in interdependent markets, to be suppliers and customers for one another, and to share technology or staff, these subunits often are prevented from making changes that would hinder integration. Likewise, subunits that are task-interdependent—for example, design engineering and production—often have established a network of practices and procedures that tie them together. Large-scale change of one unit in isolation from the other would be difficult.

Although we have presented large-scale organizational change as change in entire organizations, some subunits may be sufficiently unconstrained that they can change their character and their performance even if the corporation itself does not change as a whole. We also know that sometimes large-scale change *begins* in a subunit or in multiple subunits and that such grass-roots change can ultimately lead to organization-wide change. Consequently, executives who are implementing large-scale organizational change may find themselves focusing on different systemic levels and units of analysis.

The tactics of change, moreover, depend on the level in question. Changing a highly constrained subunit, for example, would involve a great deal of activity directed upward and laterally. The unit that is changing would have to acquire resources for change and exceptions to practices and policies and would have to work out new interfaces with other interdependent units. These developments would probably require significant changes in every other unit with which the subunit must interface. Furthermore, this change will only occur if the subunit's members develop a sense of empowerment. By initiating change in areas where previously they have received direction from above, they can develop a new understanding of their role in the organization. They can begin to see themselves as architects of their own unit, working within the organization but constantly testing the limits imposed by higher levels.

Highly constrained subunits are likely to initiate change only after encouragement or prodding from above. Generally their lack of autonomy within the system and their culture of stability make them relatively resistant to requests for change that would upset their control over their own functioning. Consequently, large-scale organizational change often begins at the top, but it must spread quickly into the operating units. Local champions of change must be imported or developed and local ''ownership'' encouraged. Large-scale change is possible for the organization as a whole only if its subunits change.

Because of the organization's strategic degrees of freedom and its ability to deal directly with financial and legal issues, there is greater variety in organization-wide change than in subunit change. Just look at the types of changes that may be adopted by a large system, such as a Fortune 500 firm, versus a plant within a firm. Small subsystems simply have fewer choices about the kinds of changes they may adopt. Plant-level systems in large corporations, for example, rarely make decisions about mergers, joint ventures, entering new types of markets, changing core technology, and so on. These and other strategic changes are generally adopted at much higher levels in the system. Therefore, to study change in whole organizations is to expand the range of changes with which the researcher must be concerned. These activities can quickly change the overall character of the corporation and provide a different context to which the subunits must adjust. Again, large-scale change in an organization entails change in many or all of its subunits.

Conclusion

Large-scale organizational changes are perhaps more frequent than one might expect. Miller and Friesen (1984) argue that organizations experience traumatic periods of revolutionary reversals accompanied by a broad range of changes, rather than slow evolution. Whatever their frequency, it is apparent that large-scale system changes are risky, hard, complex, unpredictable, and emotionally intense. All of these characteristics become more severe as the scale of the system change increases. That is, as the size of the organization grows, as the change becomes more pervasive, and as the depth of change increases, the risk, difficulty, complexity, unpredictability, and intensity of the change also become greater. A change that alters the effectiveness of Chrysler is greater in magnitude than a change that alters the effectiveness of your local Chrysler dealership. A change in the strategy, technology, reward system, and personnel at Chrysler is greater in magnitude than a change in only one of these components. A change in the management paradigm at Chrysler is greater than a change that involves the same frame of reference.

The risks of change are not mere hyperbole. In some cases, the stakes are the organization's very survival. Hannan and Freeman (1984) report that structural reorganization, which is one type of change with the potential for large-scale effects, increases organizational death rates; Carroll (1984) found that in the newspaper industry a change in the chief executive increases organizational death rates; Singh, House, and Tucker (1986) found that certain types of change in voluntary service organizations (sponsorship and service area) increased the hazard of organizational death. These results offer scant comfort to those who prefer organizational stability, however, for organizations also die because they fail to take action. The risks of change may climb as the organization's size and complexity, the pervasiveness of change, and the depth of change increase. But in this day and age, the risks of not changing may be even more serious.

References

Aldrich, H. E. *Organizations and Environments.* Englewood Cliffs, N.J.: Prentice-Hall, 1979.

Astley, W. G., and Van de Ven, A. H. "Central Perspectives and Debates in Organization Theory." *Administrative Science Quarterly,* 1983, *28,* 245–273.

Beckhard, R., and Harris, R. T. *Organizational Transitions: Managing Complex Changes.* (2nd ed.) Reading, Mass.: Addison-Wesley, 1977.

Burrell, G., and Morgan, G. *Sociological Paradigms and Organizational Analysis.* London: Heinemann, 1979.

Carroll, G. R. "Dynamics of Publisher Succession in Newspaper Organizations." *Administrative Science Quarterly,* 1984, *29,* 93–113.

Child, J., and Kieser, A. "Development of Organizations Over Time." In P.C. Nystrom and W. H. Starbuck (Eds.), *Handbook of Organization Design.* Vol. 1. New York: Oxford University Press, 1981.

Cummings, T. G. "Transorganizational Development." In B. Staw and L. L. Cummings (Eds.), *Research in Organizational Behavior.* Vol. 5. Greenwich, Conn.: JAI Press, 1983.

Cummings, T. G., and Molloy, E. S. *Improving Productivity and the Quality of Work Life.* New York: Praeger, 1977.

Cummings, T. G., Mohrman, S. A., Mohrman, A. M., Jr., and Ledford, G. E., Jr. "Organization Design for the Future." In E. E. Lawler III and others, *Doing Research That Is Useful for Theory and Practice.* San Francisco: Jossey-Bass, 1985.

Fombrun, C. J. "Structural Dynamics Within and Between Organizations." *Administrative Science Quarterly,* 1986, *31,* 403–421.

Fombrun, C. J., Tichy, N. M., and Devanna, M. A. *Strategic Human Resource Management*. New York: Wiley, 1984.

Freeman, J. "Data Quality and the Development of Organizational Social Science: An Editorial Essay." *Administrative Science Quarterly*, 1986, *31*, 298-303.

French, W. L., and Bell, C. H. *Organization Development: Behavioral Science Interventions for Organizational Improvement*. Englewood Cliffs, N.J.: Prentice-Hall, 1978.

Frost, P. J., and others. *Organizational Culture*. Beverly Hills, Calif.: Sage, 1985.

Galbraith, J., and Kazanjian, R. K. *Strategy Implementation: Structure, Systems and Process*. (2nd ed.) St. Paul, Minn.: West, 1986.

Goodman, P. S., and Kurke, L. B. "Studies of Change in Organizations: A Status Report." In P. S. Goodman and Associates, *Change in Organizations*. San Francisco: Jossey-Bass, 1982.

Hambrick, D., and Finkelstein, S. "Managerial Discretion: A Bridge Between Polar Views of Organizational Outcomes." In B. Staw and L. Cummings (Eds.), *Research and Organization Behavior*. Vol. 9. Greenwich, Conn.: JAI Press, 1987.

Hannan, M. T., and Freeman, J. "The Population Ecology of Organizations." *American Journal of Sociology*, 1977, *82*, 929-964.

Hannan, M. T., and Freeman, J. "Structural Inertia and Organizational Change." *American Sociological Review*, 1984, *49*, 149-164.

Hrebiniak, L. G., and Joyce, W. F. "Organizational Adaptation: Strategic Choice and Environmental Determinism." *Administrative Science Quarterly*, 1985, *30*, 336-349.

Huse, E. F., and Cummings, T. G. *Organization, Development and Change*. St. Paul, Minn.: West, 1980.

Huse, E. F., and Cummings, T. G. *Organization Development and Change*. (3rd ed.) St. Paul, Minn.: West, 1985.

Imershein, A. W. "Organizational Change as a Paradigm Shift." *The Sociological Quarterly* (Winter 1977), *18*, 33-43.

Katz, D., and Kahn, R. L. *The Social Psychology of Organizations*. (2nd ed.) New York: Wiley, 1978.

Kimberly, J. R. "Organizational Size and the Structuralist Perspective: A Review, Critique, and Proposal." *Administrative Science Quarterly*, 1976, *21*, 571-597.

Kimberly, J. R., and Quinn, R. E. "The Challenge of Transition Management." In J. R. Kimberly and R. E. Quinn (Eds.), *Managing Organizational Transitions.* Homewood, Ill.: Irwin, 1984.

Kolodny, H., and van Beinum, H. (Eds.) *The Quality of Working Life and the 1980s.* New York: Praeger, 1983.

Kuhn, T. S. *The Structure of Scientific Revolutions.* Chicago: University of Chicago Press, 1962.

Lawler, E. E., III. *High-Involvement Management.* San Francisco: Jossey-Bass, 1986.

Lawler, E. E., III, and others. *Doing Research That Is Useful for Theory and Practice.* San Francisco: Jossey-Bass, 1985.

Lawrence, P. R., and Lorsch, J. *Organization and Environment.* Cambridge, Mass.: Harvard University Press, 1967.

Levy, A. "Second Order Planned Change: Definition and Conceptualization." *Organizational Dynamics,* Summer 1986, *15,* 5–20.

Lewin, K. "Frontiers in Group Dynamics." *Human Relations,* 1947, *1,* 5–41.

Lundberg, C. C. "Strategies for Organizational Transitioning." In J. R. Kimberly and R. E. Quinn (Eds.), *Managing Organizational Transitions.* Homewood, Ill.: Irwin, 1984.

March, J. G., and Olsen, J. *Ambiguity and Choice in Organizations.* Oslo: Universitetsforlaget, 1976.

Meyer, J. W., and Rowan, B. "Institutionalized Organizations: Formal Structure as Myth and Ceremony." *American Journal of Sociology,* 1977, 83, 340–363.

Meyer, J. W., and Scott, W. R. *Organizational Environments: Ritual and Rationality.* Beverly Hills, Calif.: Sage, 1983.

Miller, D., and Friesen, P. *Organizations: A Quantum View.* Englewood Cliffs, N.J.: Prentice-Hall, 1984.

Mohrman, A. M., Jr., and Lawler, E. E., III. "The Diffusion of QWL as a Paradigm Shift." In W. G. Bennis, K. D. Benne, and R. Chin (Eds.), *The Planning of Change.* (4th ed.) New York: Holt, Rinehart & Winston, 1985.

Mohrman, S. A., Ledford, G. E., Jr., Lawler, E. E., III, and Mohrman, A. M., Sr. "Quality of Worklife and Employee Involvement." In C. L. Cooper and I. Robertson (Eds.),

International Review of Industrial and Organizational Psychology 1986. New York: Wiley, 1986.

O'Toole, J. *Vanguard Management.* New York: Wiley, 1985.

Ouchi, W. *Theory Z.* Reading, Mass.: Addison-Wesley, 1981.

Pennings, J. M., and Associates. *Organizational Strategy and Change.* San Francisco: Jossey-Bass, 1985.

Peters, T., and Waterman, R. H. *In Search of Excellence.* New York: Harper & Row, 1982.

Pettigrew, A. M. *The Awakening Giant: Continuity and Change in Imperial Chemical Industries.* Oxford: Basil Blackwell, 1985.

Pfeffer, J. *Organizations and Organization Theory.* Boston: Pitman, 1982.

Pfeffer, J., and Salancik, G. *The External Control of Organizations: A Resource Dependence Perspective.* New York: Harper & Row, 1978.

Porras, J., and Robertson, P. "Organizational Development Theory: A Typology and Evaluation." In R. Woodman and W. Pasmore (Eds.), *Research in Organizational Change and Development.* Vol. 1. Greenwich, Conn.: JAI Press, 1987.

Raia, A. P., and Margulies, N. "Organizational Development: Issues, Trends, and Prospects." In R. Tannenbaum, N. Margulies, F. Massarik, and Associates, *Human Systems Development.* San Francisco: Jossey-Bass, 1985.

Singh, J. V., House, R. J., and Tucker, D. J. "Organizational Change and Organizational Mortality." *Administrative Science Quarterly,* 1986, *31,* 587–611.

Thompson, J. D. *Organizations in Action.* New York: McGraw-Hill, 1967.

Trist, E. "The Evolution of Sociotechnical Systems." In A. Van de Ven and W. Joyce (Eds.), *Perspectives on Organizational Design and Behavior.* New York: Wiley-Interscience, 1981.

Weick, K. E. "Educational Organizations as Loosely Coupled Systems." *Administrative Science Quarterly,* 1976, *21,* 1–19.

Weick, K. E. "Management of Organizational Change Among Loosely Coupled Elements." In P. S. Goodman and Associates, *Change in Organizations.* San Francisco: Jossey-Bass, 1982.

Williamson, O. E. *Markets and Hierarchies: Analysis and Antitrust Implications.* New York: Free Press, 1975.

Part One

The Impact
of Environment

2

The Environment
as an Agent of Change

Susan Albers Mohrman
Allan M. Mohrman, Jr.

At this time in history, it seems almost trite to say that organizational environments have changed and continue to change both rapidly and, in many cases, radically. It is true, though. And as a consequence, many organizations have experienced a pressing need to change in significant ways. Indeed, a book on large-scale organizational change would be unnecessary if that were not the case.

In this chapter we consider a number of questions regarding the role of the environment in organizational change. First, has the environment of our organizations changed so much that a new organizational paradigm must emerge in response? Second, how are environmental changes translated into organizational change? And third, does it make sense in today's environment to concentrate on the organization as the unit of analysis or have the boundaries of organizations become so blurred that a larger unit (say, industry or society) should be the focus? This book does not pretend to resolve the questions, but the diversity of perspectives is captured in this chapter.

Time for a New Paradigm?

There is little disagreement among the contributors to this book as to *whether* environmental change has occurred. Our disagreement concerns whether the changes are pushing organizations toward a new way of organizing or whether they allow organizations to change within a well-tested range of possible designs. In the words of contingency theorists, can organizations achieve "fit" with their changing environments simply by moving along the continuum from organic to mechanistic organizational designs, or are new concepts and new ways of understanding organizations required? Are all organizations being affected similarly, or is the major change occurring in pockets of the economy? If a new paradigm is in fact emerging, do we know what it is?

One way to shed light on these questions is to examine the changes and determine to what extent they are widespread or specific and whether they are pushing organizational design in consistent or opposing directions. While we cannot claim to resolve the issue here, we can point out the trends we see and cite a few examples. We start with a brief description of several environmental trends that are causing organizational change and then examine the broad characteristics of the organizational designs that are implied. (See Table 2.1.)

Table 2.1. Environment and the New Organization.

Changing Environmental Characteristics	New Organizational Characteristics
Increasing competition	Ongoing organizational learning and self-redesign
Changing stakeholder expectations	
Technological developments	Higher levels of performance
Legal developments	Political processes for stakeholders
	Effective interfaces (external and internal)

Environmental Trends. Increasing competition is clearly the driver of a great amount of change. A number of forces are combining to create greatly increased competition—the globalization of much of the economy, the relatively flat domestic market size, deregulation, and the disappearance of protected market niches. These factors have affected a wide range of manufacturing organizations including but not limited to those whose struggles for survival are well known to us in the United States, such as steel, automotive, and consumer electronics. Many service organizations, including data processing and financial services, are likewise becoming global. In the transportation, communications, and financial services industry, among others, once protected niches are being opened to fierce competition. Other companies are finding that the days of milking high-margin products during long periods of patent protection are gone. In the defense industry, sole sourcing has practically disappeared—indeed, contractors are now being required to share proprietary technology in order to create competition. Increased competition has placed greater performance demands on almost every segment of the economy.

Changing expectations of stakeholders are putting similar performance pressures on organizations. Highly educated employees are coming to the job expecting meaningful work and a chance to participate. Shareholders are becoming more powerful and the financial markets more ruthless in their treatment of organizations that do not perform well in the short term. Customers have become more sophisticated in articulating their needs and utilizing information to determine who can best meet them. In summary, organizations are required to maintain mutually satisfying relationships with a number of increasingly sophisticated stakeholders, all of whom are necessary to the organization's ability to survive in its environment.

Technological development, particularly advances in cybernetic technologies, has spurred considerable organizational change. The ability to integrate large portions of the organization through a single computerized information system, to aggregate vast amounts of information quickly for centralized decision making, or to distribute information widely for decentralized use has created new design options. Many repetitive mechanical jobs have been replaced by robots, in turn creating more technically demanding vigilance and machine maintenance jobs. As knowledge and information work becomes more prevalent, work is more difficult to monitor and traditional means of supervision become inadequate. Closer interfaces with stakeholder groups become possible as customers have on-line access to order entry systems, companies can conduct on-line attitude surveys, and so forth. Companies marketing customized systems and value-added networks must develop overlapping boundaries with their customer organizations in order to respond to their needs— the major determinant of the product offered.

The *legal context* of organizations has been steadily changing. Legal protection of employee rights has resulted in the need for valid criteria and due process in dealing with employees. Deregulation has resulted in a rapidly changing environment that has created a great deal of uncertainty not only for the deregulated organizations but also for their customers, suppliers, and work forces. In another vein, laws encouraging joint research are encouraging partnerships and consortia as a way for companies to share the substantial R&D expenses necessary to remain in the global high-technology competition.

These four areas are not exhaustive, but they do give a sense of the direction in which the macroenvironment of organizations is moving. Above all it is clear that the causal texture (Emery and Trist, 1965) is increasingly complex and dynamic, thus demanding new and more complex responses from organizations. Some observers have pointed out that the emergence of the global economy and the capacity to integrate units through advanced information and communications technology have made the environment more interconnected. The machine model and perhaps even the systems model of organizations are no longer appropriate. Indeed, Ackoff (1981) and Mitroff (1987) argue that organizations must be based on an entirely new set of assumptions.

New Organizational Characteristics. Organizations can try to deal with the increasingly complex environment in several ways. Strategic responses may include efforts to shape a more simple environment in which to operate—by carving out a niche, for example. Organizations may also attempt to make the environment more manageable—by lobbying to change laws, for example, or by concluding long-term favorable contracts with suppliers. Organizations may also resort to internal redesign enabling them to adapt to the increasing complexity. Indeed, the dynamic nature of the environment will force most organizations to increase their internal adaptive capacity even if they are able to carve out a more simple niche and to shape their environment through such mechanisms as lobbying and forming strategic alliances. Formulating strategy and operating in such a dynamic environment require a huge information-processing capacity. In a rapidly changing environment, organizations need a design that will enable *ongoing organizational learning and self-redesign* rather than a static design optimized at a particular point in time (Cummings and Mohrman, 1987; Metcalfe, 1981).

The environmental trends mentioned above demand *higher levels of performance*. Organizations experiencing sharper competition must attain greater product innovation, cost performance, and flexibility and less uncertainty. They maintain a complex strategy and develop complex designs capable of higher standards of performance through more effective information processing (Khandwalla, 1981). This is consistent with Galbraith's notion (1973) that an organization can achieve higher levels of performance by increasing its ability to process information or by reducing the need for information by the creation of self-contained units. At the very least, it appears certain that the macroeconomic environment is pushing organizations to redesign in order to reduce slack and increase performance. Such redesigns will emphasize increased organizational integration through the creation of structures and processes that link the organization more effectively both vertically and laterally.

Diverse stakeholder pressures require higher performance as well. Such performance demands more *effective interfaces* with employees, customers, shareholders, vendors, and partners in ventures. These interfaces will be characterized by mutuality of influence rather than hierarchical power. In order to adapt to ongoing change in the environment, organizations will have to develop *political processes* enabling various stakeholders to influence decisions. Without such processes, power will be wielded by the forces that control the status quo from which the organization needs to escape (Metcalfe, 1981). Furthermore, the introduction of significant change is facilitated by the active involvement and ownership of the affected parties.

One might argue that some organizations are immune from these environmental factors and consequently will not have to change their way of organizing it. But no one is immune, because these trends are occurring throughout society and therefore touch the vast majority of organizations. The question of whether they require a change in the logic of organizing is more difficult to answer. Although it cannot be proved, it does seem that a new paradigm is required. Certainly these new organizational requirements fly in the face of the organizing principles of traditional bureaucratic structures. Most organizations have not designed themselves for ongoing changes of strategy and design; nor have they created political forums for mutual influence of multiple stakeholders. And, until recently, they have not worked very hard to reduce the inefficiencies of hierarchical control and insufficient integration of organizational components. Despite the teachings of organizational scientists about the characteristics of organic organizations and their suitability in complex environments, most organizations have attempted to create stability and predictability, to keep strategic control in the hands of the dominant coalition, and to install costly layers of management to maintain hierarchical control over organizational operations. Thus even if our theoretical frameworks have already encompassed the kinds of organizations that will survive in the new environment, a new paradigm is required.

How Does Environmental Change Become Organizational Change?

There has been an ongoing debate among organizational theorists concerning the degree to which organizations can adapt to environmental changes (Hambrick and Finkelstein, 1987). Population ecologists (for example, Hannan and Freeman, 1977, 1984) tend to stress the role of the environment in ''selecting'' those organizations that will survive and to downplay the role of purposive organizational change. Strategic choice theorists (Child, 1972; Miles and Snow, 1978; Quinn, 1980) stress the role of strategic choice in the adaptation process.

Most of the contributors to this book stand squarely in the strategic choice camp. Although our interest in creating the book came partially from our firsthand exposure to the difficulty of the change process, we do see organizational change—consider the cases of AT&T and the "Baby Bells," General Electric, and Ford, to name only a few. And yet our experience working with companies endeavoring to carry out change is that the new strategy is easier to articulate than to enact and that the status quo is extremely difficult to extinguish. Indeed, it is possible to argue that the companies cited here have not really changed fundamentally. The public press often exaggerates the extent of change.

The difficulty lies in the fact that translating environmental change into true organizational change is a multistep process. It involves registering the change, developing a strategy, designing the organization that is capable of effecting the strategy, and then implementing the design. This sequence is illustrated in Figure 2.1. Many change processes abort because the organization never begins the sequence at all; that is, it responds to pressures from the environment without assessing those pressures and formulating a strategy.

Figure 2.1 From Environmental Change to Organizational Change.

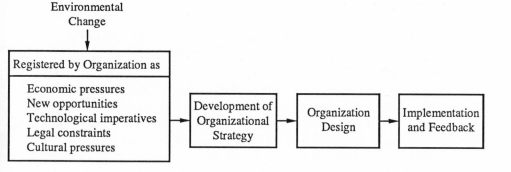

Here we ask several questions. How does environmental change become registered in the organization? How is the change process set in motion? What triggers the change process? And what has to happen internally for the organization to formulate a response?

Five change "triggers" have been mentioned by the contributors to this book: economic pressure; perceived opportunities; new technology; changing legal context; and cultural pressures as articulated by various stakeholders. Some contributors think that economic mechanisms are the principal way that environmental changes are translated into the need for change. Failure to meet targets, turnover of key personnel, declining market share, inability to generate the returns necessary to please shareholders, and difficulty obtaining critical resources are among the concrete manifestations. The organization responds by developing a strategy to regain its targeted economic performance. This strategy can have three components. First, it may be limited to "tightening the screws"—stressing economic targets, tightly controlling resources consumed through hiring freezes, head counts, budget cuts, and so forth. Alternatively, it may go further—by including special thrusts such as quality and employee involvement programs to align people behind higher performance standards. Ideally, it will include a third component—a business strategy that provides direction for an organizational redesign process. In the absence of this third component, the first two constitute superficial tampering with an organization that has not changed significantly.

Even in the absence of economic crises, organizational members often interpret environmental changes as opportunities for substantially improving the organization's performance through change. Here the trigger is not a balance sheet but a vision of what is possible by a champion who is able to set the change process in motion. The need to expand capacity, for example, becomes an opportunity to establish a "green-field site" with high-involvement practices and a sociotechnical work design. Establishing a new product line becomes an opportunity to redesign the organization into semiautonomous mini-businesses. The need to realign pay practices to fit with the changing economic environment becomes an opportunity to redesign all performance management practices to fit with the changing work force and business strategy. Such efforts flow less from a direct economic pinch than from an ongoing sense that every change presents an opportunity to create a different and more effective organization.

The introduction of new technologies can trigger more fundamental organizational change. An organization that perceives itself as computerizing operations may come to understand the power of cybernetic technologies for supporting a different logic of organizing. The push for change is less likely to come from the implementers of the new technology than from those who have learned about the potential for more effective organizational performance through localized decision making and lateral integration. Organizational change then depends on the formulation of a strategy of organization and the establishment of organizational design activities to build on the local knowledge.

Changes in the legal environment are most frequently registered by staff groups who design and implement organizational responses. Generally these responses attend to the letter of the law and the constraints of the status quo in the organization. Equal opportunity programs are an example. In many cases, the major parameters of such programs are protective measures such as quotas and the development of uniform selection processes and criteria that leave the organization fundamentally unchanged and consequently no better suited to deal with minority employees. For true organizational change, the organization must formulate a human resource strategy and go through a process to design an organization that attracts, develops, and retains qualified minorities. Digital Corporation is an example of just such a company in which the legal concept of nondiscrimination against minorities has been replaced by a corporate value that favors diversity among employees and results in active management for diversity. Legal changes can trigger fundamental organizational change if they lead to strategy and design efforts within the organization.

Finally, societal change can serve as an impetus for organizational change if it is represented by stakeholders who are able to influence the decision-making process. In Chapter Eleven,

Robert Cole argues that postwar democratization in Japan had a great deal to do with the establishment of participative quality improvement processes as an institutionalized part of Japanese manufacturing organizations. Likewise, it can be argued that the push toward more participative practices is frequently an outgrowth of the higher education and higher expectations of the work force (Cole, 1982). Again, we argue that organizational change will not occur in the absence of a process to formulate a strategy and design. In this case, a diversity of stakeholder participation is essential.

In summary, organizational change can be triggered by a number of factors: by economic difficulties; by a new leader looking for an opportunity to make a mark; by changes in the legal structure or society at large that directly affect the way the organization does its job; or by new technological tools that enable new ways of doing work. Furthermore, the fact that change is triggered does not imply that it will occur. The organization can react to the symptom and not change at all—for example, it may respond to years of escalating payroll costs by arbitrary head-count control rather than by looking at the work that is done and designing a way to do it with fewer people. Likewise, the organization may develop a strategy for dealing with the environmental change but fail to redesign itself to enact the strategy. In dealing with increasing competition from higher-quality, lower-cost producers, an organization may embark on a quality awareness program but fail to redesign the organization to facilitate quality improvement. Finally, an organization may determine a strategy and a design but fail to provide the resources and leadership necessary for implementation.

The chain of events shown in Figure 2.1 is critical to the conduct of large-scale organizational change. It demands organizational learning. Large-scale change cannot occur if the progression is incomplete and learning does not occur.

Do We Need a Bigger Unit of Analysis?

The increasing interconnections between organizations in a worldwide economy closely linked by sophisticated information technology have been pointed out by many theorists. (See, for example, Ackoff, 1981; Kilmann, 1984; and Mitroff, 1987.) We think of the steel fabricator that joined forces with its union to lobby for legislative protection against dumping of fabricated steel from foreign sources. They quickly discovered that their activity provoked a harsh reaction from their customers, who depended on cheap dumped steel for aspects of their own operations. Health care is another industry in which a large number of stakeholders are tightly interconnected in a cycle of activities that discourages unilateral action to cut costs. The competitiveness of automobile manufacturers depends on their ability to effect change in a complex network consisting of suppliers, unions, and government regulations.

In such complex networks, change in one organization is often perceived to be constrained by the actions of others in the network. Thus it makes sense to ask whether change can come in a timely and significant manner if single organizations continue to be the unit of analysis in the change effort.

Adding to the importance of this question are recent trends that tend to blur organizational boundaries. Increasingly the boundaries between supplier and customer are becoming blurred, as customer organizations begin to require certain quality control practices and efficient manufacturing processes—in some cases even stationing their employees right in their suppliers' facilities. More and more organizations are offering customer services that entail placing employees full-time in customer facilities. Joint ventures often set up overlapping organizations, as when one company performs the research and development for products that will be manufactured by another company and perhaps marketed and distributed by yet a third. Consortia and other technology-sharing arrangements such as those in the microelectronics and semiconductor industry are becoming more common. Recent examples have resulted from NASA's funding of the space station. As organizations rely increasingly on contract labor for skills they do not want to build up internally, their performance becomes intertwined with the performance of small contracting firms who train and supply part of their work force.

Efforts to improve performance in such highly interdependent networks must certainly be at least partly multiorganizational in nature. In the construction industry, which traditionally has involved a close relationship among contractors, suppliers, union halls, and subcontractors, improvement efforts have long had an industry focus. In places like Jamestown, New York, the entire community has banded together to attract business and employment opportunities by developing competitive plants. Such interorganizational improvement efforts will no doubt become more prevalent as boundaries become more permeable and organizations increasingly overlap with one another.

While we all agree that the trends described here are real, it is not always accepted that the interorganizational approach to change is desirable. The difficulty of changing even a single organization is often cited as a rationale for not expanding into a more complex area. But certainly part of the difficulty of changing a single organization lies in the fact that it is inextricably enmeshed in a larger network that multiplies the forces at work. In some ways this complexity limits the organization's freedom; in other ways it expands the scale of the change effort. Since the solutions to today's problems appear in many cases to involve network-wide action, the network may be the appropriate focus for change. At the very least, we should be looking seriously at this option to solving the complex, interrelated problems that are facing organizations today.

References

Ackoff, R. B. *Creating the Corporate Future: Plan or Be Planned For.* New York: Wiley, 1981.

Child, J. "Organization Structure, Environment and Performance: The Role of Strategic Choice." *Sociology,* 1972, *G,* 2–21.

Cole, R. E. "Diffusion of Participatory Work Structures in Japan, Sweden, and the United States." In P. S. Goodman and Associates, *Change in Organizations: New Perspectives in Theory, Research, and Practice.* San Francisco: Jossey-Bass, 1982.

Cummings, T., and Mohrman, S. "Self-Designing Organizations: Towards Implementing Quality-of-Worklife Innovations." In R. W. Woodman and W. A. Pasmore (Eds.), *Research in Organizational Change and Development.* Vol. 1. Greenwich, Conn.: JAI Press, 1987.

Emery, F. E., and Trist, E. L. "The Causal Texture of Organizational Environments." *Human Relations,* 1965, *18,* 21–32.

Galbraith, J. *Organizational Design.* Reading, Mass.: Addison-Wesley, 1973.

Hambrick, D. C., and Finkelstein, S. "Managerial Discretion: A Bridge Between Polar Views of Organizational Outcomes." In B. M. Staw and L. L. Cummings (Eds.), *Research in Organizational Behavior.* Vol. 9. Greenwich, Conn.: JAI Press, 1987.

Hannan, M. T., and Freeman, J. H. "The Population Ecology of Organizations." *American Journal of Sociology,* 1977, *82* (5), 929–964.

Hannan, M. T., and Freeman, J. H. "Structural Inertia and Organizational Change." *American Sociological Review,* 1984, *49,* 149–164.

Khandwalla, P. N. "Properties of Competing Organizations." In P. C. Nystrom and W. H. Starbuck (Eds.), *Handbook of Organizational Design.* Vol. 1. New York: Oxford University Press, 1981.

Kilmann, R. H. *Beyond the Quick Fix: Managing Five Tracks to Organizational Success.* San Francisco: Jossey-Bass, 1984.

Metcalfe, L. "Designing Precarious Partnerships." In P. C. Nystrom and W. H. Starbuck (Eds.), *Handbook of Organizational Design.* Vol. 1. New York: Oxford University Press, 1981.

Miles, R. E., and Snow, C. C. *Organizational Strategy, Structure, and Process.* New York: McGraw-Hill, 1978.

Mitroff, I. I. *Business Not as Usual: Rethinking Our Individual, Corporate, and Industrial Strategies for Global Competition.* San Francisco: Jossey-Bass, 1987.

Quinn, J. B. *Strategies for Change: Logical Incrementalism.* Homewood, Ill.: Irwin, 1980.

3

Why Organizations Change

Paul R. Lawrence

To advance our understanding and practice in regard to major organizational change, I believe we need to develop a fresh perspective on the basic question of *why* organizations change. It seems to me that change professionals are focusing too much on the questions of how and what to change. Only by digging into the *why* question can we make progress on the how and what. In this regard, I find it sobering to step back from our involvement in specific organizational change efforts and to ask ourselves what forces have been driving truly major organizational change in the past decade. I would submit that the four most powerful movers and shakers in the United States in recent years have been *technology* (integrated circuits employed in tools and in advanced information and communication systems); *global competition* (especially from the Far East); *ownership turmoil* (takeovers and leveraged buy-outs); and *new laws and legal rulings* (such as deregulation). I do not think that our usual organizational analytics and diagnostics adequately reflect these sources of change. We need to rethink our conceptual maps.

I am also concerned that analysts of change, by focusing on the how and what, may be sliding back into the search for the "one best way"—the all-purpose, ideal organization. Not long ago I was asked how I would "depict the end state (for example, in terms of values, structures, processes) that you strive to help large systems achieve.'' This question clearly implies that such an "end state" is *the* guide for a change agenda. While I believe that defining an end state in terms of values is one way to develop a change agenda, defining it in terms of structures or processes is truly dangerous. I would argue instead for sustaining a contingency approach; organizational change always involves some lack of a dynamic fit between certain elements of an organization and elements of its environment. To progress, we need to examine the sources of mismatch and use this analysis as a starting point for interventions.

I believe we have to go back to the fundamental *why* questions because as change agents we seem to be running into overwhelming new constraints to improving organizational effectiveness. Imagine what it would be like to sit down as a change consultant with a senior operating manager and some union leaders to form a partnership in building a high-commitment organization at the present time in TWA with Carl Ichan calling the shots. Or of starting afresh to build such an organization at Eastern with Frank Lorenzo in charge. What would it be like to start such a dialogue at a major oil refinery, as a colleague of mine recently did, whose distant owners have announced that it is one of the operating units that is on the auction block? Although it is sorely needed, we have trouble visualizing such a discussion getting under way at USX given their present circumstances. I believe we must struggle with the implications of these conditions for constructive organizational change even though the answers are not at all clear.

By focusing on the *why* of organizational change, I think we can also broaden our repertoire of change methods. By tending to neglect competitive forces as a cause of change, for example, I think we underutilize the social psychology of competition as a motivator of useful behavior. Likewise, by neglecting technology as a driver of change we underutilize new hardware as a leading edge for organizational change. By neglecting the legal and governmental guidelines we lose the opportunity and, at times, the necessity to renegotiate these guidelines to open the way for organizational renewal.

These observations and questions have grown out of my own recent thoughts on major organizational change. In the last decade I have largely withdrawn from action research and have looked instead at change as a researcher and theorist, using primarily historical methods. I have been seeking a broader perspective than can usually be attained by action research. This perspective leads me now to reexamine some of our basic premises about organizations and why they change.

In order to build a diagnostic framework broad enough to encompass the full range of variables influencing organizational change, I have found it valuable to think in terms of a four-ring model. This framework has the advantage that the pieces are all familiar; only their combination is somewhat new. It starts with an inner circle I call "value-adding behavior." This is defined as the everyday behavior of organizational members that consists of the transformations and the transactions that generate a surplus of outputs over inputs for the organization and its stakeholders. It involves both the *operation* of individual behavior and the *cooperation* of collective behavior. This ring is surrounded by the ring of organizational arrangements and, for the sake of simplicity, I have chosen the familiar 7-S framework (strategy, structure, systems, superordinate goals, staffing, skills, and style). The next larger ring is composed of the organization's primary stakeholders (customers, owners, employees, suppliers, community). The last ring consists of the basic drivers of change from the environment at large: social change (demographics, aspirations, cultural norms, and so forth); technological change; economic change (competition, primary demand); and political change (government rules and arrangements).

This simple framework permits an examination and classification of three basic types of fits and misfits: (1) among the seven S dimensions and their impact on value-adding behavior under four different environmental conditions; (2) among the five stakeholders in terms of contributions to and benefits from value-adding behavior; and (3) between the environmental forces and all three organizational rings. In this chapter I discuss all three types of fit and offer some hypotheses about organizational change and performance in terms of this framework. This analysis may clarify the *why* of major change in organizations in ways that carry interesting implications for the how and what questions. We begin by restating the contingency hypothesis that has evolved from the work of Burns and Stalker (1961), Leavitt (1982), Lawrence and Lorsch (1967), Thompson (1967), and Galbraith (1973).

Aligning Organizational Elements

In order to sharpen the issue between the "one best way" approach to organizational change and the contingency approach, I will state the contingency argument in a simplified style. The environment presents many opportunities, but no results will flow in terms of value-adding behavior until a matching organizational capability has been put in place. There are many fine organizations—but until they are fitted to the right environmental opportunity, not much happens. Creating the right organizational capability means fitting together all the separate elements of organizations (the seven S dimensions) into a cohesive whole. The systems must mesh with the structure; the style with the systems; the skills with the strategy. Putting together the right combination is clearly a complex, challenging process. It is made more complex by the fact that one cannot simply find a winning combination and lock it up. Since environments and organizational capabilities inevitably change, new combinations must always be found—hence the term *aligning*.

I contend that high value-adding organizations exhibit consistency or "fit" in how they align the seven S dimensions with each other and with environmental opportunities. To be more specific, the contingency hypothesis that has emerged from organizational studies can be stated in a simplified form as follows: Organizations (call them Type A) developed around a low-cost strategy to deliver standardized commodities efficiently to established and predictable users work very differently from organizations (call them Type B) developed around a differentiation strategy to deliver innovative products and services for changing environmental opportunities. Table 3.1 presents the line-up of hypothesized features of these two kinds of organizations designed to address two very different kinds of business

Table 3.1. Aligning Organizational Dimensions with Basic Strategies.

Organizational Dimension	Summary of Type A Organization Developed for Efficiency and Regularity	Summary of Type B Organization Developed for Innovation and Flexibility
Strategy	Low cost Stick to knitting Repel all competitive challenges ROI-oriented	Differentiation Search for new opportunities Cannibalize old products and markets for new ones
Structure	Centralized/functional orientation Clear vertical chain of authority for decision and communication Many explicit rules Sales and operations dominant functions	Decentralized/product orientation Network of influence and communication A few general rules Utilize projects and task forces Marketing and R&D dominant functions Growth-oriented
Systems	Top-down decision process Tight, detailed plans and budgets Specific individual/group targets Tie rewards to individual/group performance Reviews at short intervals Compete with internal comparisons	Bottom-up and top-down decision process Loose planning around objectives (MBO) General targets Compete with external comparisons Tie rewards to total business performance

Staff	Select for compliance and commitment Establish clear career ladders Tie promotion to making quotas	Select for originality and commitment Use a career maze Tie promotion to innovative results
Skills	Jobs highly specialized and tightly defined	Jobs broad and professionalized with some overlap
Style	Pride in lockstep precision Make your numbers in terms of costs, delivery, quality	Pride in being first with bright ideas Emphasize creative teamwork Reward risk-takers with soft landing for failure
Superordinate goals	Providing customers with the most for their money	Leadership in products and services (staying on the cutting edge)

opportunities. These features are presented here in an admittedly abbreviated and general form. Moreover, most environmental opportunities do not offer such clear and contrasting characteristics as I have postulated. But the hypothesis is, nevertheless, clear and testable, and furthermore it is amenable to additional elaboration.

For instance, anyone pursuing a low-cost strategy would be taking a sizable risk in assuming that current process technology and current customer requirements will persist unchanged for an indefinite period of time. It is usually prudent to develop an organizational capacity for process and product innovation. Perhaps it is a small production engineering unit or a small market development group. These units, given their purpose, could best be managed in Type B terms while the rest of the firm is run along Type A lines. This complicates the work of management: To support and sustain these differences and to integrate the new process and product changes with the old ones as needed is no trivial challenge. In a reverse image way, the same is true in a business pursuing a differentiation strategy. The search for new products and markets using innovative technology is fine, but to capitalize on an initial success at least some units in the firm need to focus on being reasonably cost competitive—usually manufacturing units and sometimes sales units. Again, the contingency hypothesis suggests that these units be managed in Type A terms, unlike the rest of the firm, and the work of management would be complicated by the need to induce the differences and integrate them.

The underlying *why* driving the search for alignment of the seven S elements is, of course, competitive *economic* pressure to improve value-adding performance. The Type A organization can best perform under conditions of simple and stable markets and technologies. I would also add that there is evidence, as indicated in Michael Maccoby's study (Chapter Seven), that a significant number of people find Type A organizations a fulfilling work environment. Type B organizations can best perform under conditions of complex and changing markets and technologies. I would argue that this general pattern holds even though Miles and Snow (1978) have shown that a few firms can survive as A Types (defenders) in a changing environment if they are internally consistent and vice versa for a few B Types (prospectors) in a stable environment. The pattern also holds even though simple and stable environments seem to be dwindling in number and even though more and more firms face competitive pressures requiring strong performance in terms of both efficiency and innovation.

Aligning Stakeholders

So that there will be no mystery about it, the underlying *why* that drives change efforts to align stakeholders with value-adding behavior is the tension between power and justice. It is the search for a distribution formula that approximately equates the outputs going to each stakeholder with their respective inputs. In the older language of Barnard (1946) and Simon (1945), it is the contribution and inducement equation; in the language of Zalenick, Christensen, and Roethlisberger (1958), is is distributive justice.

In the eighties, the balance of power among stakeholders seems to have shifted significantly toward the owners (stockholders) and clearly away from employees, both unionized and nonunion, exempt and nonexempt. The fact that competition and ownership have become international while employees and unions remain national is a major underlying reason for the shift in power. This shift is manifest in the wave of unfriendly takeovers and stockholder revolts that are driving significant changes in industry after industry. This shift is reflected in the waning power of unions and their shrinking membership. History tells us that such swings eventually generate counterforces that move back toward a balance between the inputs and outputs of all stakeholders, but such counterforces may be long delayed.

The history of the steel industry in the United States and particularly the history of U.S. Steel is informative in this regard. (For a summary of this history see Lawrence and Dyer, 1983.) For present purposes we can summarize it in three periods. In the formative growth years from 1870, when Carnegie entered the business, to 1901, when U.S. Steel was formed, Carnegie's operations set the pace of vigorous competition among many strong firms. The payouts among stakeholders were reasonably well balanced. Carnegie's policy of driving prices down and rapidly adopting such new technologies as the open-hearth furnace favored the consumer. The shareholders profited with returns on equity of between 20 and 30 percent, and these earnings were mostly reinvested. Most of Carnegie's managers rose from the ranks, and Carnegie advocated unions for the work force and pioneered the eight-hour day. So by the standards of the time even the employees were not exploited.

The steel picture changed abruptly when Carnegie retired and sold out to U.S. Steel, the new combination of the three largest steel firms. U.S. Steel started life with well over a 60 percent share of the U.S. market and competitive pressure suddenly dropped. Judge Gary, its new head, announced, ''We are perfectly safisfied to limit the amount of our business to our proportion of capacity and to do everything possible we can to promote the interests of our competitors.'' While there is no conclusive evidence of formal collusion or price fixing, a pattern of high prices remained constant over many years and profits were very high. The fortunes of employees, however, declined: The major firms combined to resist unionization, to cut wages, and to insist on the twelve-hour day. This pattern of high rewards for owners and low rewards for consumers and employees largely persisted until the unionization drives of the late 1930s. Then the unions and their members became partners in sharing the benefits of the collusive arrangements. Value-adding performance continued to lag behind the price levels at the expense of the consumer.

The final stage of steel's history started around 1960 with the steady incursion of foreign steel into the U.S. market. Innovative processes and large-scale operations gave the Japanese and other foreign producers significant cost advantages. Today, U.S. firms face extreme competitive pressure with no relief in sight. David Roderick of USX has said that American steel firms are in a ''state of accelerating self-liquidation.'' Now the raiders are offering Mr. Roderick their help in speeding up the process. None of the stakeholders are benefiting from this stage of steel's history except, for a short time, the raiders, the investment bankers, and perhaps the consumers.

This account of steel's history could be duplicated in a less extreme form in many other American industries. The point is that the pattern of power and the associated justice of contributions and inducements among stakeholders can become lopsided for extended periods. This condition seems to be associated with a drop in value-adding performance that eventually attracts higher-performing competitors. Based on these observations I would offer a tentative hypothesis: When the balance of power among stakeholders results in optimization of rewards for one or two groups at the expense of others, value-adding performance will be depressed and this will, in time, attract more effective competitors if entry is not institutionally blocked.

If this hypothesis is valid, I find its implications for current organizational change highly challenging. Employees as stakeholders—and I include managers in this analysis—always have at least latent power in organizations. Their ideas and energy are, obviously, always essential to value-adding behavior. The current intensity of international competition makes high commitment from employees especially critical. This latent power, however, is not always made manifest in effective voice mechanisms. With the decline of traditional unionism, such a condition now seems to prevail, setting the stage for change. Should we be exploring these possibilities more actively? Experiments with new voice mechanisms are, of course, being tried, but they still seem like a pale expression of their potential.

Aligning Environmental Forces

The third ring of our diagnostic framework consists of the four major environmental forces: social, technical, economic, and political. I se them as long-term drivers of organizational change, and the *why* is based on the harsh choice facing the organization: Adapt or die. Examples of these change forces appear every day in the press. I cited a few examples (integrated circuits, foreign competition, deregulation) in introducing this chapter. Here I want to clarify what I mean by the *social* change force by citing two important social changes that will be increasingly driving organizational change. It is estimated that by the year 2000 some 75 percent of the new entries to the U.S. work force will be women and minorities. To succeed, organizations must learn to manage employee diversity much more effectively than at present. A multicultural work force has great potential for generating creativity and energy, but only if it is well managed. The second social change is the pressure of rising expectations—the groundswell for a more fulfilling worklife that is stimulated by our educational system. This pressure has been well documented. It creates a dramatic mismatch between the values people bring to work and what they experience at work.

I see these four environmental forces for organizational change as problems that are waiting for change agents to turn them into opportunities. Some of this is, of course, happening, but not enough to lessen the tension. Some examples are in order.

Americans are not unique in their love affair with technology, but they do seem to slavishly follow what has been called the technological imperative. It is much easier to win if one is on the side favoring technical change rather than the opposite. This reality needs to be acted on by organizational change agents. The socio-tech approach pioneered by the Tavistock Group pointed the way to how both elements can be creatively combined to induce value-adding behavior for the benefit of all stakeholders. Their lead needs to be pursued much more vigorously and creatively than it has been. We need more efforts to extend and modify the original concepts for application to office and professional work (Pava, 1983). The problems posed by racing technology and unfulfilled aspirations can only be solved if they are joined as a shared opportunity. The power for change in low-cost computation and communication is still largely untapped.

The economic force for organizational change, in its current form of extreme pressure from foreign competitors, is also, I believe, a problem that can be turned into an opportunity. We social scientists easily fall into the bad habit, in this regard, of letting the economists define the concept of competition and dominate our thinking about it. Yes, competition does involve the microeconomics of supply and demand and optimizing pricing behavior. But competition is also a social-psychological phenomenon, a motivator of a different sort. All people, but especially Americans, love to win and hate to lose. A competitive challenge that is clearly perceived and accepted as such can unleash an amazing amount of productive energy. Perhaps sports provides the most obvious examples. Yet we students of human behavior seldom examine this human phenomenon, the competitive response, and specify the conditions under which this motivator becomes active. How can apathy or cynicism in organizations be turned into the competitive response? Why aren't we actively pursuing answers to this question? Do our values inhibit us from tapping into this energy source? If so, why? Is it because the gain sharing might not be just? Perhaps, but cannot this be creatively fixed? Is it because tapping into competitive energies is seen as manipulative? Perhaps, but only if the challenge is phony. Clearly economic competitive pressure is a real force for organizational improvement in many industries, but the competitive response is still sporadic. Is this another problem waiting to become an opportunity for change?

The steel industry provides an example of the final point I would make about environmental forces: how organizational changes are linked to the political realm. One of the conditions that can block the competitive response is the belief that the rules of the game make winning impossible. A few pages ago, we left the U.S. steel industry in a virtually impossible no-win situation. Foreign competition is so far ahead now that—regardless of the truth of claims about unfair trade practices—foreign firms now need no hidden government support to knock out virtually all of the major U.S.-based firms. The principal hypothesis coming out of the study I did on the history of seven industries (Lawrence and Dyer, 1983) was that vigorous competitive conditions provided healthy inducements to value-adding behavior but this stimulus waned if organizations faced either weak competitive pressure or extreme competitive pressure. We were tracking the social-psychological as much as the rational economic response to these competitive conditions.

Since government is the only agency in our society that can regulate competitive forces, clearly the political arena needs to be involved. Government has at its command many means to enhance competition or to dampen it. History shows that these influences may be needed on a temporary basis in certain industries to restore the vigorous market competition that induces value-adding behavior. This argument cannot be developed in depth here, but we can add it to our list of problems waiting to be turned into opportunities. Would it stretch the role of organizational change agents beyond reason to suggest they could be of value where new ground rules need to be invented and negotiated between business and government? Can they be agents, for instance, in the creation of joint R&D ventures among competitors? Can they perform as third-party facilitators in arranging for temporary government support in exchange for a realistic plan of organizational renewal to which all stakeholders are committed? Many of the problems of U.S. firms are not going to be solved unless someone can orchestrate change programs at this level.

I began this chapter by calling for a reassessment—a stocktaking of the state of efforts to change and improve organizational effectiveness. I called for an examination of the *whys* of organizational change and introduced the four-ring framework as an analytic tool to this end. It provides a means of clarifying and restating the contingency view of organizational change with various misfits as the driver of change. We have seen how mismatches can occur among the elements of the 7-S framework, among stakeholders, or between the factors in all four rings. My hope is that this examination of the *whys* of organization change has stimulated fresh ideas and has renewed energies for addressing the questions of *what* organizational changes should be espoused and *how* constructive change can be induced.

References

Barnard, C. *The Functions of the Executive.* Cambridge, Mass.: Harvard University Press, 1946.

Burns, T., and Stalker, A. *The Management of Innovation.* London: Tavistock Press, 1961.

Galbraith, J. *Designing Complex Organizations.* Reading, Mass.: Addison-Wesley, 1973.

Lawrence, P., and Dyer, D. *Renewing American Industry.* New York: Free Press, 1983.

Lawrence, P., and Lorsch, J. *Organization and Environment.* Boston: Division of Research, Harvard Business School, 1967.

Leavitt, H. "Unknown Organizations." *Harvard Business Review,* July–August 1982, 8890–8898.

Miles, R. E., and Snow, C. C. *Organizational Strategy, Structure, and Process.* New York: McGraw-Hill, 1978.

Pascale, K., and Athos, A. *The Art of Japanese Management.* New York: Simon & Schuster, 1981.

Pava, C. *Managing New Office Technology.* New York: Free Press, 1983.

Simon, H. *Administrative Theory.* New York: Free Press, 1945.

Thompson, J. *Organizations in Action.* New York: McGraw-Hill, 1967.

Trist, E., Higgin, G., Murray, H., and Pollack, A. *Organizational Choice.* London: Tavistock Press, 1963.

Zalenick, A., Christensen, C., and Roethlisberger, F. *Motivation, Production, and Satisfaction of Workers.* Boston: Harvard Business School, 1958.

4

From Recovery to Development Through Large-Scale Changes

Jay R. Galbraith

A great deal of practical and academic interest is currently focusing on changing our large institutions. In the past, industrial change took place through the birth and death of firms. But recently the birth and death process has been replaced by bailouts, chapter 11, turnarounds, corporate raiders, and mergers. Institutions are not allowed to die but are revamped, revitalized, reoriented, and reorganized.

Executives such as Lee Iacocca at Chrysler and Sanford Sigaloff at Wickes have demonstrated that there is a private, intuitive fund of knowledge about how to revive existing institutions, but there is still no body of tested, public knowledge about this important subject. In this chapter, I examine the attempts of American manufacturing enterprises to recover from global competition and an overvalued dollar in the first half of the 1980s. All these firms discovered that sustainable competitiveness requires more than laying off workers, closing plants, and reducing layers of middle managers. Competitiveness demands redevelopment, revitalization, and renewal. Thus in analyzing four manufacturing companies that are attempting to recover and redevelop, I describe the processes involved in taking a manufacturing enterprise from recovery to development in today's environment.

Large-Scale Change

The scholarly study of large-scale system changes and their management presents a definitional problem. The first aspect of the problem is to identify the level of analysis. A case in point is the American Can Company, now called Primerica. Viewed from the level of the corporation, the changes since 1980 have been enormous. American Can has sold off all its paper, metal, and plastic packaging businesses and reinvested in various financial services companies and specialty retailing businesses. Its stock has more than tripled and its CEO is on the cover of *Business Week*. When viewed from the perspective of society as a whole or from the level of a business unit, however, the change has been small. The ownership has been reshuffled, but the same business units exist. Business units have more or less access to capital; different leaders and constituencies hold power; but the same assets are producing the same products. And when the change is viewed from the floor of a divested can plant or an acquired insurance office, the ownership change is a nonevent. The work force and salespeople carry out the same day-to-day activities. So when addressing large-scale changes in an organization, the target level must be identified. Here I am addressing the corporation as a whole.

The other issue is what kind of change constitutes a large-scale system change? In one sense organizations are always changing. New products are introduced and old ones are phased out. But these are "normal changes" that are handled through routine procedures for adaptation. The changes of scholarly interest are those that are not normal and therefore are not handled by applying procedures from the organization's current repertoire. Usually there are vested interests in the status quo that not only blur the need to adapt but resist any efforts to do so. Here the changes of interest are those that must be made to happen to a large organizational unit. Somebody must prevail over the vested interests in the status quo.

Corporate-level changes, forced by corporate management, are now occurring. Technology, in the form of increasingly large-scale integrated circuits, is forcing Hewlett-Packard's management to scrap the tried and true autonomous division for more centralized cooperative efforts to sell systems rather than disconnected products. Deregulation forced AT&T's management to lead a change to a more market-oriented and competitive organization rather than a monopoly.

On other occasions more predictable organizational changes result from changes in corporate strategy. Chandler's case studies (1960) describe the transformation of companies to the divisionalized form when diversifying from their core business. Other studies show the predictable stagewise development of new enterprises (Greiner, 1972; Galbraith, 1982a). These predictable changes can be planned and anticipated and the groundwork laid more easily than for other changes. They should, in short, be more manageable.

The changes of interest here are those recently undertaken by mature American manufacturing firms. In the late 1970s and certainly the 1980s, these firms were faced with lower-cost (and often higher-quality) global competitors. For part of the period the overvalued dollar magnified their cost problems. This situation was neither easily anticipated nor easily controllable. Change has been a significant test for corporate managements. In order to bring costs into line, most companies have made tough decisions about layoffs, pruned corporate staffs, reduced managerial levels through early retirements, and closed inefficient plants. All have learned, however, that they could not become more competitive merely by closing plants. They had to do things differently and revitalize the company. The cutbacks, moreover, did nothing for the revenue side of the equation. Many companies have recovered their cost competitiveness and now seek new revenue sources. The question at General Electric is: How do you grow the top line? They are all seeking new sources of business development.

This study examines four companies—General Electric, General Motors, Westinghouse, and TRW—to see what strategy and organizational changes they have taken to recover and to develop their organizations. After cutting costs, what next? The changes at these mature, successful enterprises certainly constitute large-scale system changes. In this study we will first examine the process of change at General Electric and then extract lessons from all four cases.

The Change Process at General Electric

The change process at General Electric started with the appointment of Jack Welch as chairman in 1981. Welch was selected to be an instrument of change. GE had missed out on semiconductors and computers in the 1960s and 1970s. They had to get back into the technology race with integrated circuits. Welch was an engineer, an innovator, and a person who was comfortable with technology. He built the plastics business in GE and had a reputation for working with the Central Research Labs. He was an operating manager and a complete contrast to Reginald Jones, his financially oriented predecessor. Moreover, he was only forty-five years old. If Welch chose to stay, he could run GE for the next twenty years.

Initial Moves. Welch initially set out his thoughts about future directions. He said GE was too diverse and too complex to have a corporate strategy. But his thoughts would constitute what leadership theorists call a vision (Bennis and Nanus, 1985). The vision came from his technical background, his view of the future, and an immediate need to communicate with the investment community.

General Electric had always been more popular with management theorists than with Wall Street investors. Even though GE's profits had improved during the 1970s, the stock price did not. Investors regarded GE as a conglomerate. This meant that diversification had not only protected GE from falling profits but also prevented it from experiencing rising profits. And with so many different businesses (forty-three of them), GE could not be good at all of them. The financial analysts pressed Welch for a strategy for GE. He did not believe that one could be articulated for the whole company. But the combination of certain other actions gave him a means to communicate what GE was all about.

Welch believes that the 1990s will be a period of slower growth. When combined with rapid changes in technology and markets and the continuing evolution to a global economy, he sees a period of very intense competition. The winners and losers will be clearly identified. To survive profitably, a business must have a significant competitive advantage. Welch therefore challenged all of GE's business units to be either number one or number two, in terms of market share, in their industry or show some special capability. If it could not, the business unit would be sold, combined, or closed.

One of the first units to feel the pressure of the new criteria was Utah International, which had been bought in a hotel room by Reg Jones in the 1970s. The raw materials businesses of Utah International were seen to be low growth, low margin, and high capital. Before the decline in oil prices, Utah International was sold for a hefty sum.

After the sale, Welch found a useful way of classifying GE's businesses in terms of three circles (Figure 4.1). He felt

Figure 4.1. Welch's Vision of General Electric.

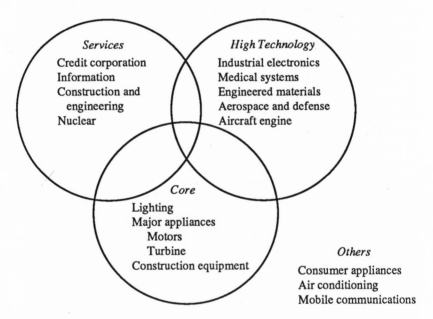

he could communicate better with the financial analysts by saying that GE is not a conglomerate but concentrates on three basic areas: its electrical products core, high-technology businesses, and services. Some fifteen businesses that were number one or two in their industries were listed inside the three circles. The businesses that were not number one or two were listed in a column outside the circles signifying their questionable status.

The three circles with the number one and two businesses have become the means by which Welch's vision is communicated inside and outside of General Electric. Being number one or two has become a standard of performance for all businesses at GE. This standard was needed because General Electric did not lose billions of dollars prior to Welch's appointment. He faced the difficulty of creating a sense of urgency in order to bring about change. The businesses outside the circle began to feel the urgency.

The circles also became a device for discussing the future portfolio. The service and high-technology areas would become the sources of future growth. They are the areas where the United States has an advantage in worldwide competition. The U.S. economy is becoming more service-oriented, and services are less subject to foreign and especially Japanese competition. Welch's intent is to reduce the percentage of business attributable to the core manufacturing businesses. These mature businesses will be supported to maintain their positions by R&D investments for new products and new process technologies; capital will be invested to support automation and cost reduction; but emphasis on the core will be reduced. In 1980 the distribution of profits was 46 percent core, 31 percent high technology, and 23 percent services. In mid-1986, after the RCA acquisition, the distribution was 22 percent core, 40 percent high technology, and 38 percent services.

The vision has been communicated many times through its execution. Acquisitions and investments have been made in the service and high-technology areas. Less effective businesses have been sold or closed. By 1985, a total of 120 plants, operations, and divisions had been sold, consolidated, or closed. These actions generated about $3.5 billion in cash. Many of the businesses that were sold or closed were consumer product divisions. With the sale of the raw material commodities and small consumer appliances, GE is less diverse and concentrates on big ticket products and services sold to institutional customers. The pressure to reduce costs and become more competitive has resulted in a reduced payroll. Overall the salaried work force has been reduced by 13 percent and the hourly work force by 18 percent. The corporate staff has been reduced from 2,500 to 2,100.

In summary, Welch has launched GE in a new corporate direction portrayed by the three circles. He has fundamentally altered the business mix and reduced diversity through acquisitions and divestitures. Because of his insistence on being number one or two, a number of misfits and low performers have been sold, closed, or consolidated with other operations. Welch has also made a series of changes to the organization. Again the intent is to become more competitive. He likes to use the phrase "lean and agile." The implication is that a competitive organization in today's and tomorrow's environment must be quick-acting and less bureaucratic.

The corporate structure has been changed several times. The first moves were continuations of GE's sector organization. General Electric has always led American enterprise in structural changes. In the late 1960s GE initiated the strategic business unit organization. This form was based on organizing around logical economic entities rather than size of a department. The number of building blocks went from 250 to 43. In the late 1970s, all business units, independent of size, reported to a level between the office of the chief executive and the business units. This level was the sector level. Initially Welch added additional sectors in order to collect and highlight all the high-technology businesses and the materials and service businesses. These moves gave structural priority to businesses that Welch wanted to grow and moved some of his supporters into the inner circle.

The subsequent structural changes have been aimed at eliminating the sector level. The number of businesses has been declining as those that are not number one or two are sold or combined. In 1985, Welch finally eliminated the sector position by forming a four-person Chief Executive Office (CEO). Welch does not want a filtering layer between the executive office and the business. He wants frequent direct contact between the CEO and the business to enable fast action. He was also able to eliminate previous competitors for chief executive and thus consolidate his power.

The CEO is being shaped to reflect Welch's style. Each member is responsible for several businesses and several staff units. All members are to be corporate in their orientation and compensation, however. The group of four is to act very much as a team. They meet often on short notice and coalesce to a position. Welch leads the discussions in an open problem-solving style. The teamwork and openness are fostered by the lack of an immediate management succession issue. The CEO meets regularly in reviews and information-sharing meetings; it meets quarterly to get a view of the earnings and financial situation. About twice a month, the CEO meets to review a business—its strategy, budgets, and management staffing plus specific issues that Welch wants discussed. The CEO exercises strategic control, financial control, and control over management talent. In 1986, Welch increased the product development budget in Medical Systems; he wanted them to devote more energy to new products.

The pressure to be lean has had an effect on the businesses. They are reorganizing and becoming more functionally organized. The functional organization allows consolidation and fewer people. As a result, there is a greater orientation toward product management and matrix organization in order to achieve sharper focus. They too are reducing levels and people to meet standards set by the CEO.

Welch has made substantial changes to the management systems. The old planning system was formal, had many reviews, and was run by the strategic planning department. One of his first changes was to eliminate most of the planners and transfer more decisions to the business managers. Now there is a system of operating plans that are reviewed by the CEO, but they can be changed when required rather than waiting for a year to pass. The result is more responsive and quicker decisions as well as more ambitious and realistic plans. Welch has doubled the approval authority for expenditures to make the businesses quicker-acting and more autonomous.

Welch has changed the nature of the reviews, as well. Before, they involved sixteen to eighteen people; now a review is conducted by the CEO and the strategic business unit (SBU) manager in a small room. These reviews are organized around problem-solving discussions rather than presentations. The reviews are directed to issues that Welch wants discussed.

The change in the budgetary and planning systems is typical of the general move to consolidate and differentiate. The forty-three SBUs are being consolidated as losers are sold, closed, and consolidated. The businesses then report directly to the CEO. On the other hand, each business is given the freedom to organize according to its marketplace, not according to GE practice. Businesses are to organize to beat the competition. They should pay people and give titles according to the industry's competitive practices. The decision process should fit the timing requirements of the business. The planning and budgeting processes at GE are tailored to the individual business's needs. A business is now measured on how well it competes; before, it was whether you met your budget. Now an operating plan is put in place for one year or until the environment changes, at which point a new plan is drawn up.

The reward system too is being changed. Welch is offering financial incentives tailored to the business situations. He wants to use more bonuses and fewer salary rewards. To promote risk taking, Welch is trying to reduce punishment for failures on new ventures that can be viewed as ''near misses'' or ''good tries.'' When one project was canceled, he rewarded the people for a good effort and publicized the event in the company and the press.

Welch is acting in other ways as well. He is encouraging quantum change, not incremental. This takes place through the review of the business plans. He himself suggests changes and encourages a more vigorous stance. Things move faster today. The major appliance group reorganized and completely changed its factory in a year and a half. They dropped the breakeven point by 25 percent. Welch rewarded and encouraged this bold action.

The role of corporate staff has also changed—no more monolithic systems that apply to all businesses. Today systems are tailored to the business practices of the industry. Staff is composed more of advisers and supporters of the businesses than of controllers. The staff feels the fundamental tensions of one company with diverse businesses. Thus GE is decentralizing and adding much more direct contact with the CEO. Ironically, the businesses themselves are centralizing and consolidating.

Welch also is pushing for the use of new technology. He wants quantum change through new technology. In promoting the use of the Corporate Research Laboratories, he himself conducts business managers through the labs and promotes contacts and transfers. Research has been expanded and the funding increased.

Career paths, too, are being changed. Before, people moved often and across businesses. Now Welch is championing longer stays in a job and in the same business until later in the career. He has also gone outside for talent in some businesses. His intent is to increase the number of outside managers. These are major culture changes. Candidates are now being selected on how well they meet the challenge of the job; before, it was more important to see if they had the right background. There will be more cross-functional moves within a business, and, with fewer layers, there will be more lateral moves. The career system is being thoroughly revamped.

In summary, the structure is being changed to reduce levels. The businesses are being reduced in number and report directly to the CEO. Businesses are moving to functional organizations and consolidating. Corporate staff has been reduced from 2,500 to 2,100. Overall, the salaried work force has been reduced 13 percent and the hourly work force 18 percent. A new planning and budgeting system that responds to the environment and changes when the world changes has been implemented. The process requires more interaction between the businesses and the CEO. People are measured against competitors, not last year's budget. A risk/reward system that grants large rewards for large risks and does not punish reasonable failures has been installed. The decision process moves much faster.

Most of these changes are still taking effect. Not everyone likes the new GE; some people have left. Welch and the CEO take every opportunity to communicate their views in open sessions. A three-page document detailing "Values We Share" has been created by the CEO and circulates throughout the company. They use Crotonville, the company's training center, for discussion purposes. Welch himself invests two hours with every management course that goes through Crotonville. He sees Crotonville as a source of cohesiveness for the company. He wants it to be the finest business education facility in the world and to lead in training leaders as opposed to managers. At the moment, Welch and his staff are trying to define the kind of person needed in the 1990s. They want Crotonville to base its training on this definition.

Probably the most powerful change tool being used by Welch is the executive succession process. Changes in a unit begin when an executive who believes in Welch's program is moved into a position of leadership. One executive was wondering why there was such a fuss about Jack Welch's change program. Then his division got a new manager out of the Welch mold and things started to happen. Since Welch may be in a position of leadership for quite a while, developing and promoting executives who fit his vision may be the most powerful means to foster and sustain the changes he has initiated.

The Results. In terms of large-scale systems change, GE has been significantly altered by the succession of Jack Welch. Today the business mix favors services and high technology. Profitability has increased. Although revenues (not including RCA) are constant, profits are up over 40 percent from 1981. All this has been accomplished by throwing every lever Welch could get his hands on. He has articulated a new strategy and made acquisitions, divestitures, investments, and consolidations to effect the new direction. He has changed the organization's structure, review processes, planning processes, careers, performance standards and measurements, compensation policy, and the executive development system. He is working on the company's shared values. Change, it appears, is not implemented by changing one particular policy but by changing all of them when the opportunity presents itself. Each and every change, however, is consistent with the three-circle strategy and with each other. All changes lead the organization in the same direction.

The changes at GE confirm the strategy and organization models that follow the Leavitt diamond (Leavitt, 1965; Galbraith, 1987), shown in Figure 4.2. Leavitt thinks most organizational change efforts are too narrowly focused. In changing task performance, managers and consultants often use a structural approach, an approach based on a technology such as computers, or a human systems approach like those advocated by organizational development theorists. Each of these approaches is promoted by specialists to the exclusion of the others—a narrow focus that leads to less effective changes. Leavitt's point is that successful change involves changes to the structure, the technology, and the human system simultaneously. Elaborations to the model have included additional factors and the proposition that all the factors must be changed in a consistent and congruent manner. The idea is that an effective organization is one whose strategy, structure, decision systems, and human systems are all in alignment.

Figure 4.2. The Leavitt Diamond.

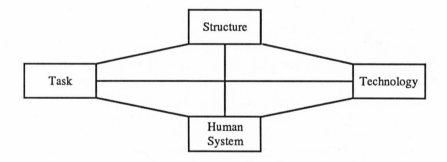

Anyone who reads about General Electric is immediately struck by the presence of Jack Welch. His actions are supporting evidence for the proponents of the transformational leader and the centrality of leadership (Bennis and Nanus, 1985). He has articulated a vision. His actions are consistent with the vision and help to communicate it even more clearly. He has provided the consistency and clarity of direction that is needed in turbulent times.

The GE case is somewhat consistent with Quinn's notion (1980) of strategic change occurring by a process of logical incrementalism. He says that strategic changes do not follow a well-laid-out plan as suggested by the classic strategy formulation literature. Instead strategic changes follow from precipitating events like oil crises that are totally unforeseen and whose implications at the outset are unknowable. Given the lack of data and understanding, CEOs set only general goals and directions. They then move incrementally and opportunistically as events unfold. Each incremental act—investments, divestitures, acquisitions, organizational restructurings—moves the company closer to its general goal and creates information to clarify the way for the next incremental steps. Each incremental act takes place somewhat independently of others led by different groups. They are not formally tied together by an explicit plan. Quinn argues that this is a logical way to proceed when faced with unknowable futures.

In some ways, Welch confirms the model with a sequence of incremental acts. He does respond to opportunities like the RCA acquisition. Yet Welch is more logical in his approach than he is opportunistic. An enormous amount of effort went into screening all acquisition candidates, such as Hughes Aircraft, prior to buying RCA. The only precipitating event appears to be the arrival of Welch himself. He wants GE prepared for the 1990s before a billion-dollar loss forces a need to change. Welch himself may be the difference.

In summary, GE's changes are quite consistent with current theories of strategy and organization. In one sense, this congruence is unfortunate. Case studies that do not conform can reject a theory, but consistent ones cannot confirm it. Thus an inconsistency might lead to new ideas and a reformulation of theory.

Recovery

The determination to become more competitive is continuing at GE, but new sources of revenue are replacing cost competitiveness as the number one priority. General Electric has done a reasonably good job of recovering and becoming cost competitive. The same can be said for Westinghouse and TRW but not for GM, which continues to have higher costs than its American counterparts. General Motors responds, however, by referring to its reorganization costs and its expensive approach of launching new products in short time frames. In any case, GM can be disputed as a recovery case.

All of the firms including GM have acted in similar ways to cut their costs and become more competitive. They have reduced employment through layoffs and early retirements. They have closed inefficient plants, combined operations, increased spans and reduced levels of management, reduced corporate staffs, run with leaner staffing patterns, shifted manufacturing offshore, and sold their less desirable businesses. Some companies launched corporate-wide productivity and quality programs. Usually a staff unit was created at corporate level that funded demonstration projects, ran courses, and spread ideas. After a few years the staff groups would disappear and migrate into the business units.

All four companies employed automation and robotics but to different degrees. General Electric created showcase plants at the Louisville major appliances factory and the Erie locomotive works. Both were cost-reduction approaches to demonstrate that Rust Belt and Frost Belt unionized plants can be made competitive; both were featured in Fortune's ten best plants in America. General Motors has been the heaviest investor in new automated technology. Indeed, GM has invested so heavily in automation that it has bought into or joint-ventured with its equipment suppliers. Whether it will be successful, though, is still in doubt. Some say GM has spent too much on unproved technology. (Its Fremont, California, plant, which is run by Toyota, is more productive with conventional technology.) General Motors says it is looking ahead and investing for the long term.

All four organizations have tried new high-involvement work systems (Lawler, 1986), but mainly in new plants where the effort could start from scratch. General Motors and TRW have launched corporate efforts in this area. GM and the UAW have been pursuing a quality-of-worklife program for some time.

Despite its success and the general success of the new plants, the use of participative work systems has been limited; more effort has gone into automation. Nevertheless, there is untapped potential here.

One reason for the limited use of high-involvement plants is their confinement to new plant start-ups. Although older plants and older managements are seldom redesigned, some change attempts and ideas are being tried. One organization with extensive experience in high-involvement work systems at new plants was going to simulate a start-up at an old plant. They planned to shut down the plant for about three weeks so that employees would get three weeks of training to acquire the knowledge and skills to work in the new system. As many physical alterations as possible would be made to the old plant including painting it a new color. New management from high-involvement plants plus some workers would be brought in. Workers who wished to opt out could be sent to other plants, be outplaced, or take early retirement. The revised plant would start anew at the end of the three weeks as if it were a start-up.

A similar approach was taken to an entire division at Westinghouse. The divison was considered ''sick'' throughout the company. There were conflicts between departments, between sites, between union and management. Then, during a low-demand period, 100 managers were put on task forces to plan moving the division to a new site and starting fresh. A Florida site was selected by one task force. The northern unionized plants were closed and work was transferred to nonunion southern factories. The divison was reorganized from two profit centers to a single functional one, and selected people moved to the new Florida site. The divison is now staffed at 70 percent of its former level and waiting for sales to increase again.

Joint ventures and cooperative arrangements are seldom used for recovery. At Westinghouse, however, one of its power generating businesses has an arrangement with Mitsubishi Heavy Industries. The two partners agreed to produce major components of a large capital-intensive product at the site with the lowest cost. Some are now made by Westinghouse and sent to Japan; others are made by Mitsubishi and sent to the United

States. Both companies do their own assembly, distribution, and servicing. Auto companies in Europe have been coproducing capital-intensive items like engines in order to get better than break-even volume. This practice is less extensive in the United States, however, and may be illegal in some cases.

The largest recovery effort yet is taking place at GM's Saturn project. Originally a five-car project, Saturn began when every design attempt at a small car totaled $2,000 more than the Japanese manufacturing cost. Roger Smith encouraged fresh thinking about a new plant, but present labor agreements represented constraints and some 30 percent of the costs are in the distribution system. Finally Smith decided not on a new plant or a new division but a new company. As a result Saturn now has a separate, high-involvement labor agreement. The new company can be financed separately. The information system is to allow a two-week delivery cycle. It is to establish a new dealer network. Since dealers can have smaller showrooms and inventories, they now can locate in shopping malls and other high-traffic areas. The emphasis on robotics has been reduced but is still extensive. The original publicity for Saturn is gradually being replaced with a more realistic set of expectations. Putting the publicity aside, Saturn is to be a laboratory for new approaches to manufacturing and distributing cars and a training ground for new managers. Graduates of the Saturn program may be its most important product.

In summary, these manufacturing firms have followed the traditional but difficult approaches to becoming more competitive. They have reduced employment, reduced management levels, and reduced corporate staffs. When these reductions are extensive, they force new ways of doing things. Investment in automation and robotics and, to lesser extent, employment of high-involvement work systems have also been used to make factories more productive. Programs for productivity improvement, quality, and quality of worklife have been adopted by some firms. Their success has been mixed. Joint ventures for coproduction of components have not been extensively used. While the biggest changes are taking place at new plants, some attempts to simulate start-ups are taking place at existing facilities.

The most daring attempt to do things differently is GM's Saturn program. The formation of a separate company and Smith's protection have freed it from the vested interests of the bureaucracy. Whether Saturn is successful or not, much should be learned from the venture.

Development

With recovery under way, the four manufacturing firms analyzed here are seeking new sources of development. Others, like the oil companies, have given up on diversification and are restructuring and shrinking their operations. Unlike the oil companies, though, the manufacturing companies are seeking ways to improve the top line or revenue side of the equation.

All four companies, but to various degrees, are applying portfolio approaches. The low-growth, low-return businesses are being sold, closed, combined, or scaled back. The higher-growth, higher-return businesses are being expanded through investment and acquisitions. Even in low-growth but good-return businesses, some product areas are growing. TRW has achieved some growth in rack and pinion steering for small cars, power steering, and seat belts even though the automotive market as a whole has not been growing. The portfolio approach has brought improved profitability but flat or negative growth. Hence the firms are searching for alternatives to shrinking.

The obvious growth producer is acquisition. In the case of these four firms, they must make large acquisitions in order to make a substantial improvement. General Electric and General Motors have both followed the big acquisition trail. General Electric has bought RCA and several financial services companies; General Motors has acquired EDS, Hughes, and some mortgage banking companies. Most of these acquisitions have been controversial, however.

The financial community is very negative on conglomerate acquisitions. They think they can diversify their own portfolios. They want to see acquisitions where the corporation brings value added and not just more overhead. The GE merger with RCA has been questioned. Originally, analysts said that GE simply saw a good deal for its money. Others saw the combination as paying less taxes because their credit operations had extensive investment credits. General Electric defends its purchase by saying that RCA fits its three-circle strategy: RCA's high-technology defense businesses fit nicely with GE's own aerospace and defense group; the NBC subsidiary is a prize service business. Moreover, both service and defense are less vulnerable to Japanese competition and both can provide cash for global battles in power generation, jet engines, and medical systems. RCA was probably a good buy for GE because all of these reasons are true. The misfits from RCA have been sold; the others must become number one or two.

General Motors has had more difficulty explaining its acquisitions. They have been accused of making conglomerate acquisitions and of paying too much. GM's response is that EDS and Hughes are agglomerate acquisitions—that is, the acquisitions are meant first of all to provide the technology to upgrade GM's core automotive business and secondarily to provide a diversified earnings stream. In fact, all of GM's acquisitions, joint ventures, and minority investments outside of financial services are in vendors supplying new technology to them. The idea is that since the vendor will supply GM first, the vendor will get smarter and more capable because GM has enormous state-of-the-art problems. Then, having trained the vendor, GM will profit from it secondarily by selling the more valuable vendor or by capturing earnings as the vendor sells its capability to the rest of American industry. It is not a bad strategy since GM selects the best vendor, works with it as a customer, gets top priority initially, and gives it a competitive advantage. Subsequently GM can profit from either its sale or future profits.

The big acquisition route is limited. Big acquisitions in the companies' core businesses may not exist, they may be unattractive, or they may be disallowed for antitrust reasons in a post-Reagan environment. Acquisitions outside the core are often viewed negatively by the financial community, which can make the acquirer itself a future target of acquisition. This negative view is based on the poor track record of companies making conglomerate acquisitions. Westinghouse illustrates the dilemma. They are still gun-shy from an acquisition binge in the 1970s. As yet they have no vision for the future on which to base a major acquisition. If big acquisitions are limited, then where are the new developmental opportunities? All the companies have reacted similarly. They have selected high technology and services as their new growth areas.

Services

The service area is being pursued vigorously by all four companies. They say that the United States is becoming a service-based economy and services are local businesses and therefore less subject to foreign competition. The companies already have experience with services. They are offering the services now as part of their product offering. Services such as repair have been part of product support. They have not been sold to make money in their own right. That is the change. The services are to become money-making businesses and a new source of growth.

The financial service subsidiaries are the best example and an indicator of the potential for development. All four companies started financial subsidiaries to provide easier financing for credit customers and distributors of the companies' big-ticket products. The subsidiaries proved to be competitive against other financial institutions. The combination of deregulation of financial services, tax law advantages like investment credits, and the decline or sale of core businesses drove the companies to free the subsidiaries from product support and to make them stand-alone businesses. They have been very successful and GE Credit has been outstanding. It has made numerous acquisitions in insurance and in investment banking (Kidder, Peabody). It provides a whole menu of financial services to other institutions.

The success of financial services has prompted the companies to free up other services like maintenance and repair of the companies' products. Originally, these were product support activities to help sell more products and provide service during warranty periods. At GE some of the services came into their own after the sale or closure of the manufacturing business they were to support. GE Information Services has grown from the time-sharing service bureaus that GE retained after selling its computer business to Honeywell. The nuclear services were retained after the manufacture of nuclear equipment was stopped with the decline of the nuclear utility plants. The service has been expanded to include maintaining the plant, replacing equipment, holding spare parts inventory, coplanning additions, and disposing of wastes. These services have been successful also. But the successes have been earned. The new strategies require new organizations.

The establishment of service businesses increases the diversity to be managed in the companies. Diversity requires more decentralization and differentiation of policy. Even at GE, which has experience at managing a wide variety of businesses, differentiation was difficult. In financial services titles, salaries, and benefits are different from those of manufacturing businesses. The personnel function prefers a uniform policy for equity purposes and ease of administration. If managers move among the businesses, a call for uniformity is usually made. Welch's new policy is to differentiate according to norms and practices in the industry. He wants the businesses to be competitive, not uniform. The change for corporate staffs is enormous. They move from control and review functions to consulting and servicing business units. The business unit administers the compensation program and corporate staff consults on how to differentiate it.

Service businesses also require different performance measures. Usually manufacturing businesses are measured on return on assets (ROA) or return on sales (ROS). Service businesses have fewer assets and look good on ROA but not so good on ROS. Again more flexibility and differentiation in the management and financial system are required if the new source of growth is to succeed. Some computer companies with less experience at managing diversity have been unsuccessful with their service and computer retail businesses.

The real difficulty, however, comes about when management wants to free up the service from its product support role but the manufacturing business wants to keep the service as a vertically integrated portion of the product offering. Often the product management wishes to offer the service at a discount in order to sell the product. It is impossible for the service unit to serve two masters. It is important to be clear about the role of the service business. One company says it is to serve the product first and then make money. The solution is to separate the service unit from the product unit while keeping a subunit within the service business that is dedicated to the company's product. A central staffing function can avoid duplication. Some definition of territory is also needed. In one company the product unit serves the customer while the product is still under warranty; after warranty, the bid competition begins.

The separation is needed in order to build a service business with its own compensation, performance measures, business strategy, and organization. It may need to negotiate a different labor agreement. The competitors in services are often local mom and pop operations. Wages based on manufacturing master agreements may make the service noncompetitive. The business may start to service competitors' equipment. Thus numerous occasions for conflict will arise. Top management must be active in the separation process. Otherwise the service business will not provide a source of growth and will remain a captive of the product business.

Thus the use of service components to provide a source of development requires a separation from the product businesses which created them. Separation can occur by selling or closing the product operations or by placing the service in a separate structure. Then the compensation, performance measures, union contracts, and so on must be tailored to the service business. There is bound to be resistance from the product business and uniformity-conscious corporate staffs. The leadership must protect the new businesses and manage the conflict. The corporate office must be capable of managing diversity and be flexible in its style.

Organizations such as General Electric are going a step further. Some customers buy equipment and use the services of several business units. The thought occurred to GE of treating these major accounts differently. Why not service them from one point? In fact, why not let GE do all the servicing of all the equipment at a customer site? So GE is exploring the establishment of relationships with major customers to provide an extensive service and maintenance contract.

The changes here are enormous. The customer is not used to the new relationship. The customer's unions will see a loss of jobs. The customer's plant managers may see a loss of autonomy. The GE service units themselves are used to thinking in terms of repair transactions, not long-term relationships. There is always the problem of cooperation among business units. The change process requires a pilot project with an understanding customer and an evolutionary movement to a major account unit that draws on existing service units.

The freeing up of service components has considerable potential as a source of new revenue growth for manufacturing firms. The success of financial services is a case in point. The other services will require a more differentiated and decentralized organization. The most difficult cases occur where the manufacturing unit is still healthy and wants to maintain the service as product support. The next step is to combine various services and form a relationship with large customers. All these new thrusts are good ideas, but they all require large-scale system changes like those used in recovery.

Technology

The other area that is being promoted for development is high technology—businesses where the United States is seen to have an advantage over lower-wage countries. As a result the four companies analyzed here are investing in the business units in their portfolios that are based on high technology. They are pursuing new products in the conventional way. The problems occur when pursuing new technologies that have not been mastered by the business units.

The companies are pursuing all avenues in order to generate and acquire new technologies. They are investing in their own R&D labs, too, but these investments are coming under more scrutiny. All of them are using university contracts, joining research consortia, and using licenses. Some are forming joint ventures. General Electric, Westinghouse, and Toshiba have a venture in power semiconductors. Toshiba provides the technology and Westinghouse and GE furnish the distribution and customers. The product is made in an old Westinghouse plant. The ownership is 40 percent GE, 40 percent Westinghouse, and 20 percent Toshiba. Most companies have venture capital funds to invest in new technologies and a clearinghouse for taking minority investments in start-ups. As at GM, many investments are made in start-up vendors. After choosing the best vendor, the company invests in it. The companies will continue to search in all areas for new technology.

The real problem lies in taking advantage of the technologies that are found. If the technology fits an existing business, the company is faced with a problem of technology transfer. If the technology is the foundation of a new business unit, the company is faced with an internal start-up venture. The track record of large corporations in these two areas is poor. If technology is to be a developmental source, companies will have to improve their implementation of technology transfer and internal start-ups. The companies analyzed here publicly emphasize their handful of successes in technology transfer but complain privately about all of the failures. General Motors largely justifies its acquisition of Hughes on the transfer of Hughes' technology to GM's Delco Divison. TRW and Rockwell have been trying for years to transfer state-of-the-art technology from their defense groups to their commercial groups, but the results have been disappointing.

There are several reasons for the lack of transfer. Some technologies are not applicable to commercial use. Others are applicable but fail to be adapted to commercial priorities. In defense applications, performance is paramount and cost secondary. While some commercial applications are similar, costs are much more important throughout the commercial world. Scientists are less interested in cost reduction. The technologies are often not proprietary because the government owns the patent.

Some hot technologies are kept secret or restricted by the Defense Department. But even with these barriers, firms are ready to try again and are putting a great deal of effort into it.

Technology gets transferred by transferring people and having peer-to-peer discussions among technologists. TRW is working hardest to make transfers happen. They are transferring people at a controlled rate from their defense electronics centers to commercial centers like the one for electrohydraulics. Joint centers are being created for specific technologies. Incentives are being created for managers to transfer technologies, information, and people. Some people are sent into defense specifically to bring technologies out. Management is devoting time and attention to the issue. Although it is still too early to judge the results, many American manufacturing firms are trying a number of practices to increase their odds at technology transfer.

Internal start-up experience is just as bad as that for technology transfer. Most companies are designed for ongoing operations, not entrepreneurial start-ups (Galbraith, 1982a). Big companies have trouble managing small start-ups. They give them too much autonomy and then too little. They do not have the patience to fund the start-up for the eight years it usually takes to build a profitable new business. They throw too much money too fast at the fledgling enterprise. General Electric committed all of these sins in trying to create the Factory of the Future business. Their robotics business may yet be successful, though, since it has been scaled back and redefined. Thus despite the current effort at intrapreneurship, no organization, with the possible exception of 3M, is consistently effective at using internal start-ups to employ new technology. I have dealt elsewhere with the question of how to design an organization that can innovate (Galbraith, 1982b).

Conclusion

American manufacturing firms have been going through large-scale system changes at the corporate level. These changes are the direct result of global competitive forces augmented by an overvalued dollar and a recession. All the firms analyzed here initially responded to the pressure by trying to recover competitiveness in their core business. Invariably recovery meant cost reduction and quality improvement. Most companies did the obvious first by reducing management and staff, laying off workers, and closing inefficient plants. Then they began more fundamental changes like those described in the section on General Electric. These other changes involved changing the existing organization, discarding pieces that were regarded as unrecoverable, and adding new pieces for the future.

The large-scale system changes needed to make an organization more competitive were illustrated by Jack Welch's actions at General Electric. At GE the recovery is still taking place, led actively by Welch. He has created a sense of urgency, he has articulated a vision for GE in the 1990s, and his actions have been consistent with the stated direction.

Change happens when it is attacked on multiple fronts. Welch, for example, has changed structure, planning and budgeting processes, management review, compensation structure, career paths, and now the value system. These changes will be perpetuated primarily through control of the management succession process. The key appears to be the consistent direction of each and every change. All are aimed at creating a more competitive enterprise.

The manufacturing enterprises that have recovered or at least have breathing room because of better economic conditions and a lower-valued dollar are now entering a new phase. How do they develop new sources of revenue to replace divestitures and closures? It will be interesting to see if the same leaders who have created recovery can create development. Here Welch has been less successful. Revenue has been added through acquisitions but not yet through internal growth. Danforth of Westinghouse has been masterful at recovery but has not attempted development. Smith at General Motors appears to have ideas of new development but has not led the tough decision making to recover the core business. The two problems appear to call for two different types of leadership. Recovery is a tough road. It requires a lot of stomach. It is not fun. Growth is fun. Leaders must be tough and persistent to force real change. Development, on the other hand, requires vision and future perspective. It requires selection of growth modes. It is more open and experimental. People must be sold on new directions. Although there is no reason why the same manager cannot lead both campaigns, it appears that they have not. Perhaps the leader's style must match the type of change.

References

Bennis, W., and Nanus, B. *Leaders.* New York: Harper & Row, 1985.

Biggadike, R. "The Risky Business of Diversification." *Harvard Business Review,* 1979, *57* (3), 103.

Chandler, A. D. *Strategy and Structure.* Cambridge, Mass.: MIT Press, 1960.

Galbraith, J. R. "The Stages of Growth." *Journal of Business Strategy,* Summer 1982a, 70–79.

Galbraith, J. R. "Designing the Innovating Organization." *Organizational Dynamics,* Winter 1982b, 5–25.

Galbraith, J. R. "Organizational Design." In J. Lorsch (Ed.), *Handbook of Organizational Behavior.* Englewood Cliffs, N.J.: Prentice-Hall, 1987.

Greiner, L. E. "Evolution and Revolution as Organizations Grow." *Harvard Business Review,* 1972, *50* (4), 37–46.

Lawler, E. E., III. *High-Involvement Management.* San Francisco: Jossey-Bass, 1986.

Leavitt, H. "Applied Organizational Change in Industry." In J. March (Ed.), *Handbook of Organization.* Chicago: Rand McNally, 1965.

Quinn, J. B. *Strategies for Change: Logical Incrementalism.* Homewood, Ill.: Irwin, 1980.

Part Two

The Impact
of People

5

The Actors
in Large-Scale
Organizational Change

Thomas G. Cummings
Allan M. Mohrman, Jr.
Ian I. Mitroff

This part of the book is concerned with the actors involved in large-scale organizational change. Typically referred to as ''stakeholders,'' these individuals and groups include those who have a vested interest in the change process and its outcomes, such as managers, employees, owners, and consultants. In Chapter One we proposed three dimensions of large-scale organizational change: size, depth, and pervasiveness. Each dimension presents its own set of issues regarding the actors in the change.

The size of the organization signifies the sheer mass of people who potentially could participate. Since size correlates with complexity, we can expect these actors to represent several levels of hierarchy and multiple units and subsystems, along with multiple views of the world.

The depth of the change is important to the participants. Shallow changes—in authority and communication structures, reward systems, job descriptions, among others—might require new behavior, skills, knowledge, and understanding. Deep changes involve feelings and values; the unconscious, latent, and tacit ways of behaving; and the (mostly unarticulated) culture of the organization.

91

Figure 5.1. Pervasiveness of Change and the Actors Involved.

Scope of Change

	Internal	Whole Organization	Beyond Organization
Every/All	Everyone connected with changing subsystems and units	All organizational members	All organizational members and environmental stakeholders (including consultants)
Key/Limited	Key people representing changing subsystems	Key members of organization (leader)	Key organizational members and environmental stakeholders (including consultants)

Stakeholder Participation

There are two directions in which change can pervade the organization. These are captured in Figure 5.1. As discussed in Chapter One, change can affect only part of the organization, it can affect the entire organization, or it can even extend beyond the organization itself. The second direction of pervasiveness involves the stakeholders; this is equivalent to the social matrix of the new paradigm. Do the participants in the change process include everyone within the scope of the change or do they include only the key players? All change efforts must ultimately end up in the upper-right-hand cell of Figure 5.1 because, in the final analysis, everyone affected by the change will, by definition, be participating in it. Nevertheless, the starting point for most change efforts is in one of the cells of the lower row. Usually these key actors are already in positions of authority.

In contrast to smaller, more routine forms of organizational change, large-scale change tends to involve multiple stakeholders. This follows from the simple fact that such change has to reach many levels and parts of the organization as well as significant elements of the environment. Because members from these different levels and parts have the power to support or undermine the change, their participation in the change process is critical for success. Obviously, the greatest degree of change is that in which all the members of an organization and its environment participate at both the surface and deep levels. That is, they not only change the products of their interactions but they also change themselves. Changing organizations means both changing individuals and altering the ways they relate.

In considering the actors involved in large-scale change, at least three key issues emerge: the role of leadership in initiating and directing change; the management of individual differences among participants; and the role of consultants in facilitating change. In the following sections we examine these issues one by one.

The Leadership Role

There is a widespread belief that large-scale organizational change must be managed from the top of the managerial hierarchy (Tichy, 1983; Nadler and Tushman, 1987). Institutional leaders are responsible for the strategic direction of the firm. They make big decisions about corporate strategy, culture, technology, structure, and human resource systems, as well as decisions about aligning those dimensions with each other. Because large-scale change invariably entails making significant changes in these organizational dimensions, corporate leaders need to initiate and direct the change process. They need to provide a clear vision of the organization's future, a vision that embodies the values the organization is trying to enhance through change. Top leadership is particularly crucial when the organization is experiencing problems and there is ambiguity and conflict among stakeholders regarding causes and solutions. Such direction can reduce uncertainty about the corporation's goals. It can energize and focus motivation for change. It can signal to stakeholders the need to resolve conflicts and to support change actively in the right direction.

The role of corporate leaders in directing large-scale change rests on a common assumption, often implicit, about leadership—that top managers really matter in determining organizational actions and outcomes. The belief that chief executives have the power to initiate strategic changes is typically taken for granted in the literature and among specialists in large-scale change. This view has received mixed support, however, from organization theorists and researchers. Indeed, there has been a long-standing debate among researchers about the extent to which corporate leaders make a difference in organizational functioning. Those supporting a "strategic choice" perspective argue that top leaders have substantial freedom to adapt the organization to its environment and even to change the environment itself (Andrews, 1981; Child, 1972). "External control" advocates, on the other hand, say that organizations are inertial and chief executives are severely constrained in making strategic changes by both environmental and organizational forces (Hannan and Freeman, 1977; Salancik and Pfeffer, 1977). Given the evidence supporting both sides of the debate, surely the issue about whether corporate leaders make a difference should be considered an empirical question rather than an implicit assumption.

In large-scale change situations, then, it seems wise to assess corporate leaders in terms of the discretion they have in making such changes. Situations can be expected to vary considerably in affording chief executives latitude for action. Research suggests that at least three forces determine the amount of leeway executives have in making strategic changes: the environment, the organization itself, and managerial characteristics (Hambrick and Finkelstein, 1987). By examining variables falling into these categories, one can arrive at an empirical evaluation of whether or not corporate leaders should be able to initiate and direct large-scale changes. A leader might have considerable discretion, for example, when the environment involves high market growth and few legal constraints. On the other hand, discretion might be limited because of the organization's age, size, and a well-established culture. Finally, leaders might enjoy more discretion if they have a strong power base, high aspirations, and a high tolerance for ambiguity. When the configuration of these elements constrains latitude for managerial action (as is frequently the case in large-scale organizational change), the role of leadership in large-scale change may be negligible. Opportunities for significant change may require loosening the major constraints—by replacing senior management, for example, or entering a different environment.

When leaders get involved in large-scale organizational change, they find the issues very different from those arising from limited efforts. Large-scale change transcends the authority of any leader. While limited change may be driven by the authority of the leader, in large-scale change the bases of authority themselves change. A leader promoting large-scale change is putting her or his role at risk. Success in this situation depends on the leader's ability to establish a new power base that drives the change and is strengthened by the change itself.

Managing Individual Differences

In considering the diverse actors involved in large-scale organizational change, the issue of individual differences invariably arises. People can vary on a number of characteristics that can affect reactions to change, such as values, psychological needs, social character, and worldviews. These differences can influence people's motivations to change, how change is planned and executed, and what organizational features are considered desirable.

Contingency views of organizational change suggest that specific changes as well as the change process itself must match people's personalities, needs, and values if they are to accept them (Cummings and Srivastva, 1977; Nadler, 1981). A common prescription, for example, is to tailor the organizational changes to fit the needs of managers and employees. This matching is considered a rational process of analyzing needs and values and then choosing appropriate changes. It may be more political than rational, however, in large-scale change situations. Here multiple stakeholders are involved in the change process—increasing the likelihood that there will be differences in needs and values among the participants. There is evidence to suggest that organizational change programs may be unable to satisfy all these diverse values, and consequently there may be conflicts over whose needs and values should govern the change process (Cummings, 1981). Such conflicts cannot be resolved through rational methods; it takes political bargaining among the stakeholders. This requires making trade-offs among the diverse needs and values, resulting in organizational changes that are compromises among the stakeholders or favor one set of actors over another.

The political nature of large-scale change argues strongly for a participative change process to manage individual differences among actors (Cummings and Mohrman, 1987). Involving multiple stakeholders in the change process increases the likelihood that important individual differences will be exposed and resolved. It can help stakeholders articulate different needs and make explicit the values involved in the change. Authoritarian change processes, by way of contrast, tend to follow a limited range of values, often resulting in strong managerial and technical imperatives in changing organizations. The needs and values of other potential stakeholders, such as employees and customers, are either neglected altogether or taken into account after the change program has been designed and is being implemented.

The Consultant's Role

The role of consultants in large-scale organizational change is still being formulated. As practitioners from a diversity of backgrounds and perspectives have gained experience with large-scale change, a number of role demands unique to these contexts have emerged. (See, for example, Cummings, Mohrman, Mohrman, and Ledford, 1985; Argyris, Putnam, and Smith, 1985.) These role requirements have to do with forming the consulting relationship, facilitating organizational learning, and applying relevant skills and expertise.

Consultants must establish effective relationships with organizational members if they are to facilitate change. The consulting relationship forms the basis for mutual understanding and influence among the parties; it serves as the medium for gaining access to relevant information providing appropriate help for change. The quality of the consulting relationship determines whether participants understand the situation well enough to design and implement organizational changes and whether they are receptive to one another's ideas.

Because large-scale change involves multiple stakeholders, consultants must establish relationships with a diversity of individuals and groups interested in the change process. They can help form the different parties into an effective communications network that explores and resolves differences about goals and innovations to achieve them. Creating such networks can be a harrowing process, particularly when the participants have divergent values and views of the situation. These differences can place opposing demands on consultants. Indeed, the different parties may view the consultants as simply another stakeholder with vested interests in the change process. To gain widespread acceptance, consultants may have to appear neutral to the different parties; they may have to show their openness to diverse values and perspectives while resisting the tendency to choose sides. Achieving such neutrality may require considerable political acumen. It may also demand a networking ability as well as a willingness to invest in relationships with potentially long-term commitments and psychological intensity.

Large-scale change generally requires considerable organizational learning. Since knowledge about organizational design and improvement provides only general prescriptions for change, participants must learn how to translate that general information into the new behaviors implied by the changes. Moreover, large-scale change is increasingly aimed at helping organizations gain the capacity to improve themselves continually. Managers and employees are becoming involved in solving organizational problems and improving the performance of their work units. They are learning how to develop themselves and their work groups. All this means that consultants will need to work themselves out of their roles by helping the organization acquire the capacity to continually change. It also means that organizational members will need to adopt the consultant role so that the organization can continually learn, improve, and change.

The sheer diversity of relevant consultation skills strongly suggests that the era of the single consultant may be over. Rather, teams of consultants with a variety of skills and expertise may be necessary for large-scale change projects. Team members can be expected to specialize in particular skills and knowledge, and the team's ability to interact among themselves and with other stakeholders will determine their effectiveness.

Although a consultant team is ideal, in reality different consultants are usually brought in by different clients within the organization. Ideally they should team up and orchestrate their efforts, but often they are only vaguely aware, if at all, of one another's existence. If there is to be any teaming, therefore, it must be designed as part of the change effort.

The presence of consultants begs the question "who is the client?" In large-scale organizational change there is no ready answer. Any organizational group—top management, a functional department—that originates change must at some point realize that, as part of the organization, they too must change. Precisely at this moment the consultant needs to proceed as though some larger entity is the client—the organization itself or even the organization's environment. In fact the term *client* loses its meaning entirely as the consultant too becomes involved in the change process.

References

Andrews, K. *The Concept of Corporate Strategy.* (Rev. ed.) Homewood, Ill.: Irwin, 1981.

Argyris, C., Putnam, R., and Smith, D. *Action Science.* San Francisco: Jossey-Bass, 1985.

Child, J. "Organization Structure, Environment and Performance: The Role of Strategic Choice." *Sociology,* 1972, *6,* 2–21.

Cummings, T. "Designing Effective Work Groups." In P. Nystrom and W. Starbuck (Eds.), *Handbook of Organizational Design.* Vol. 2. Oxford: Oxford University Press, 1981.

Cummings, T., and Mohrman, S. "Self-Designing Organizations: Toward Implementing Quality-of-Work-Life Innovations." In R. Woodman and W. Pasmore (Eds.), *Research in Organizational Change and Development.* Vol. 1. New York: JAI Press, 1987.

Cummings, T., Mohrman, S., Mohrman, A., and Ledford, G. E., Jr. "Organization Design for the Future: A Collaborative Research Approach." In E. Lawler and others, *Doing Research That Is Useful for Theory and Research.* San Francisco: Jossey-Bass, 1985.

Cummings, T., and Srivastva, S. *Management of Work.* La Jolla, Calif.: University Associates, 1977.

Hambrick, D., and Finkelstein, S. "Managerial Discretion: A Bridge Between Polar Views of Organizational Outcomes." In B. Staw and L. Cummings (Eds.), *Research in Organizational Behavior.* Vol. 9. New York: JAI Press, 1987.

Hannan, M. T., and Freeman, J. H. "The Population Ecology of Organizations." *American Journal of Sociology,* 1977, *82* (5), 149–164.

Nadler, D. "Managing Organizational Change: An Integrative Perspective." *Journal of Applied Behaviorial Science,* 1981, *17,* 191–211.

Nadler, D., and Tushman, M. *Strategic Organization Design.* Glenview, Ill.: Scott, Foresman, 1987.

Salancik, G., and Pfeffer, J. "Constraints on Administrator Discretion: The Limited Influence of Mayor on City Budgets." *Urban Affairs Quarterly,* 1977, *12,* 475–498.

Tichy, N. *Managing Strategic Change.* New York: Wiley, 1983.

6

Leadership for Organizational Change

David A. Nadler
Michael L. Tushman

The increasingly competitive environment has demanded that many large organizations undergo significant and profound change. These major organizational transformations appear to be necessary for those who would remain as major players on the world industrial and commercial stage. The management of large-scale organizational changes, therefore, has become a critical task.

There is a growing body of observations and knowledge about large-scale planned organizational change. (See Goodman and Associates, 1982; Kimberly and Quinn, 1984; Nadler, 1981.) Virtually all of those who have written about large-scale change have in some way cited the issue of leadership. It appears that significant and profound organizational change cannot happen without a certain type of executive leadership. The leader is a critical player in the drama of organizational change.

This chapter lays out an approach to the question of leadership and organizational change. Our aim here is to build a framework for thinking about the effective leader of change. We draw from two sources: close consulting work with leaders attempting major changes (see Nadler, 1987) and macrolevel analysis of leadership and organizational changes in several different industries (see Tushman and Romanelli, 1985; Tushman,

1986). In the first section, we present some basic thoughts and terminology about organizational change and discuss the general importance of leadership. After describing a commonly held view of the nature of effective leadership in change—the magic leader—in subsequent sections we expand the notion of the magic leader and propose a role for leadership beyond the magic leader. In the final section we discuss some implications for organizational change management.

Organizational Change and Reorientation

Although organizations go through change all the time, the nature, scope, and intensity of organizational changes vary considerably. In other words: A change is not always a change. One way of thinking about the differences among changes is to think about the varying types of planned organizational changes along the following dimensions:

- *Strategic and incremental changes.* Some changes in organizations, while significant, affect only certain elements of the organization. The fundamental aim of such change is to improve the efficiency or effectiveness of the organization, but within the general framework of the strategy, mode of organizing, and values that already are in place. These changes are called *incremental changes.* Other changes have an impact on the whole system of the organization and end up fundamentally redefining what the organization is or changing the basic framework of organizing, including strategy, structure, people, processes, and (in some cases) core values. These changes are called *strategic organizational changes.*
- *Reactive and anticipatory changes.* Many organizational changes are made in direct response to an external event. These changes are in some way forced upon the organization—it *must* change. These changes are called *reactive.* There are times, however, when organizational change is initiated not because of the need to respond to a contemporaneous event, but rather because certain individuals believe that initiating such change in advance of future events will provide competitive advantage. These changes are called *anticipatory.*

Figure 6.1. Types of Organizational Change.

	Incremental	Strategic
Anticipatory	Tuning	Reorientation
Reactive	Adaptation	Re-creation

When these two dimensions are combined, a basic typology of different changes emerges (see Figure 6.1). Change that is incremental and anticipatory is called *tuning*. These changes are not system-wide redefinitions but modifications of specific components, and they are initiated in anticipation of future events. Incremental change that is initiated reactively is called *adaptation*. Strategic change initiated in anticipation of future events is called *reorientation;* change introduced in response to immediate demands is called *re-creation*. (For a detailed discussion of this framework, see Nadler and Tushman, 1986.)

Research on patterns of organizational life and death in several industries has provided insight into the patterns of strategic organizational change (Tushman and Romanelli, 1985). Here are some of the key findings:

- *Strategic organizational changes are necessary.* These changes appear to be environmentally driven. Various factors—competitive, technological, legal/regulatory, and so forth—drive the organization (either reactively or in anticipation) to make the changes. Organizations that do not change do not survive.
- *Re-creations are risky.* Re-creations are riskier endeavors than reorientations. The research indicates that fewer than one

in ten re-creations succeed. Those that do succeed usually entail changes in the senior leadership of the organization, frequently involving replacement from the outside.

- *Reorientations are associated with success.* When reorientations are initiated in advance of external events, success (defined as continued organizational survival and in most cases continued growth) is more likely. Again, however, many of the successful reorientations also involve change in the CEO and executive team. At the same time, a number of reorientations occur with the same leadership team, and these are usually among the most successful.

The role of leadership varies considerably in these different changes. Most incremental changes can be managed by the existing management structures and processes of the organization, in some cases with special "transition structures" appended (Beckhard and Harris, 1977). In these situations, a variety of different leadership approaches and styles may be effective, depending on how the organization is normally managed and led. In the strategic changes, however, the management process and structure itself is the subject of change, so it cannot be relied on to manage the change. Moreover, the organization's definition of effective leadership may also be changing as a consequence of the reorientation or re-creation. In these situations, leadership becomes a critical element of change management.

Within this context this chapter focuses on the role of leadership in strategic organizational change—in particular, the role of leadership in reorientations. The reason for this focus is that re-creations often fail and are frequently characterized by the replacement of leadership. Thus the key challenge for current organizational leadership is to learn how to initiate, lead, and manage reorientations.

Why is leadership so essential to reorientations? It appears that certain aspects of reorientation depend upon the leader. The first is *strategic anticipation*. Reorientation requires that somehow the organization must be able to anticipate that the conditions for strategic change will arise in the future and to determine the effective responses to that change. (What are the key strategic and organizational moves that will enable an organization to be an effective competitor?) Unless the leadership becomes involved in this anticipation, no change will be initiated. Second, reorientation requires a *created sense of urgency*. Since, by definition, the need for change is not apparent to everyone, energy has to be mobilized to stimulate behavior. Usually, only the leadership can create such a sense throughout the organization. Third, reorientation requires effective *creation and management of pain*. Urgency frequently results from pain (current or anticipated). Pain, however, can motivate both functional and dysfunctional behavior. Again, only the leadership has the capacity to create pain and to shape the responses to pain by providing direction. Finally, reorientations are effective when people perceive the required change to have *centrality*—to be truly critical to the basic business and strategic issues of the organization. Centrality, if not apparent, can only be defined by the leadership. (For more discussion of principles for managing reorientations, see Nadler, 1987.)

It is understandable, therefore, why no successful reorientations occur without a major role being played by the organization's leadership—either the current leaders or new leaders brought in from the outside. The question, then, is this: What is effective leadership in these situations?

The Magic Leader

While the subject of leadership has received a lot of attention over the years, leadership during periods of change has only recently begun to be examined as a specific question. (See Burns, 1978; Bennis and Nanus, 1985; Tichy and Devanna, 1986.) What emerges from various discussions of leadership and organizational change is a picture of the special kind of leadership that appears to be critical during times of strategic organizational change. While various words have been used to portray this type of leadership, the label "magic leader" is used here. The term *magic* refers not to something mystical or illusory, but rather to a special quality that enables the leader to mobilize action within an organization and sustain that action over time through personal actions combined with perceived personal characteristics. In many cases this is manifested by the development of an intimate bond between the leader and people in the organization. Successful strategic changes appear to be characterized by the presence of such a magic leader.

At the core of this concept is the model of the charismatic leader. This is not the popular version of the charismatic leader (the great speech maker, the television personality, and so on) but rather the result of recent work to identify the nature and determinants of a particular type of leadership that appears able to bring about changes in a person's values, needs, or aspirations. Research on charismatic leadership (Berlew, 1974; House, 1977; Bass, 1985) has identified this type of leadership as observable, definable, and having clear behavioral characteristics.

Building from the general concept of charismatic leadership, what in practice characterizes the magic leader of organizational change? We have developed a first-cut description of the leader in terms of the patterns of behavior that he or she seems to exhibit. Three major components of behavior—envisioning, energizing, and enabling—appear to characterize these leaders.

Envisioning is the first component of magic leadership. This involves the creation of a picture of the future that people can accept and which can generate excitement. By creating vision, the leader provides a way for people to develop commitment, a common goal around which people can rally, and a way for people to feel successful. Envisioning is achieved through a range of different actions. Clearly the simplest form is through articulation of a compelling vision in clear and dramatic terms. The vision needs to be challenging, meaningful, and worthy of pursuit, but it also needs to be credible. People must be able to believe they can succeed in their pursuit of the vision. Sometimes the vision is communicated in other ways, as through the leader expressing expectations and personally modeling behavior and activities that are consistent with or symbolic of the vision.

Energizing is the second component. Here the role of the leader is the direct generation of energy—motivation to act—

among members of the organization. How is this done? Different leaders energize in different ways, but some of the most common include demonstration of their own personal excitement and energy, combined with the leveraging of that excitement through direct personal contact with large numbers of people in the organization. They express confidence in their own ability to succeed. They find examples of success and use them to celebrate progress toward the vision.

Enabling is the third component. Here the leader's role is to help people to act or perform in the face of challenging goals. Assuming that individuals are directed through a vision and motivated by the creation of energy, they then may need emotional assistance in getting the tasks accomplished. This enabling is carried out in a number of different ways. Magic leaders demonstrate empathy—the ability to listen to, understand, and share the feelings of those in the organization. They express support for people. Perhaps most important, the magic leaders tend to express their confidence in the ability of the people in the organization to perform effectively and meet the challenges.

Assuming that magic leaders act in these ways, what functions are they performing that help bring about change? First, they provide a psychological focal point for the energies and aspirations of people in the organization. Second, they may serve as the embodiment of some type of organizational "ego ideal." They represent what the organization hopes to become. Through their personal effectiveness and attractiveness they build an intimate bond between themselves and the organization. Thus they can become a source of sustained energy, a hero with whom people can identify.

Limitations of the Magic Leader

Even if one were able to do all the things involved in being a magic leader, it still might not be enough. In fact, our observations of people who fit the general class of magic leaders indicate that there are a number of inherent limitations to the effectiveness of the magic leader, many stemming from the risks associated with leadership that is built around one individual. Some of the key problems are as follows:

- *Unrealistic expectations.* In creating a vision and getting people energized, the leader may create expectations that are unrealistic or unattainable. This tactic may backfire if the leader cannot live up to these expectations.
- *Dependency and counterdependency.* A strong, visible, and energetic leader may spur different psychological responses. Some people may become too dependent on the leader, and in some cases whole organizations may become dependent. They stop initiating actions and always wait for the leader to provide direction. They may become passive or reactive. At the other extreme, some may be uncomfortable with a strong personal presence and spend a lot of time and energy demonstrating how the leader is wrong, how the emperor has no clothes, and so forth.
- *Reluctance to disagree with the leader.* If the leader is personally the focus of energy, then the leader's approval or disapproval becomes an important commodity. In the presence of the strong magic leader, people may become hesitant to disagree or confront the leader. This may, in turn, lead to conformity or group thinking.
- *Need for continuing magic.* Magic leaders may create a trap for themselves because of the expectation that the magic will continue unabated. This may cause the leader to act in ways that are not functional or (if the magic is not forthcoming) cause a crisis of credibility.
- *Potential feelings of betrayal.* If things do not work out as the leader envisioned, then the potential exists for people to feel betrayed. They may become frustrated and angry, and some of that anger may be directed at the person who created the expectations in the first place.
- *Disenfranchisement of next levels of management.* The rise of a magic leader may cause the next levels of management to feel disenfranchised. They may lose the ability to lead because no direction, vision, exhortation, reward, or punishment is meaningful unless it comes directly from the magic leader himself. The magic leader thus may end up undermining middle management.
- *Limitations of the magic leader's range.* When leadership is built around one individual, the ability of management to deal

with different issues is limited by that person's time, energy, expertise, and interest. This situation is particularly problematic during periods of change when different issues present themselves and demand different competencies (markets, technologies, products, finance). Different strategic changes make different managerial demands and call for different personal characteristics. Finally, there may be limits to the number of strategic changes that one individual can lead over the life of an organization.

In light of these risks, it appears that the magic leader is a necessary but not a sufficient component of the leadership required for organizational reorientation. There is a need, therefore, to move beyond the magic leader.

Instrumental Leadership

The description of the magic leader outlined here is not fundamentally unique or novel. As mentioned earlier, a number of different observers of leadership have described this phenomenon. The three components—envisioning, energizing, and enabling—are simply one way of describing what these leaders do and how they do it.

Given the risks of magic leadership, a growing number of executives fit the description but nevertheless fail to initiate or sustain change. Apparently, effective leaders of change need more than just magic. Effective reorientations also seem to call for another type of leadership—one that focuses not on exciting people and changing their goals, needs, and aspirations but on making sure that people throughout the organization indeed behave in the ways needed for the change to occur. The role of leadership is to clarify required behavior, institute measurement, and administer rewards and punishments so people realize that behaving in ways consistent with the change will help them achieve their own goals. Thus we will call this type of leadership *instrumental leadership,* since it focuses on the management of structure to create individual instrumentalities. The basis of this approach is in expectancy theories of motivation, which propose that people will act in ways they perceive as instrumental for acquiring valued outcomes (Vroom, 1964; Campbell, Dunnette, Lawler, and Weick, 1970). Leadership, in this context, involves the managing of environments to create conditions that will motivate the required behavior (House, 1971; Oldham, 1976).

In practice, instrumental leadership of change involves three elements of behavior. The first is *structuring*. The leader invests time in creating structures that make it clear what types of behavior are required from people. This involves setting goals, establishing standards, defining roles, and similar activities. In reorientations it involves detailed planning: What will people need to do, and how will they be required to act during different phases of the change? The second element of instrumental leadership is *controlling*. This involves the creation of systems and processes to measure, monitor, and assess both behavior and results and to administer corrective action. (See Lawler and Rhode, 1976.) The third element is *rewarding*, which includes the administration of both rewards and punishments contingent upon the degree to which behavior is consistent with the requirements of the change.

Instrumental leadership focuses on the challenge of compliance. The magic leader excites individuals, shapes their aspirations, and directs their energy. In practice, however, this may not be enough to sustain patterns of desired behavior. The followers may be committed to the vision, but in time other forces may influence their behavior, particularly when they are not in direct personal contact with the leader. This is particularly relevant during periods of change when the formal organization and the informal social system may lag behind the leader in the types of messages communicated and the types of behavior that are rewarded. Instrumental leadership is needed to ensure compliance consistent with the commitment created by magic leadership.

The Role of Mundane Behavior. Typical descriptions of both magic and instrumental leaders tend to focus on significant events, critical incidents, and grand gestures. Indeed, our vision of the change manager is frequently exemplified by the key speech or big public event. While these are important arenas for leadership, change is frequently managed through an accumulation of minor patterns of activity that have been called mundane behavior (Peters, 1978). The use of mundane behavior involves the sending of signals by the leader through everyday actions as opposed to grand gestures. Through relatively unobtrusive acts, the leader can shape the patterns of events that people see. Here are some examples of mundane behavior that can have a great impact:

- Allocation of time and calendar management
- Shaping of physical settings
- Control over agendas of events or meetings
- Use of events such as lunches and meetings
- Summarization—post hoc interpretations of what occurred
- Use of humor, stories, and myths
- Small symbolic actions, including rewards and punishments

All these examples suggest ways that the leader can use specific episodes of day-to-day behavior to send signals about what issues are important, to indicate desirable behavior, and to create patterns and meaning out of the various transactions that make up organizational life.

The Complementarity of Leadership Approaches. Effective organizational reorientation requires both magic and instrumental leadership. Magic leadership is needed to generate energy, create commitment, and direct people toward new objectives. Instrumental leadership is needed to ensure that people really do act in a manner consistent with their new goals. Either style alone is insufficient for the achievement of change.

The complementarity of leadership approaches (House, 1987) and the necessity for both creates a dilemma. Success in implementing these approaches seems to be associated with the personal style, characteristics, needs, and skills of the leader. Thus a person who is adept at one approach may have difficulty executing the other. Magic leaders, for example, may have problems with the tasks involved in achieving control. Many magic leaders have narcissistic tendencies, and in fact a certain degree of narcissism may be necessary if they are to be effective. The problem is that these leaders are frequently motivated by a strong desire to be loved by those around them. They therefore have problems delivering negative messages, dealing with performance problems, or creating situations where they may be likely to be the object of displeasure. The implication is that only the truly exceptional leader can cover the range of both approaches. While such leaders do exist, an alternative may be to involve others in leadership roles in order to complement the strengths and weaknesses of the individual leader.

The limitations of the individual leader (of either type) pose a significant challenge. Magic leadership has a broad reach. It can influence many people, but it depends on the frequency and intensity of contact with the individual leader. Instrumental leadership too is limited by the degree to which the individual leader can structure, observe, measure, and reward behavior. In large organizations, these limitations constitute significant problems for achieving reorientation. One implication is that structural extensions of leadership need to be created in the process of managing reorientations (see Nadler, 1987). A second implication is that human extensions of leadership need to be created to broaden the scope and impact of the leader's actions. This leads to a third aspect of leadership and change—the extension of leadership beyond the individual leader (that is, the creation of institutionalized leadership).

Institutionalizing the Leadership of Change

Given the limitations of the magic leader, the challenge is how to broaden the range of individuals who can perform the critical leadership functions during periods of significant organizational change. There are three leverage points for the extension of leadership—building the senior team, broadening the senior management, and developing leadership throughout the organization.

Leveraging the Senior Team. Those who report directly to the individual leader—the executive or senior team—are the first logical place to look for opportunities to extend and institutionalize leadership. Development of an effective, visible, and dynamic senior team can be a major step in getting around the problems and limitations of the individual leader. Several actions are important in building the senior team as an effective element of leadership in reorientations:

- *Visible empowerment of the team.* A first step is the visible empowerment of the team. This is equivalent to anointing the team as an extension of the individual leader. There are two different aspects to this empowerment: objective and symbolic. Objective empowerment involves providing team members with the autonomy and resources to serve effectively as leaders of elements of the reorientation. Symbolic empowerment involves the creating and communicating of messages (through information, symbols, and mundane behavior) telling the organization that these executives are indeed extensions of the leader and, ultimately, key components of the leadership as an institution. Symbolic empowerment can be done through the use of titles, the designation of organizational structures (office of the chairman, executive committee), the visible presence of individuals in ceremonial roles, and so forth.
- *Individual development of team members.* Empowerment will fail if team members are not capable of picking up the mantle or leveraging their anointed status. A major problem in having these people lead the organization through change is that the members of the senior team are frequently the product of the very systems, structures, and values in need of reorientation. Participating in the change (and, more important, leading the change) may require a significant switching of cognitive gears. It demands that the senior team members think very differently about the business and also about managing. A big problem in many reorientations is getting senior team members to deal effectively with increased ambiguity and uncertainty. This need for personal change at the most senior level has implications for the selection of

senior team members. It also may mean that one role of the individual leader is to coach, guide, and support executives in developing their own personal leadership capabilities. Team members should not be clones of the individual leader; they should be able to initiate credible leadership in a manner consistent with their own personal styles. Ultimately, the leader must deal with those who are unwilling or unable to make the personal changes required to participate in leading the reorientation.

- *Composition of the senior team.* Since the senior team must serve in the leadership of change, it may become necessary to change the composition of that team. Different skills, capacities, styles, and value orientations may be called for. In fact, most successful reorientations involve significant changes in the makeup of the senior team. This may require exporting some people and importing others—frequently people from outside the organization or at least outside the coalition that has traditionally led the organization.

- *Inducement of strategic anticipation.* A critical issue in organizational reorientations is strategic anticipation. By definition, a reorientation is a strategic organizational change that is initiated in anticipation of external events that may demand strategic change later on. Reorientation occurs because the organization's leadership thinks it can gain competitive advantage from initiating the changes earlier rather than later. The question is: Who is responsible for anticipating external events and ultimately deciding that reorientation is necessary? In some cases, the individual leader does this, but the task is enormous. Here the senior team can be helpful because as a group it can scan a greater number of events and think more imaginatively about the environment and the process of anticipation. Successful companies create conditions where anticipation is likely to occur. They invest in activities that are likely to improve anticipation such as environmental scanning, probes inside the organization (frequently on the periphery), and frequent contacts with the outside. The senior team has a major role in initiating, sponsoring, and leveraging these activities.

- *The senior team as a learning system.* For a senior team to benefit from involvement in the leadership of change, it must become an effective system for learning about the business, the nature of change, and the task of managing the change. The challenge is to bond the team together while at the same time preventing insularity or an inward focus in the team. The dark side of such team structures is that they become isolated from the rest of the organization; they develop patterns of dysfunctional conformity, avoid conflict, and in time develop patterns of learned incompetence. All of this undermines the team's ability to engage in effective strategic anticipation and provide effective leadership of the reorientation process. One way to avoid such an outcome is to work hard to keep the team an open system receptive to ideas and information from outside. This can be accomplished by creating a constant stream of events that expose people to new ideas—inviting speakers or visitors to meet with the team, arranging visits by the team to other organizations, ensuring frequent contact with customers, and planning "deep contact" in the organization (informal and nondisruptive regular data collection through personal contact at breakfasts, focus groups, and the like). A second approach involves shaping and managing the internal group process of the team itself—by ensuring effective group leadership, building team members' skills, creating management discipline, acquiring group problem-solving and information-processing skills, and ultimately creating norms that promote effective learning, innovation, and problem solving.

As a final note on senior teams, keep in mind that frequently there are significant obstacles to developing effective senior teams to lead changes. The issues of skills and selection have been mentioned, but more important is the question of power and succession. A team is most successful when there is a perception of a common fate. In short: People have to believe that the team's success will, in the long run, be more salient to them than their individual short-run success. Often this can be accomplished through appropriate structures, objectives, and incentives. When there are pending decisions to be made concerning senior management succession, however, the quality of collaboration tends to deteriorate significantly and effective team leadership of change becomes problematic. The implication is that the individual leader needs to manage the timing and process of succession so that the team continues to work together effectively and the situation does not create conflicting (and mutually exclusive) incentives.

Broadening Senior Management. A second step in moving beyond individual leadership of change is the extension of leadership beyond the executive and the senior team to include the senior management of the organization. This group would include people one or two levels down from the executive team. Ranging in size from 30 to 120 people, this group is in fact the senior operating management of most sizable organizations and is regarded as senior management by most employees. However, in many cases (particularly during times of change) they do not feel like senior management, and thus they are not positioned to lead the change. They feel like participants (at best) and victims (at worst). This group can be particularly problematic since they may be more embedded in the current system of organizing and managing than some of the senior team, they may be less prepared to change, they frequently have modeled themselves to fit the current organizational style, and they may feel disenfranchised by the strong executive team set above them (particularly if that team has been assembled by bringing in people from outside the organization).

The task, then, is to make this group feel like senior management, to get their commitment to the change, and to motivate them to work as an extension of the senior team. Although many of the implications are those mentioned above in relation to the top team, here there are problems of size and a lack of proximity to the magic leader. Part of the answer is to get the senior team to take responsibility for developing their own teams as leaders of change. Other specific actions may include:

- *Rites of passage.* Creating symbolic events that help these people to feel part of senior management.

- *Senior groups.* Creating structures (councils, boards, committees, conferences) to maintain contact with this group and again signify their participation as members of senior management.
- *Participation in planning change.* Involving these people in the early diagnosing of the need to change and the planning of change strategies associated with the reorientation. This approach is particularly useful in getting them to feel they are managers of the change rather than its victims.
- *Intensive communication.* Maintaining a constant stream of open communication to and from this group. It is the lack of information and perspective that disenfranchises these people psychologically and makes them feel excluded.

Developing Leadership in the Organization. A third opportunity for enhancing the leadership of reorientations is through the organizational structures, systems, and process for the development of leadership. These aspects frequently lag behind the reorientation, when they should be in tune with strategic anticipation. The management development system of many organizations frequently creates managers who fit well with the organizational set that the leadership seeks to change. The implication is that there must be strategic and anticipatory thinking about certain aspects of the leadership development process:

- *Definition of managerial competence.* The first step is determining the skills and capacities needed to manage and lead during the reorientation period and after. Factors that have contributed to managerial success in the past may represent the seeds of failure in the future.
- *Recruiting managerial talent.* Reorientations may require the organization to find new sources for acquiring leaders or potential leaders. Senior managers need to be involved in the process of recruiting and hiring. Because of the lead time involved, managerial recruiting has to be approached as a long-term task (five to ten years).
- *Socialization.* As people enter the organization and move into positions of leadership, deliberate actions need to be taken

to teach them how the social system of the organization works. During periods of reorientation, the socialization process must lead rather than lag behind the change.

- *Management education.* Reorientation may require managers and leaders to use new skills, competencies, or knowledge. This need in turn creates a demand for effective management education. Since recent research indicates that internal management education may have less impact on the development of effective leaders than their job experiences, exposing people to external settings or ideas and socializing them may be more useful than trying to teach them to be effective leaders and managers.

- *Career management.* Research and experience indicate that the most potent factor in the development of effective leaders is the nature of their job experiences. The challenge is how to ensure that people get the appropriate experiences. Preparing people to lead reorientations may mean a major rethinking of the types of experiences that people need (by situation and problem rather than by function or discipline). It may require designing processes to ensure that people get the right experiences, sharing the burden of career management between the organization and the employee, and, finally, balancing current contribution with investment for the future when placing people in job assignments.

- *Seeding talent.* Developing leadership for change may also require deliberate leveraging of the available talent. This implies thoughtful placement of individual leaders in different situations and parts of the organization, the use of transfers, and the whole notion of strategic placement.

Summary

We have outlined a way of thinking about leadership of strategic organizational change and, in particular, the task of building effective leadership for reorientations. Our starting point was that there are different types of organizational change that make different demands and pose different challenges. In strategic organizational change (and, in this case, reorientations) the role of leadership is central and an absolutely critical condition for success. We have tried to define what is required and to expand the view of what is involved in the leadership of organizational change.

At the broadest level, we argue that we must deal with three basic issues: *excitement* of the organization and individuals to change through the concept of the magic leader, *control* of behavior through structuring, controlling, and rewarding, and finally *institutionalization* of leadership by moving beyond the individual leader and focusing on the senior team, the senior management, and the question of leadership development through the organization. Leadership is an issue that has stimulated years of study and still eludes our full understanding. Leadership and organizational change pose even greater challenges for understanding. The task is critical, however, if we are to learn how to build more effective organizations.

References

Bass, B. M. *Performance Beyond Expectations.* New York: Academic Press, 1985.

Beckhard, R., and Harris, R. *Organizational Transitions.* Reading, Mass.: Addison-Wesley, 1977.

Bennis, W., and Nanus, B. *Leaders: The Strategies for Taking Charge.* New York: Harper & Row, 1985.

Berlew, D. E. "Leadership and Organizational Excitement." In D. A. Kolb, I. M. Rubin, and J. M. McIntyre (Eds.), *Organizational Psychology.* Englewood Cliffs, N.J.: Prentice-Hall, 1974.

Burns, J. M. *Leadership.* New York: Harper & Row, 1978.

Campbell, J. P., Dunnette, M. D., Lawler, E. E., and Weick, K. *Managerial Behavior, Performance, and Effectiveness.* New York: McGraw-Hill, 1970.

Goodman, P. A., and Associates (Eds.). *Change in Organizations: New Perspectives on Theory, Research, and Practice.* San Francisco: Jossey-Bass, 1982.

House, R. J. "Path-Goal Theory of Leader Effectiveness." *Administrative Science Quarterly,* 1971, *16,* 321–338.

House, R. J. "A 1976 Theory of Charismatic Leadership." In J. G. Hunt and L. L. Larson (Eds.), *Leadership: The Cutting Edge.* Carbondale: Southern Illinois University Press, 1977.

House, R. J. "Exchange and Charismatic Theories of Leadership." In A. Kaiser, G. Reber, and W. Wunderer (Eds.), *Handbook of Leadership*. Stuttgart: C. E. Poeschel Verlag, 1987.

Kimberly, J. R., and Quinn, R. E. *New Futures: The Challenge of Managing Corporate Transitions*. Homewood, Ill.: Dow Jones–Irwin, 1984.

Lawler, E. E., and Rhode, J. G. *Information and Control in Organizations*. Pacific Palisades, Calif.: Goodyear, 1976.

Nadler, D. A. "Managing Organizational Change: An Integrative Perspective." *Journal of Applied Behavioral Science*, 1981, *17*, 191–211.

Nadler, D. A. *Organizational Framebending: Principles for Managing Re-orientation*. New York: Delta Consulting Group, 1987.

Nadler, D. A., and Tushman, M. L. *Managing Strategic Organizational Change*. New York: Delta Consulting Group, 1986.

Oldham, G. R. "The Motivational Strategies Used by Supervisors: Relationships to Effectiveness Indicators." *Organizational Behavior and Human Performance*, 1976, *15*, 66–86.

Peters, T. J. "Symbols, Patterns and Settings: An Optimistic Case for Getting Things Done." *Organizational Dynamics*, Autumn 1978.

Tichy, N. M., and Devanna, M. A. *The Transformational Leader*. New York: Wiley, 1986.

Tushman, M. L. "Patterns of Organizational Re-orientation." Paper presented at the University of Pittsburgh Conference on Large-Scale Organizational Change, 1986.

Tushman, M. L., and Romanelli, E. "Organizational Evolution: A Metamorphosis Model of Convergence and Reorientation." In B. M. Staw and I. L. Cummings (Eds.), *Research in Organizational Behavior*. Greenwich, Conn.: JAI Press, 1985.

Vroom, V. H. *Work and Motivation*. New York: Wiley, 1964.

7

Social Character and Organizational Change

Michael Maccoby

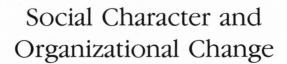

The global market demands that companies produce new, higher-quality products and services. America needs better, more cost-effective services in health, education, and policing. To achieve these goals, business and bureaucracies must eliminate expensive levels of administration and balance control with self-management. Employees must not only work hard but care about cutting costs and satisfying customers. Managers must not only be administrators but also entrepreneurial leaders.

Generally, executives and researchers approach change by focusing on investment, product strategy, technology, organizational roles, structures, and measurement. As I work with businesses and government attempting to adapt to the new environment, I focus on the values and relationships that must also change, and I have tried to integrate them with the other, more easily measurable factors. In this chapter I explain my approach to studying values at work and describe their importance in the case of the Bell System.

Starting in the late 1960s, I began to study the social character of managers and engineers who create new electronic technology at the Bell Labs and other high-tech companies. The managers I interviewed were designing work relations for others. I asked: Did they think about the impact of their work on other people? What motivated them, and how did their own work affect their values? More than 250 managers from ten companies participated in the study because they, too, were intrigued by these questions and hoped that a psychoanalytic exploration would help them understand themselves better and become more effective managers.

Corporate Character

In my book *The Gamesman* (Maccoby, 1976), I outlined four variations in corporate social character and described their influence on organizational behavior. I called these types the Craftsman, the Jungle Fighter, the Company Man, and the Gamesman, terms the high-tech managers were able to use to describe differences in motivation among themselves. The *psychostructure* of a corporation is formed through a process of social selection. Managers tend to rise to the level where character fits the role. These character types have both positive and negative potentials. The positive side is productive and flexible; the negative side is defensive and rigid. Formative experiences and current opportunities determine which side will be expressed. When there is a good fit between the requirements of work and values, people become successful, respond to opportunity, and gain the incentive for positive development. When conditions no longer allow a type to adapt, negative traits become stronger. People feel frustrated, unappreciated, resentful, defensive. Consider, for example, the hardworking, self-reliant farmers who, no longer able to compete against large agribusinesses, become increasingly isolated, angry, and paranoid about the politicians and bankers they blame for their disaster.

Craftsmen value making, building, designing high-quality computer programs or technical systems. They tend to be responsible, self-contained, prudently conservative, and paternalistic. Craftsmen fit easily into a system of masters and apprentices. As leaders, they tend toward perfectionism and seek the one best way to do things. They find it difficult to delegate, for they want to control the whole process and infuse it with their high standards. Craftsmen want to make money, but they are motivated even more by the problem to be solved, the challenge of the work itself, and the satisfaction of creating something of quality. They want to stay with the project from conception to completion, but may not care what use is made of their creations. They can also be uncooperative and unresponsive to the necessity of making a product that does not fit their personal concept of excellence.

Many Craftsmen fit comfortably into expert bureaucratic roles. But as markets, technology, and employees' values change, negative traits emerge more intensely. This is especially the case for Craftsmen in leadership positions. Their emphasis on personal control and one-best-way to do things limits their ability to make use of employees' knowledge.

Jungle Fighters live in a psychological world where they see everyone as either predator or prey. Bold and entrepreneurial, they value survival skills and power. At their best, like the lion, they defend their workplace families. Protectors at the top can create freedom for front-line employees, but Jungle Fighters at middle levels resist sharing power and block the open exchange of information.

Company Men value harmony, cooperation, and identification with the organization. They are other-directed careerists who climb the corporate ladder by making themselves useful to bosses. They flourished in the age of rapid growth of fat American corporations. Typical Company Men are from large families and adapt to the corporation as if it were a new family mediating paternal and fraternal demands for the good of all. At best, they are institutional loyalists who support leadership and defend corporate values. At worst, their drive for consensus and fear of conflict drags the organization toward mediocrity, and their drive for status makes them into turf-oriented bureaucrats. As corporations struggle to become lean and competitive, the negative side of the Company Men is fueled by fear of the future and by confusion about their roles.

Gamesmen are highly competitive people who love change and want to influence its course. They like to take calculated risks and are fascinated by technique and new methods. They see a developing project, human relations, and their own careers in terms of options and possibilities, as if they were games. Their characters are collections of near-paradoxes understood in terms of adaptation to the needs of the business. They are detached and playful, but compulsively driven to succeed, team players but would-be superstars, team leaders but often rebels against bureaucratic hierarchy, tough and dominating, but fair and unprejudiced.

In *The Leader* (Maccoby, 1981) I contrasted the detached, deal-cutting Gamesmen, who were managing America into industrial decline, with the creative Gamesmen-Innovators who were stretching themselves to become developers of organization, people, and new uses of technology. I described pioneers in creating cooperation and involving all employees in management. In *The Leader* I also predicted the emergence of a new social character for whom the dominant meaning of work is self-development. Since writing that book, I have interviewed many self-developers at work and, through surveys, I have charted the growth in their numbers in *Why Work* (Maccoby, 1988).

During the past five years, my colleagues and I have interviewed and surveyed people at all levels of business and government about the values that motivate them at work. On the basis of more than 300 interviews and over 3,000 questionnaires we have named new types according to their positive motivating values: *Expert, Helper, Defender, Innovator,* and *Self-Developer.* These new types are broader than those of *The Gamesman* and make it easier to see that people can express a combination of these values. Experts include Craftsmen; a subgroup of Helpers are Company Men; lionlike Jungle Fighters are a type of Defender; creative Gamesmen are Innovators.

Transforming the Bell Bureaucracy

In 1977, the management of American Telephone and Telegraph Company invited me to lecture to its corporate policy seminar on the Bolivar Project as the first successful American union/management effort to improve the quality of working life. However, most Bell System managers were not interested in the small auto parts factory in Bolivar, Tennessee, where Harman

Industries and the United Auto Workers had developed their model for the auto industry. They wanted to hear me talk about *The Gamesman,* which had been published a few months before and which spoke to their immediate concerns. Identifying themselves as Craftsmen-Experts and Company Men (there were few women) dedicated to a spirit of service, they felt threatened by the newly recruited Gamesmen-Marketeers who were ridiculing their style. They wanted advice on how to deal with them. Only a few recognized that the traditional Bell System managerial character was too cautious and inflexible for a fast-arriving competitive market.

Among the latter was Rex Reed, Bell System's vice-president of industrial relations. He also saw the need for a new approach to management that would make better use of people. He believed that the Bolivar Project and the subsequent quality of worklife experiment at the GM assembly plant in Tarrytown, New York, were promising models for the Bell System. His team had surveyed Bell employees over a five-year period and found disturbing trends. Although satisfied with pay and benefits, and proud of their service to customers, both workers and supervisors were unhappy with new technology and what they considered oppressive supervisory control. They felt they were overcontrolled, pushed around, not listened to, and that the spirit of service was being eroded by the expert drive to cut costs and automate work.

AT&T had subcultures. The elite experts of the Bell Labs valued science and rationality, collegiality and conviviality, as they built the technology that, combined with sophisticated operating and management systems, provided high-quality, widely available, reasonably priced, and reliable telephone service. Unfortunately, it also required extensive controls over the people who made it work. Legions of dedicated Company Men in the Bell Operating Companies implemented policy created in the labs. They determined Bell System practices that were sent throughout the country. Managers read these directives and transmitted orders. A worker sitting at a computer was told how to sit, where to put his pencil, and what to do.

The very strengths of the system were its weaknesses. Uniformity of policy, standardization, and technology-driven, top-down control created economies of scale—and a culture of level consciousness, rigid regulation, Bell-shaped heads with internal regulators that censured new ideas.

A salesman from a computer company confessed that he kept a set of calling cards with different titles on them to present to Bell System managers. Bell vice-presidents would talk only to the same rank from another company, and so on down the hierarchy. New ideas received a hearing only if offered by certified experts approved by Bell Labs.

Right before divestiture, an anonymous gallows humorist circulated a six-page Bell System Burial Plan. The Kafkaesque plan described eligibility (''the company believes, without reservation, that all employees deserve the right to die and therefore deserve appropriate disposition'') and benefits depending on level. First-level managers were entitled to a burial ceremony with beer party at the nearest volunteer fire department, VFW Post, or Knights of Columbus meeting hall. The executive level got a wine and cheese party in the executive dining hall and were laid to rest in burial containers including a ''Mr. Coffee, carpet at least three inches thick, and burial companions of choice.'' In between were carefully graded alternatives. This humor was not only a critique of the bureaucratic mind, it also expressed a sense of tragedy and mourning concerning the breakup of the system and the fragmenting of relationships that had provided the best telephone service in the world.

This expert-dominated system built on supreme rationality sometimes produced absurd irrationalities. Drivers in Manhattan and Casper, Wyoming, were allotted the same amount of time to park their trucks. In Cleveland, the computer determined that operators who arrived at 8:00 A.M. should take a break at 8:15 because that was the time the phone traffic was lightest. When the workers then asked to come in at 8:15, they were told it would be against the rules.

Managers felt powerless to change things. The demand for uniformity and reliability created a culture of anonymous authority. The rules and measurements were the authority. Success depended on working the system, giving your manager what was required and measured, not what *you* considered reasonable or right.

Managers moved up the ladder by getting measured results based on meeting budgets (learn how to ask for more than you need, budget, and never spend over, even if spending would increase revenue and profit), doing well on customer audits, and fulfilling management-by-objectives (MBO) demands that might put participation in the community fund on the same level with cutting costs. Unlike a business that gives service to gain profits, Bell System managers thought of profits as a means to giving good service. Their real customers, the ones they had to satisfy, were not the users of telephones but the rate commissions that allowed a fixed profit over whatever costs AT&T could persuade them to accept.

To make the system work more effectively, lower-level managers needed sometimes to challenge the anonymous authority of expert systems and affirm common sense. A few Innovators did, but most were themselves Experts in awe of the superior scientific experts of the labs, locked into the system not only by interest but also by their social character.

One 33-year-old midwestern clerk, a Self-Developer, expressed her feelings of resignation and fear, similar to those I had heard from many employees: "Most of all, I dislike the poor relationship between management and subordinates. I don't like tiers, class structure, or higher and lower. I dislike that greatly."

When I asked "How would you like work changed?" she responded: "More technical thinking, decision-making work. Now my work is repetitious and doesn't require brains. I'm looking for more advanced or involved responsibilities. This is an office where there's a lot of technical knowledge to be known, it's a state-of-the-art office. I could do financial reports or learn more about different machines. Programming, other functions, different jobs that I'd assist someone in and further my knowledge. Some days aren't filled. At one point, they seemed to say, 'Perhaps we could let her in on some of these things.' But they're so cautious.

"It's hard to define where my role ends and someone else's begins. Times I feel confident and do it, yet some little man in my head is saying, 'You're stepping out of bounds.'

Personally, I feel capable of taking on more work, yet I know this is not how it's done. The bottom line, when somebody is dumped on, it's the little person who gets the biggest scolding. If you step out of bounds, you blow it. Bell has written everything down, just like the military.

"I had a dream that I was sitting at this computer. I had input information that was incorrect. It came back saying, 'This information is incorrect.' Then the printer starts spitting out, 'This is incorrect. You did it intentionally.' Then the printer and computer grew larger than life and spoke, 'You are in trouble!' I saw myself become quite distressed. I screamed and hollered that it wasn't true. It was a nightmare.

"In the actual situation in the office, they looked for a motive for why the error was made. I had input the data and they made me feel I had done it intentionally. It took them two or three weeks to find the error, which was in the data I had been given."

In January 1978, Reed invited me to meet with the presidents of the twenty-two Bell System companies and top AT&T executives to present new approaches to raising morale and improving service. Those present agreed they should moderate the rigid bureaucratic system, but there was no consensus about how to do so. Before competition and divestiture had forced a new outlook on management, their concern was as much humane as economic. They mentioned their own work history, how some had started as linesmen or clerks, and had moved up with the help of friends. "Working for the Bell System has been more than making a buck," one said. "We have the obligation to make it a good place to work for others. Everyone should feel important, respected, needed."

This meeting stimulated experiments in participative management, but most were without union involvement. In fact, some middle managers I met in regional operating companies got angry when I suggested they should cooperate with the union. Relations between the Communications Workers of America (CWA) and AT&T had been stormy in parts of the country. Strikes had caused violence and bitter feelings. The processing of grievances was a sizable business itself keeping hundreds of managers and union officials employed. Although relationships at the top, particularly between Reed and CWA President Glenn Watts, were cordial and respectful, at lower levels there was considerable distrust.

As in many American companies, mangement tended to view the union as a symptom of failure to create a good workplace. Bell System managers were proud of their achievement—building a great company, providing universal service—and of Bell Labs' role in creating new technology. In the view of executives, management was identified with science and productivity, while the union represented unproductive politics. Yet managers and workers in the operating companies shared strong values of service, technical craftsmanship, and pride in the company. In contrast to other industries, where workers and managers may come from different cultural backgrounds, in the Bell System they often came from the same family. But top management's sense of superiority seemed to divide union and management, obscure the shared values, and impede productive cooperation.

In the spring of 1978, Robert H. Gaynor, vice-president of AT&T Long Lines (the long-distance company), began a change project with his managers in Kansas City. Gaynor, an innovative leader in shifting AT&T to a more market-oriented business, believed that this could not be achieved by decree, that managers had to analyze the changing market together and persuade themselves that competition required new approaches. After I had given a talk to his management group based on interviews with first- and second-level managers, Gaynor hired me as a consultant to the change project. Through interviews with their peers, a research team of AT&T managers in Kansas City defined the problems: the need for innovative leadership as opposed to turf-oriented administrators; the need for measurements and control systems more supportive of teamwork; and the burden of a planning process which, like that of most large companies, was mainly extrapolation from past demand according to future demographic trends. The managers believed the planning process should become more strategic, making use of what they were learning from customers, to determine how they would allocate resources. They should start thinking about satisfying customers rather than extrapolating market trends based on past sales.

Most managers believed change was essential, but they were anxious that AT&T's positive values—the spirit of service, high standards, integrity, and technical excellence—be preserved in the new corporate culture. They questioned the integrity of companies they saw condoning lying or misleading customers in order to make a sale. I was asked to help create more open and participative management, starting with Gaynor's relationships with his direct subordinates. By January, 1980, we had improved management teamwork and had also learned that participative management required competent leadership. Without a leader to defend clear goals and values, participative decisions would become compromises, balancing interests at the expense of the whole. The managers decided that good leaders made use of subordinate information, encouraged constructive criticism, consulted on decisions, gave reasons, but did not take votes. Good leaders provided help to subordinates. Leadership was in this sense good bureaucratic administration befitting a monopoly, not yet the entrepreneurial leadership demanded by competition.

We had also addressed organizational problems such as bad measurement systems that allowed one department to gain points by cutting costs and withholding new equipment from another at the expense of increased revenue. But the participative process had not yet reached the worker level and did not yet include the union.

In January, 1980, Ronnie J. Straw, director of research at CWA, called and asked if I would advise the union on how it should approach AT&T to gain greater participation in management. The CWA wanted to explore a range of possibilities from membership on the AT&T board to shop floor participation. Was I interested?

Very much so. I believed the CWA under Watts was an exceptionally forward-looking union; under his leadership members had supported technological advances that improved productivity. But the union was dissatisfied for some of the same reasons that had moved Rex Reed. I had read in the newspapers that its members were disaffected by new technology and were asking union leadership to do something about job stress. I believed that a strong, informed CWA would both further the interests of its members and put pressure on the Bell System to improve its management. Both union and management could benefit from the project I was being asked to undertake.

But I was an AT&T management consultant. Watts would have to decide whether or not he trusted me. Moreover, I would not take the job unless it was approved by Reed. There were two reasons for this: First, I was uncertain about the ethics of bringing knowledge of Bell System management to the union; and second, I wanted to keep alive the chance to work with both parties on the development of participative approaches.

Watts liked the idea that I was familiar with the Bell System; it would save time. I wouldn't have to learn from scratch. Furthermore, John Carroll, CWA executive vice-president, had attended the AT&T corporate policy seminar at which I urged management to cooperate with the union, and he had supported the Bolivar model. Reed had no objections. He agreed that a stronger, more knowledgeable union would push management to improve whereas a weaker, more reactive union would be less able to understand and support change.

To maintain membership today, unions must be competent service businesses. The best ones are also more than this—democratic clubs that provide fraternity, mutual aid, a sense of community beyond economic self-interest. Union leaders feel they are part of a movement for greater justice, but unless they satisfy their member customers, they will go out of business. And workers want to participate in management.

More than 80 percent of AT&T employees surveyed in 1981 and 1983, and again in 1985, indicated they would volunteer to join problem-solving teams. A Harris Poll commissioned by the AFL-CIO in 1984 indicated that one reason workers are disaffected from unions is that they believe union leaders block participation in such teams.

Like oligopolistic American companies, big unions became complacent and bureaucratic during the fifties and sixties, the period of U.S. domination of industrial markets. Like a culture of noncommissioned officers in the military, CWA mirrored the hierarchy and status consciousness of Bell System management. To support bottom-up change, it had to become involved in new approaches to improving the quality of working life and its leaders had to learn new skills.

To develop a strategy for CWA, I proposed that Straw and I together interview union leadership about what changes they would support. A few years before, the union had hired a consulting firm to advise it on becoming more effective. The consultant had written a report criticizing the union hierarchy and suggesting structural changes, but the report was filed away unused. Proposals for change are a likely threat to those who are adapted to and benefit from the status quo. I wanted CWA to own the study and the strategy, which meant that its leaders had to participate from the start.

Straw and I and others (including Charles Hechscher and Richard Balzer) interviewed the union executive board and more than 100 local officers from all over the country. We asked Reed and his aide Gene Kofke to find examples of what they considered the best participative management projects at AT&T, and then we asked local union leaders to evaluate them. In this way, I hoped to begin shaping models for change that had been invented and already tested within the system.

A consensus emerged: The union leaders believed that in recent years management had tightened to prepare for deregulated competition; workers believed they could give better service with less monitoring (both electronically listening to operators and supervisory policing of workers in offices, trucks, and switching plants).

Union officials reported a number of attempts to improve morale through increased participation, but they were usually short-lived. Very few of the attempts tried to involve the union. Some had actually caused grievances when "participation" resulted in actions considered in violation of the contract. In the "Five-Minute Solution," for example, Mountain Bell management videotaped operators who were asked to criticize co-workers who came late and were slower in processing calls.

The local presidents we interviewed did not favor union participation on the AT&T board. They questioned the business competence of union leaders, and some felt the union was already too close to management. They were skeptical of joint committees that had done little in the past. They liked the idea of a quality-of-worklife program in offices and garages, based on the Bolivar model and its development at GM and the UAW at the Tarrytown assembly plant. In fact, CWA leaders in Detroit were currently taking part in joint initiatives of this sort and were enthusiastic about the results: Grievances had been reduced and workers felt more respected.

When I reported these findings to the union executive board in July 1980, Watts asked me to draft an article for the contracts he was then negotiating with Reed. I recommended joint sponsorship of participative experiments. The final agreement included a national committee with the following function:

- Developing and recommending principles and objectives relative to working conditions and service quality improvement that will guide experiments or projects such as quality circles, problem-solving teams, and the like, in various work stations. These should be designed to encourage teamwork, to make work more satisfying, and to improve the work operation.
- Reviewing and evaluating programs and projects that involve improving the quality of the work environment.
- Arranging for any outside consultants it feels are necessary to assist it, the expenses to be shared equally by the company and the union.

The national committee first met in the fall of 1980. It could agree neither on principles nor on a strategy. Some management members wanted to take a relatively passive role, supporting whatever Bell local companies initiated. They viewed quality-of-worklife (QWL) programs as a step toward healthy decentralization and wanted to avoid the traditional AT&T role of control. The unions distrusted this laissez-faire measure because it legitimized approaches they considered antiunion;

they were getting messages from local leaders that participative programs were causing problems. If the national committee was not to direct the QWL programs, CWA members wanted it at least to control the quality of the programs and set minimum standards. Unsure of what to do, the union proposed that I be retained as consultant to the committee. Management resisted the idea.

The debate was not so much about my competence as about the committee's role. AT&T had no objection to my continuing as a consultant to its management. When they agreed to hire me on the national committee, it was a decision to be more active centrally and to give the union more power. If one of two parties is stronger, as was AT&T compared to CWA, hiring a third party paid equally by both inevitably increases the status and power of the weaker. Once I was hired, however, Reed defined my role as helping to develop the change strategy and creating a corps of internal consultants so that AT&T would not have to hire outside consultants who might bring in approaches that undermined the union/management cooperation.

We organized a series of meetings with union and company labor-relations leaders, where I described the quality-of-worklife process, its potential benefits and risks, and the skills and relationships necessary to make it work. The process was meant to make the company more competitive and the union more effective in serving members. But to succeed, I argued, both union and management had to change. Management had to share power and information, and the union had to learn more about the business, work cooperatively to strengthen it, and agree that ongoing QWL projects would not be held hostage during unrelated conflicts. Quality-of-worklife projects should not be a substitute for collective bargaining but a development of bargaining into issues of mutual benefit.

At these meetings, union and management groups then caucused separately to discuss what they wanted from QWL projects and what they thought the other side wanted. Then they shared their hopes and suspicions. There was high trust in some companies, especially where top managers had discussed technology changes and ways to reduce grievances with union leaders. In other companies, there was little trust. Even where top leaders had created a good relationship, lower levels might be wary. Some managers were insecure, overcontrolling, or insultingly paternalistic; some union leaders wanted to make all deals themselves and feared giving more power to members who might criticize them or discover they did not need either managerial or union bosses.

In later meetings, Richard Walton and I facilitated efforts by top union leaders and operating executives to develop shared visions of work. Our strategy for the first four years was to support leaders from union and management who volunteered to begin the process. As a result of these efforts, a training package was developed and we held experience-sharing meetings to showcase successful projects and draw lessons. Research by an internal union/management team and by outside academics (sponsored by the U.S. Department of Labor) proved useful to demonstrate the value of QWL programs and to show that they required leadership and resources to produce results (U.S. Department of Labor, 1985).

By January 1, 1984, when the Bell System was broken up into AT&T and seven regional operating companies, a final survey of employees indicated that more than 90,000 of the million employees were involved in QWL activities, and labor/management cooperation had survived a strike in 1983. This breakup of the Bell System was traumatic, especially for the many expert Company Men who had adapted so well to the monopoly system. There were deep feelings of loss, resentment against leaders they felt had let them down, and fear of the future. In the upheaval of divestiture, some promising beginnings of participation ground to a halt. In other places, experimentation had gone far, especially when pushed forward by market forces. The Innovators, Self-Developers, and Helpers responded with particular enthusiasm to the new opportunities.

A thirty-year-old Helper/Self-Developer in the Midwest describes how the process increased her sense of confidence, competence, meaning, dignity, and motivation: "The QWL Clerical Committee brought us administration people a lot closer together, and it opened up some eyes among managers that the clerks were taking a more positive approach to their jobs because of it. Personally, it helped me learn how to communicate with peers and management. I'm not so afraid now. I feel more at ease. . . . I've changed. Someone made a comment: 'Linda, you look different. Your eyes, you seem older or wiser.' I thought about that. Being involved has helped me. I'm more outward, that's the biggest thing. I've always been impressed with QWL, but the Clerical Committee gave me the opportunity to make all the administrative jobs better. I felt good in helping make someone's job easier.''

I am continually impressed and moved by seeing insecure people gain competence and confidence to speak out, question inefficiency, propose and justify new approaches. Within the QWL process, people who have been made to feel inferior by the sorting process of school and bureaucracy, the narrow jobs, expand in mastery and sense of personal value.

The market-driven, automated-service workplace requires that workers have the capability and freedom to solve problems where they occur—to satisfy customers—without waiting for hierarchical approval. The QWL process supports this change and moves management from the philosophy of One Best Way, determined at the top, to many ways of making company strategy work. It moves from the idea of one big Bell Lab brain controlling the system to the notion of many individual brains creating a customer-responsive human network that learns.

Typically, these participative programs have started with a first generation of worker committees that deal with bottom-up concerns. Unless these committees evolve into a second generation where management starts delegating from the top downward, the worker groups go no further than solving problems that make work more bearable (moving desks, getting a Coke machine, flexitime), but not more interesting or more efficient. In the second generation, the process of delegating to teams starts at the top and includes teams of managers as well as workers (Maccoby, 1986). At the office level, employees not only propose ideas, but they also address managerial problems. They are told what needs to be done, but they themselves determine how to do it and what it will cost. In the process, they begin to redesign roles, rules, and measurements.

In one Michigan Bell office, a team did away with unnecessary documentation and saved the company over a million dollars a year. In Florida, a team of network employees determined their own schedule and decided how they will solve problems for customers. Another example was a hotel and billing office in Tempe, Arizona, with 120 operators. Through the QWL process, the operators ran the office. Although some workers (especially Self-Developers) were enthusiastic about self-management, more traditional types missed having supervisors to reward and encourage them (and perhaps also to serve as a target for frustration). Furthermore, the QWL committee found it difficult to deal with disciplinary issues. The one manager complained that her phone rang day and night with requests to solve problems. From the Tempe experience, AT&T management and union organized an operator office in Denver with one manager to thirty-five operators and more training in self-management.

An even more advanced ''technoservice'' workplace is American Transtech, a fully owned AT&T subsidiary that evolved from the Stock and Bond Division through a quality-of-worklife process that transformed roles, reward systems, and the computerized system. At Transtech, front-line teams set their own schedules and within guidelines decide how to satisfy customers. They are encouraged to propose business ideas and, in some cases, try them out. They regularly see the financial results of their work and have monthly reports on profitability. Part of their compensation is profit sharing. The role of managers is to serve as resources, facilitators, and educators at the first level and entrepreneurs or service-providers (marketing, advertising) on higher levels.

Although Transtech is not unionized, the model is applicable to cooperative union/management projects. Its organization is similar to that proposed by a General Motors/United Auto Workers team for its Saturn plant in Tennessee. In the plans for that plant, union stewards will become team facilitators and local UAW officials will participate on management's business strategy team.

In unionized companies, such a process requires support by competent, informed union leadership. In second-generation

QWL projects, local union presidents meet regularly with district managers to plan together how to implement technology, force changes, and conduct training. Ideally, national leadership participates in such planning at the corporate level. This is now happening in various parts of AT&T. Stimulated by the QWL concept, CWA discovered that its own staff echoed some of the same complaints as did Bell employees—overcontrol, lack of respect, need for more training. The union leadership asked me to help initiate an internal QWL process in order to strengthen its ability to serve its members.

AT&T Adapts

While the Regional Bell Operating Companies held onto their monopoly control of local telephone service as they also moved out into competitive ventures, AT&T faced competition across the board. It was forced to change in order to cut costs and satisfy customers. At AT&T the market requires work to change in two major ways. First there are the changes at the front line with over 9 million daily interactions between customers and operators, service techs, sales and billing people. Customers are satisfied, efficiency is gained, and costs are cut when employees are free to respond and make decisions without asking permission. This requires that employees replace their bureaucratic compliance with business understanding. Levels of hierarchy are costly and interfere with communication, both from strategists at the top and from the front line up. Front-line employees learn the skills of communication and teamwork through QWL programs and quality training. Second, big customers demand complex, customized products and services. To provide them, AT&T must develop teamwork that breaks down barriers between marketing, development, service, and legal turf. Again, new skills of team building and conflict resolution are required.

Driven by these market demands, AT&T has worked at developing various approaches to organization, rewards, and measurements. Managers who were promoted because they were expert administrators now understand that they must learn to be entrepreneurial leaders. To aid this process, I have served a number of managers as organizational strategist, facilitator, and researcher. Using interviews and questionnaires to focus on management style and values, I have participated in designing and evaluating new approaches to organization.

The leading edge at AT&T has been the innovative Gamesmen who were frustrated in the conservative bureaucracy, along with the new breed of employee whose goal at work is continual self-development. Many of the operators, clerks, and secretaries who first volunteered for the QWL approach saw it as a means to self-development. The resistance to change has come mainly from Expert-Administrators who cling tightly to protective bureaucratic systems.

The uneven process of change causes complex human problems, however. Where the first generation of QWL has taken root, it is run by union and management facilitators who become a new interest group. Some of them resist the development of the second generation of participative management in which the supervisor becomes the facilitator-educator. Furthermore, the values of this resource group are typically those of the antihierarchical Helper who sees managers as cold, detached, status-conscious Experts who do not care about people. Such polarization can be avoided only when line managers take responsibility for the change process.

Some managers who recognize the need for change have rejected the QWL process as too bureaucratic and too dependent on union cooperation. Instead, they have introduced similar training through Quality Circle (QC) programs. This has caused those union leaders who support QWL to react strongly and has led to a reaffirmation of a new combined QC/QWL initiative.

The whole relation between union and management is being redefined in the Bell Companies and AT&T. Glenn Watts led his union almost as a division of the Bell System. He retired in 1985 and his successor Morton Bahr must deal with AT&T and independent Bell Operating Companies in a more deregulated marketplace. These companies are not all alike in their managerial philosophy and relationship to the union. While some have continued to develop the cooperative relationship (AT&T, Pacific Bell, and Pacific Northwest Bell are notable examples), others have started nonunion subsidiaries or tried to substitute management-controlled programs for QWL.

The 1986 strikes at AT&T and some of the operating companies caused resentment and further slowed progress. So have massive layoffs at AT&T, which have broken an implicit psychological contract based on employment security. In restructuring, AT&T is defining a new psychological contract based on reciprocity rather than paternalism. This relationship includes company commitment to continued training that allows employees to maintain their marketability. (A step in this direction was the joint AT&T/CWA Alliance, funded to retrain workers.) In return for employees' taking more responsibility to cut costs and satisfy customers, they need to share equitably in company success.

Correspondingly, the union cannot expect management to develop a consultative relationship if union leaders withdraw from cooperative projects over unrelated issues of collective bargaining. The union must recognize that these programs serve its members and that its role is to make sure they are carried out in a way that protects members' interests in terms of employment security, opportunity, fair rewards, and the quality of working life.

Conclusion

My work with large organizations in the process of change has involved an unorthodox mixture of research and participant consulting. This combination has the advantage of providing in-depth knowledge of organizations and actors. It has the disadvantage of clouding objectivity. Since researchers want the project to succeed, they tend to overvalue the actors who share their goals and undervalue those who do not. Given this weakness, it is essential to make one's own values explicit, to maintain a critical attitude toward one's judgment and findings, and to welcome independent evaluation and criticism from colleagues.

Much of the original impulse for change at Bolivar (Macy, Lawler, and Ledford, 1978), AT&T, and other organizations I have worked with comes from strong union leadership with humane motives shared by top management: to make work more satisfying and to alleviate job pressures caused by technology. Improved productivity and union/management cooperation have been by-products of these efforts. Even when QWL projects in the Bell System showed gains in organizational effectiveness, this was not a compelling reason for all of management to jump on the bandwagon. Most managers did not believe the environment required these changes. Furthermore, QWL did not attract many of them. It did not feel right. It threatened them. In terms of social character, participative approaches did not mesh with the Expert's values of control and predictability. But the changing environment of international competition, the demands for customized service, and computerized technology now require organizational change. What was created largely from humanitarian motives becomes necessary for economic adaptation.

Social character is a significant factor in the process of change. It is a force *for* change as people whose social character bridled against the organization now feel liberated; it evokes resistance *against* change in those who were well-adapted and now feel stressed. Not everyone is satisfied with change. Some find it extremely frustrating.

To be a useful analytic tool, social character must be integrated with a holistic approach combining market and organizational strategy. Change today typically requires new behavior from employees. This involves changes in structures, roles, and incentives. But by themselves these factors may not be sufficient to shape behavior. Decentralized teamwork, responsiveness to customers, innovative leadership—all may require a change in values and style. This raises the question: How can people change the quality of their relationships at work? Where we have observed such changes, the following conditions have been met:

- There has been committed leadership presenting a compelling new business strategy, a vision that requires changing organization and work relationships. Leadership models new relationships.
- Everyone is encouraged to participate in the implementation of change and there is a spirit of continual improvement.
- There has been an open dialogue about values in relation to change. This process puts pressure to change on those people whose personal values do not support the organizational implications of the market strategy.

- Measurements and rewards are designed to support the desired values.
- Coaching and training are provided for those at all levels who want to change their style, but inevitably, some middle managers either opt out or are replaced.
- Successes, even small ones, are celebrated.

Even when these conditions are met, the change process is difficult and requires a critical mass of committed leaders at every level. The larger the organization, the greater the opportunity for individual managers to hold out—and the more important it becomes for top management to communicate the urgency for change, to lead the process, and to require that everyone be involved in the strategic dialogue.

I believe these dialogues are most effective when they include social and human, as well as economic and technical, considerations. In such a process, conflict is inevitable—not only because of different interests but also because of different values, especially the Helpers and Self-Developers challenging the Experts and vice versa. By transforming conflict into constructive dialogue about how to serve customers more effectively *and* make work more satisfying, leadership can gain greater involvement and support for change.

References

Maccoby, M. *The Gamesman*. New York: Simon & Schuster, 1976.

Maccoby, M. *The Leader*. New York: Simon & Schuster, 1981.

Maccoby, M. "The New Generation of QWL." *QWL Resource Bulletin*, Vol. 3, No. 1, January 1986, 1–3.

Maccoby, M. *Why Work: Leading the Next Generation*. New York: Simon & Schuster, 1988.

Macy, B.A., Lawler, E. E., and Ledford, G. "The Bolivar Quality of Work Life Experiment." Unpublished manuscript, 1978.

U.S. Department of Labor, Bureau of Labor-Management Relations and Cooperative Programs. *Quality of Work Life: AT&T and CWA Examine Process After Three Years*. Washington, D.C.: Government Printing Office, 1985.

Part Three

Strategies
for Large-Scale
Organizational Change

8

Interventions That Change Organizations

Susan Albers Mohrman
Allan M. Mohrman, Jr.
Gerald E. Ledford, Jr.

What techniques and strategies are appropriate for large-scale organizational change—that is, for fundamental change of complex organizations? Do they exist? What differences do the size of the system and the scale of change make? Do pervasive changes require different techniques than targeted innovations? These are questions for which there are, at best, only partial answers.

Choice of Interventions

Two decades ago Chin and Benne (1985) proposed a typology of strategies for deliberate changing. They saw the typology as relatively inclusive, and the strategies seemed to apply to all levels of social systems. Their aim was to capture the fundamental strategies of deliberate change that had been used throughout recorded history. These three basic strategies are rational-empirical, normative-reeducative, and power-coercive.

Rational-empirical strategies have their roots in the Age of Enlightenment. They include approaches that use logic, the scientific method, research and development, and rational argument

145

to drive change. Heavy reliance on expertise and the dissemination of information is typical. These approaches appeal to the rational aspects that underlie utilitarian approaches to organizing (Etzioni, 1961; Katz and Kahn, 1978). They are based on the assumption that if rational-empirical strategies can uncover better explanations of reality and its cause-effect relationships, people will change their behavior and the ways they organize in order to advance their own self-interest.

Normative-reeducative strategies approach change as a matter of getting the participants to adopt new patterns of behavior by engaging them in activities that lead them to adopt a different set of norms or beliefs about the situation. In this category fall various organizational development (OD) techniques, which aim at increasing problem-solving capacities and fostering growth and development, and organizational design approaches that communicate new relationships and structures. This kind of strategy acts on a different source of behavior in organizations. Much of what people do in organizations has nothing to do with objective reality, as it might be discovered using a rational-empirical approach. Rather, it is based on the common beliefs, values, and norms that people hold. These are the normative aspects of organizations (Etzioni, 1961; Katz and Kahn, 1978). Normative strategies work on a fairly deep aspect of organizational change.

As the name implies, *power-coercive* strategies focus on the power and influence that can be used to create change. Various political approaches apply here, including both revolutionary strategies and reliance on legitimate sources of power, such as organizational position. This category also includes charismatic leaders who use the power of their personality to bring about change. Power-coercive strategies aim directly at the political dynamics that drive organizational behavior. Many approaches to organizing are based on people's political nature. Bureaucratic behavior, for example, is governed by establishing and granting authority based on position. Expertise, money, information, and physical might are alternative sources of power and influence. Power-coercive strategies aim to change organizations either by realigning power relationships or by using power to force other changes.

As we have pointed out, each of these approaches to changing organizations is closely tied to a basis of organization: utilitarian, normative, or political. This relationship raises two questions. First, should the approach to change be congruent with the current model of organizing? For example, will a change strategy that works in organizations that are normatively bound and characterized by a high degree of trust (Ouchi's "clans," 1981) also be effective in organizations where people are linked primarily through their self-interest and norms of exchange (markets) or through notions of legitimate power (bureaucracies)? Second, will the change approach predetermine the outcome for the organization—such that, for example, a coercive, top-down strategy will create an authoritarian organization, not an organization characterized by mutual influence and participative practices?

It is tempting to answer both questions in the affirmative. In some ways, however, the questions are simplistic and misleading. Katz and Kahn (1978) point out that no organization is purely utilitarian, normative, or political; rather, all these dimensions of organizational behavior are interwoven simultaneously. Any change effort will therefore need to deal with all three aspects. Moreover, fundamental organizational change may be aimed at altering the norms and assumptions underlying all three dimensions. The nature of legitimate power, for example, may change from level in the hierarchy to appropriate expertise. The calculation of self-interest may change from individual to collective gain. Rational-empirical approaches may be expanded beyond the issue of technology to include organizational structure and human resources. Normative behavior may change from a reverence for the past to a search for creative change. In each case, interventions and designs that are planned to fit the needs of the current organization may unwittingly reinforce the past and discourage the behavior necessary to accomplish the desired changes.

Typologies such as the one developed by Chin and Benne should not be misconstrued to suggest that one or another approach is sufficient to effect change in a complex organizational system. Change strategies must be multifaceted and consequently able to address the multiple models and realities that exist in the organization. Moreover, they must reinforce and serve as models for the desired behavior. This is a tall order fraught with contradiction and ambiguity.

The different change strategies may nevertheless be useful in different types of organizations. Perhaps the dominant basis of organization may suggest which strategy is to be favored in a particular case. Power-oriented strategies, for example, may be more successful in changing organizations based on political assumptions; perhaps the surest way to change market-based organizations is to change the ground rules for exchange (for example, by changing the reward system). Conversely, large-scale organizational change that is strong in the depth dimension (see Chapter One) may be more likely to succeed if the strategy for change differs from the basis of organization. Organizations based on power, for example, may change least if one charismatic leader replaces another and most if they come to resemble markets or clans through changes in organizing arrangements that make leaders less central and powerful.

Levels of Analysis

In the interventionist's toolbox are approaches that deal with individual, group, organizational, and transorganizational change. Similarly, design elements and the dynamic organizational processes occur at all four levels. Training and development interventions, individual incentive programs, and psychodynamic processes take place at the individual level. Team building, self-managing work groups, and group decision-making processes are team phenomena. Organization-wide survey feedback, policies, gain-sharing plans, and the political collective bargaining process are at the organizational level. Transorganizational approaches (Cummings, 1984) include combinations of organizations—as when quality programs go beyond the boundary of the organization and make demands on suppliers or when communities band together around plant closings. The same questions can be asked here as were asked before: Is there an appropriate focus, does the focus determine the outcome of the change effort, and can there be multiple focuses?

The contributors to this book all believe in approaching organizational change as a multilevel phenomenon. After all, there are individuals, groups, and organization-wide phenomena in all organizations, and a fundamental systemic change will require behavioral changes at all three levels. Nevertheless, several flags of caution should be raised. First, interventions at different levels of analysis can contradict or support one another. A fixed-pie, individual-level incentive system, for example, can reverse the positive impact of the creation of teams at the group level. Team building that stresses the need for cooperation and openness can be offset by organization-wide centralization of decision making and formalization of control processes.

Moreover, it is easy to think that change is occurring at multiple levels when in fact only one level is being affected. Organization-wide training programs, for instance, may have some impact on individual skills and knowledge; the planners of change, however, may believe that because it is being done throughout the organization, it is having organization-wide impact. This may or may not be the case. It all depends on how the training is being done and whether the skills and knowledge are being utilized and reinforced back on the job. Team building with the top management and creating a vision for the organization may be intended to have organization-wide impact. Depending on subsequent interventions, however, it may in fact be an intervention limited, at most, to one group within the organization: the top team. And although creating opportunities for multistakeholder decision making between union and management is essentially an organization-wide phenomenon, management may mistakenly believe they have given increased political power to employees as individuals.

In summary, large-scale organizational change must occur at multiple levels of analysis, but changes at these multiple levels must be carefully orchestrated to ensure that they do not work against one another. Furthermore, it is important to recognize that change activities directed at one level of analysis will spill over and have an impact at the other levels.

Number of Change Levers

Large-scale change, as we have noted, involves changes in multiple subsystems of the organization. Both the design of the organization and the political and normative processes are altered. Individuals, groups, and the organization as a whole will behave and perform differently. It is far easier for change agents to help new organizations develop innovative design features, political processes, and norms than it is to transform an old organization. In a mature organization all design features and processes are part of the status quo and often congruent with one another. Behavior in a well-established setting is determined by numerous forces that are often redundant in their consequences. Therefore, change in one feature alone cannot yield the performance improvements that are demanded of many organizations today.

This line of reasoning argues that the more levers that are utilized—that is, the more variables that are altered—the more likely it is that new behavior patterns will emerge. At the very least, there may be a critical mass of changes required to set up momentum for change. Not much research has been done on this issue, and clearly a number of questions need to be explored. Even so, it is possible to speculate, based on experience, about some potential considerations.

There are limits, it seems, to the number of interventions that an organization can sustain and benefit from, and, moreover, there are certain conditions under which multiple interventions may be more likely to work than others. For example, a start-up involving a large number of nontraditional features may surpass people's ability to learn the necessary skills, internalize the altered norms, and accept the new political processes. Thus our experience suggests that interventions must be staged so that the organization's learning capacity is not overwhelmed. Further, the organization's ability to implement multiple changes is limited by such resources as time, money, and energy.

Under some conditions, multiple interventions might actually sabotage the change process. This would be true if they moved the organization toward a different set of outcomes or way of functioning and thus acted against one another. If deep-seated resistance and anxiety are not dealt with early in the process, multiple interventions may create more apparent change than real change, which can be expected to lead to a great deal of skepticism in the organization. Such skepticism will certainly work against the ultimate goal. These and other considerations suggest how much we still have to learn about large-scale system change. They also lead us to the next consideration: how to sequence various changes and interventions.

Sequencing of Interventions

The literature tends to deal with sequence as stages of the change process. This book's contributors, however, disagree about whether it is possible to prescribe a sequence for interventions and a path along which change should proceed. Perhaps neatly packaged change programs do not fit with the reality of organizations. The change process may vary, depending on the deep-seated worldviews and values held within the organization, the levels of awareness of various organizational and environmental issues, and the political system in place.

A related issue concerns the extent to which the organization should understand the change process in advance versus an approach in which the change agent decides what the organization needs, often without trying to bring the organization to understand the dynamics from the change agent's viewpoint.

Another perspective is that change is neither a neatly planned process nor a gradual development of the deep-seated processes within the organization. Rather, it is a series of small steps that are incremental and opportunistic, gradually changing the character of the organization. Perhaps all the change agent can do is help the organization take advantage of the opportunities that arise.

Again, large-scale organizational change is probably a combination of all these perspectives. Perhaps it can be described as a theoretical sequence that will not be realized unless the worldviews of the participants and normative and political processes are dealt with effectively and greatly enhanced by opportunistic moves.

There is widespread agreement in the book that, in the early stages of the change process, organizational members have to accept a vision of where the organization is trying to move. One observer describes this as achieving an image of the change that has centrality for the organization. It works best when it captures what the organization and its members valued in the past and serves as a rallying point given the organization's new mission and technology.

References

Chin, R., and Benne, K. D. "General Strategies for Effecting Change in Human Systems." In W. G. Bennis, K. D. Benne, and R. Chin (Eds.), *The Planning of Change.* (4th ed.) New York: Holt, Rinehart & Winston, 1985.

Cummings, T. "Transorganizational Development." In B. Staw and L. Cummings (Eds.), *Research in Organizational Behavior.* Vol. 6. Greenwich, Conn.: JAI Press, 1984.

Etzioni, A. *A Comparative Analysis of Complex Organizations.* New York: Free Press, 1961.

Galbraith, J. *Organization Design.* Reading, Mass.: Addison-Wesley, 1973.

Katz, D., and Kahn, R. L. *The Social Psychology of Organizations.* (2nd ed.) New York: Wiley, 1978.

Kilmann, R. H. *Beyond the Quick Fix: Managing Five Tracks to Organizational Success.* San Francisco: Jossey-Bass, 1984.

Leavitt, H. "Applied Organizational Change in Industry." In J. March (Ed.), *The Handbook of Organizations.* Chicago: Rand McNally, 1965.

Lewin, K. *Field Theory in Social Science.* New York: Harper & Row, 1951.

Mohrman, S. A., and Cummings, T. G. *Designing High Performing Systems.* Reading, Mass.: Addison-Wesley, 1989.

Ouchi, W. G. "Relationship Between Organization Structure and Organization Control." *Administrative Science Quarterly,* 1981, *22,* 95–113.

Ouchi, W. *Theory Z.* Reading, Mass.: Addison-Wesley, 1981.

Pettigrew, A. M. "Contextualist Research: A Natural Way to Link Theory and Practice." In E. E. Lawler III and others,

Doing Research That Is Useful for Theory and Practice. San Francisco: Jossey-Bass, 1985.

Porras, J. I., and Robertson, P. "Organization Development Theory: A Typology and Evaluation." In R. W. Woodman and W. A. Pasmore (Eds.), *Research in Organizational Change and Development.* Greenwich, Conn.: JAI Press, 1987.

Quinn, J. B. *Strategies for Change: Logical Incrementalism.* Homewood, Ill.: Irwin, 1980.

Tichy, N. M. *Managing Strategic Change.* New York: Wiley, 1983.

Tichy, N. M., and Devanna, M. A. *The Transformational Leader.* New York: Wiley, 1986.

9

Meta-Praxis:
A Framework for
Making Complex Changes

Will McWhinney

The fervor of the 1960s reawoke hopes that we could create major changes—improvements—in the ways our societies operate: in social relations, in international relations, in the organization of education and work, and in our beliefs about humanity's capacity for achievement. The spirit of revolution animated almost every aspect of human endeavor. New politics, new psychologies, and new social technologies arose—all supporting change. The spirit appeared in so many fields that one cannot identify the single authentic root. Rather, one can find many roots of the movements that arose to overcome social injustice and evoked dreams of a better way of life if not actual utopias. This chapter presents new perspectives on the continuing quest for a higher quality of life in social organizations, particularly the organization of work. It is a search for methods to produce large-scale sustainable changes in the institutions of industry, commerce, education, political administration, and, ultimately, those that support the transformation of humankind.

This quest is as ancient as history. History itself contains many tales of efforts to improve the quality of the secular or sacred life in institutions and in society at large. Thus, in the late

154

1960s, there were innumerable theories, examples, and practices available to us through which we might develop large-scale change efforts in organizations. In many cases the drive was economic, but more commonly it was based on a social or political cause—the desire to reestablish equity between the dominant cultures and depreciated minorities, the desire to achieve the full human potential, or, simply, out of the creative spirit of managers and entrepreneurs, it was a drive to produce more effective social instruments (for example, using the practice of sociotechnical systems and group facilitation). It did seem possible to achieve a sustainable improvement in the quality of working life, providing personal, social, and economic good. The optimism came in part from our success in creating microcosmic prototypes, exemplars that we imagined would spread across to the giant organizations of Western industrial society.

By 1970 there were a number of such prototypes. Most widely publicized were various sociotechnically designed plants such as Volvo plants in Scandinavia and the Pet Food plant in Kansas. Many of these prototypes were successful—so successful economically that Procter & Gamble kept its green-field, open-system production factories under tight wraps to prevent competitors from recognizing the competitive advantage of high-performing factories. These plants appeared then to be the forerunners of whole companies, of industrial and political empires being transformed into exemplary organizations and communities.

I, as well as many others involved in creating such organizations, got high on the possibilities. These open-system organizations, however configured, provided for participation in decision making, for work patterns designed in response to people's needs for social interplay, for power sharing, and for great economy. They were, it seemed then, the foundation of efficient social democracies in the workplace. And some of these plants do continue to operate, more than fifteen years later, at high efficiency and with outstanding humanity. But we still have a long way to go. There has been little spread of the initial work—few of these leading organizations have permitted these models to be replicated even within their own boundaries. It is instructive to note that effective organization of the famous Ahmedabad weaving shed experiment similarly persisted, but there was no success in attempts to replicate it (Miller, 1983).

There were questions even in the first quality of working life (QWL) conference in 1972. From the beginning we saw difficulties in spreading the model to all forms of work or institutions; it was clear that not all employees would participate in humanistic approaches to designing their environments. We also recognized that only in a few cases have the workers come to control significant resources and opportunities. For all our sense of boundless possibility, there were easily apparent limitations and skeptical queries came from all sides—students of the labor movement and experts on religious communities, technologists, economists, and managers all expressed doubt or outright opposition. My own skepticism arose as I recognized that there were few situations in which one could successfully introduce the open-system and similar models of future organizations. As we moved into the disillusionments of the 1970s—the losses in Vietnam and the various energy crises—the lack of models for self-sustaining large-scale change in the quality of working life became even more evident. It was obviously easier to start such changes than to sustain them. While there has been a slow change toward the better, we still are not assured that the trend is either broad or permanent. In recent work developing a high-QWL work site within the Walt Disney Company, I had occasion to study the organization's background. It was a bit sobering to find that the participative, semiautonomous organizational form we were implementing had been specified by Walt Disney himself in the company's organization manual, dated 1941! The form had long ago disappeared from that organization.

It would be unduly pessimistic to say there has not been some success. Rather, there has been a noticeable shift in the way most American organizations are operated, a shift which in total effect has been massive. Few organizations can sustain what is now called a ''Japanese'' style of work organization, however, or worker control through employee stock-option programs (ESOPs) or similar devices for participation in ownership. Some suggestions of how to take the next step are now coming from a few industrial organizations and community projects that approach social change through concepts of *network formation* (for examples see Trist, 1986) and *organizational transformation* (Levy and Merry, 1986). As useful as these approaches have been, they have been formulated from established modes and encounter all the limitations thereof. One thing we have recognized from the failure to achieve significant changes in particular industrial and other organizations is this: The very richness of mankind that we wish to preserve assures us that no single approach using the present-day range of strategies will ever have pervasive application. We must respond to the issues of large-scale change with a far more complex strategy than we envisioned in the ebullient movements of the sixties.

The concepts introduced here are directed toward a new level of the practice of social change—toward a praxis based on *emergent operations* that go beyond a focus on either structure or process. Rather it points toward methods based on understanding the interaction of the concepts of reality and the selection of the criteria for action.

Meta-Praxis

A theory of practice—that is, a *meta-praxis*—has become a necessity if we are to achieve large-scale changes in society. A meta-praxis helps us select the paths of resolution that will be effective in resolving complex issues and producing large-scale, or *systemic,* change. We have in any situation a great range of possible routes to effecting change. In trying to revitalize a political state, for example, we might choose to induce a violent revolution, seek some sort of amelioration, do a technocratic redesign, reform the constitution, or produce a cultural transformation under a charismatic leader or a socially conscious political party. The choice of path establishes the logic of change, the depth of its impact, and the style if not the personage of the leadership. The particular choice controls the pace and extent of change as well as the involvement of the stakeholders and neighboring powers. Each occasion of change, be it the systemic changes involved in personal therapy or the reconstruction of great multinational corporations, can be approached with many different strategies. The dictates of the strategy along with the history of the system and the accidents of the moment indicate both the next steps and the general flow of the change process.

A meta-praxis provides a catalogue of change theories, putting our familiar practices into a matrix through which we can systematically explore them. This organizing process shows that there is a vast range of strategies seldom considered by practitioners, strategies that provide capabilities beyond those in which most have been schooled and gained competence. Having a catalogue of practices protects us against routinely falling back upon the familiar approaches and opens us to emergent concepts through which to understand change.

This concept of meta-praxis I introduce here arose from my dissatisfaction with the methods of resolving complex issues—issues that, whether for individuals, social systems, or loose communities, call for major redefinitions and systemic changes. I take as a fundamental premise a humanity that is highly differentiated with regard to each person's beliefs in what is *real*—that is, how the world operates, what power we have to influence its course, what the relations among its parts are, and so on. Each of us has such a basic belief in what is real that it is impossible to conceive that others live in a different reality. Further, I propose that these ontological differences either reproduce or are correlated with a great many other differences in human behavior that are critical to the design of change efforts. The selection and implementation of modes that respond to these differences is the foundation of a reinterpretation of strategies of change at the level of individuals as well as large systems. In particular, the change issues comprehended by this meta-praxis include:

- The meaning of change itself, as it differs among elements of the population. The different ways people view change is one of a number of important qualities on which people differ that are correlated with the maintained realities.
- The goals of change and the criteria related to these modes of resolution.

- The tools—that is, the general *modes*—that can be used to produce change in a system.
- Leadership and governance and their relation to the modes of change.
- Alternative paths of change including the distinct points of entry.

Meta-praxis, by its nature, transcends the criteria by which we induce change. It does not pursue truth, it does not establish scientific fact, it does not lead to social or political equity. Nor does it lead to any of the other goals usually sought in social change. It is a self-reflexive work in which the practitioners themselves strive to keep in touch with the relevant environments and the multiple realities of the systems within which they are practicing and work to encourage such awareness in the client systems. The goal of meta-praxis, then, is to see that the designer (the consultant), the designing (the process or structure), and the designed (product or service) should operate in harmony.

This meta-praxis, for all its organizing power, is not sufficient to respond to all the *dynamics* of change. Specifically it does not include propositions concerning the boundary conditions, the system's history, and the effects of coupling among systems. (Brown, 1980, provides an excellent discussion of change projects with different degrees of coupling.) These properties, as well as the distribution of beliefs about reality, have to be specified in order to produce an operational practice.

The presentation of the meta-praxis in this chapter is organized as follows:

- *Alternative realities*—describing the ontological source of difference and conflict
- *Modes of resolution*—describing the basic methods of change
- *Leadership*—showing its association with the realities and their modes

These three elements provide the basis for the meta-praxis. Some concepts of its use, built on this base, are described in the two final sections:

- *Paths of resolution and change*—illustrating the concept of a path with the archetypal open-system planning model
- *The four games of chess*—a representation of the meta-praxis via a metaphor that provides an easy way to relate the praxis to applications

Figure 9.1 illustrates the development of a change effort, beginning with an assessment of realities, the specific system dynamics, and boundary conditions, all of which are necessary to make strategic choices.

In this presentation of meta-praxis the topics are necessarily treated summarily and numerous figures are used to suggest topics that go beyond the limits of this chapter. The brevity will provide at least a quick overview of meta-praxis for some readers, others will find it a basis for developing their own applications. While the main focus of this presentation is on organizational change, the concept is equally suitable for considering change in individuals and in communities and other social units.

Alternative Realities

The original drive for a meta-praxis grew from questions of how we choose approaches for resolving complex issues. In the search for theories of resolution, I developed an underlying structure that explained the choice of method in terms of the ontological view held by the individual or organization making the choice. This structure derives from the work of Lawrence LeShan published in his *Alternative Realities* (1976). He hypothesized, and I have further confirmed, that at least within Western cultures people hold individually to a few distinct beliefs about reality. These beliefs are deeply held and are probably maintained from birth with only minor changes due to one's maturing and to pressures from one's culture. Further, each society reinforces a limited set of beliefs. These limitations on the view of reality may themselves be maintained over a whole historical epoch.

From within a society that strongly maintains a given worldview (a more encompassing term than *reality*), it is hard to

Figure 9.1. Meta-Praxis: Choosing the Engagement.

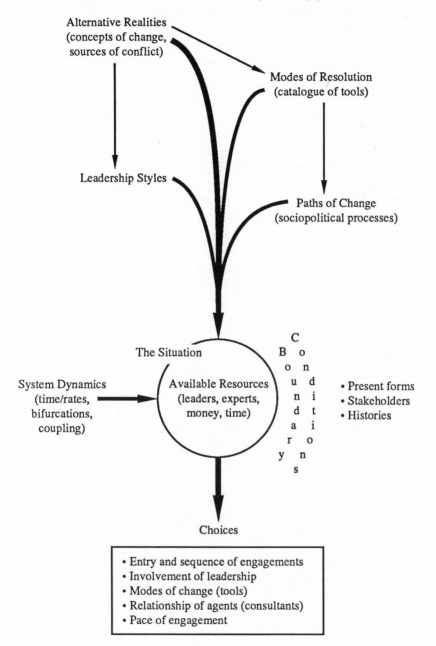

take seriously views of reality that presume fundamentally different concepts of the basic *onta* of existence. Our scientific worldview, the grand paradigm of the Age of Reason and the Industrial Age, proclaims reality to be expressed in distinct physical entities characterized by mass, color, density, surface, stability, and so forth. It recognizes change by measuring these qualities. But if we look more carefully at the way we operate, we also (and consistently) recognize the fundamental nature of *values*. Thus a "thing" does not exist unless we have some use or place for it—unless we place a value on it. A chair, for example, exists not because of its chemistry but because we have a use for it and having a name allows us to communicate to others about that which is useful; that is, the reason for the concept of chair is so I can talk to you about it. With such a worldview, changes are made by the assertion of value for some phenomenon—by calling a particular configuration of wood and cloth a chair, for example, or by calling the half-empty glass "half-full." The difference is significant. Such changes, for example, are not subject to the laws of conservation as are those in the physical reality; an individual or society can create or destroy a value at will. In Western society today there is an ambiguous mix of bases by which we determine what is real and what is good and how things are changed and how the world should be controlled.

LeShan identified four concepts of reality based on historical and psychological insights. To further delineate their qualities, I developed a model through which the properties of these realities can be derived. The model is expressed as a field in two dimensions selected to separate the four realities. The first is the *monistic-pluralistic* dimension (see Figure 9.2). Properly there are only two points on this dimension, for it is the dichotomy of the one and the many, but I am treating it as varying continuously from the extreme belief that "all is one" to the other extreme that the universe is made up of an infinity of distinct things and energies. The second dimension is *freedom of will*—the freedom to make the world the way we wish it to be. At one extreme is the belief that there is no freedom whatsoever—everything is predetermined by a supreme being or by natural laws. Such a conept of reality may be held by a deeply spiritual

Figure 9.2. Alternative Realities.

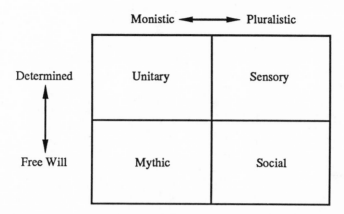

person as well as by an empirical scientist. At the other extreme is solipsism. More moderate are the beliefs of the charismatic leader and the assertive personality who believe that much can be achieved by their willpower. We can envision degrees of belief in free will along a continuum between the extremes.

The quadrants of the space defined by these two dimensions represent four different realities with intermediate strength of beliefs lying between the extremes. The characteristics of these four realities can be deduced more or less formally from their positions on the underlying dimensions. A great many personal characteristics can be derived from the model, providing rich descriptions of the stereotypical person who has chosen or was born to live within one of the realities. An extensive list of characteristics is provided in Figure 9.3.

No one can live and behave exclusively within any one of the reality positions; there must be some admixture of determinism and free will and some practical realization of plurality. The beliefs, attitudes, and behaviors of every person or society derive from combinations of realities.

To provide the reader with a more immediate sense of these distinct worldviews I characterize each reality in terms of five aspects that are particularly relevant to understanding the ways in which a person holding these beliefs responds to change: (1) concepts of change, (2) modes of action, (3) criteria for

Figure 9.3. Characteristics of Alternative Realities.

Unitary		Sensory
	← – – – – – – Deterministic Behavior – – – – – – +	
Everything is one; boundaries are arbitrary. Space and time are a continuum. Events simply are. No involvement in past or future.	CONNECTIVITY	All objects are separable. They affect each other by direct contact and according to general laws. Time and space are separate dimensions.
No free will; no doing or wishing to do. Things that happen, happen.	WILL	No free will, though there are alternative paths one can follow.
Going with the flow.	ACTION	Anticipation allows selection among features.
Direct experience of oneness; knowledge is gained by direct intuition of oneness. Senses provide only false information.	SOURCES OF KNOWLEDGE	All valid information comes directly or indirectly via the senses. All is testable and verifiable.
No meaning to causality since it is all one. Central question: What?	CAUSALITY	Cause precedes effects. Action occurs only through physical forces and contact. Central questions: How? How to?
Connectedness, serenity, joy, peace. No existential anxiety or aloneness.	EMOTION	Groundedness, confidence, well-being from taking action. Fear of death.
No moral opportunity. A single-valued world. Divisiveness is the only evil.	MORAL JUDGMENT	No moral judgments. Criterion: Does it work?
"We know we are at home in the universe."	SOURCES OF MEANING	Workability: "I can see the effects." Grounded in facts.
Experienced only as cleansing of what is.	CHANGE	Selecting among established futures.
Relativistic physics, law, maintaining authority structures, devotion.	USES	Survival, creature comforts, everyday commerce. Empirical science and technology.

Mythic (Monistic)		Social (Pluralistic)
Any part can stand for any whole. No difference between objective and subjective or between things and symbols. Once a connection is established, no space/time separation.	CONNECTIVITY	Separable entities but boundaries are chosen according to purpose.
All connections start with acts of will. All things have power (mana) to create connections among anything in the universe.	WILL	Free will in each sentient being. Everything can affect everything else so at the level of the cosmos there is predetermination.
Proactive; self-starting.	ACTION	Interactive; transformational.
Oneself (since all can be created by one's intention).	SOURCES OF KNOWLEDGE	Through observation, but also through direct awareness as part of a whole. (Recognizes the possibility of ESP, etc.)
All is willable. No accidents; everything has meaning. Nothing is falsifiable. Central question: Do I want it?	CAUSALITY	Strong focusing can bring to bear forces of the cosmos onto a local situation. Central questions: Why? How?
Playfulness, capriciousness, humor, and power to create.	EMOTION	Awe, humility, majesty, greatness. Love and anxiety; can't fully experience oneness.
Total moral responsibility for one's acts since others are not recognized as active agents. No concern for wishes of others.	MORAL JUDGMENT	Since we can choose, we are subject to moral and ethical demands: golden rule. Recognizes the morality and rights of the other.
The creative potential of the living will. Life and death are phases of one's being.	SOURCES OF MEANING	Own choice in articulating a moral world. Awareness of separation and integration.
No change, just creation.	CHANGE	The normal interactive modes produce change.
Play, art, dreaming, invention. Taking charge—charisma.	USES	Inquiry, philosophy, policy, ethics. Social organization.

choosing an action, (4) sense of responsibility, and (5) relations to other people. In the following paragraphs I present these and a few additional characteristics for each of the four basic realities.

Sensory. I begin with the sensory reality, for it is the most familiar. It is what we (educated Westerners) most often associate with the term *reality*. It is the belief system that allows us to have confidence in the permanence of "stuff" and the common laws of nature. It is essential to our bodily survival and our creature comforts. We find the sensory belief among empirical scientists and engineers as well as in the athlete, the gourmand, and the practical person on the street—all those who are primarily interested in sensing and engaging with that which is "out there."

- *Concepts of change.* In the extreme form of the sensory reality there is no possibility of making changes—it is all predetermined. There is no reason why an organization or society would wish to redirect its course. For the practical sensory person, change is reification, making what must be made in the pursuit of the technological imperative. To do anything else would be inefficient and ineffective.
- *Action mode.* Action is paradoxical; it serves to cause that which will happen anyway. In less extreme form action is drawn out of anticipation of what will be.
- *Criterion.* Does it work?
- *Responsibility.* Without free will, there is no moral responsibility. However, the observed behavior supports the drive of a technological imperative to do what must be done.
- *Relation to others.* The basic relation is one of use. A relation is chosen on the basis of how well it contributes to one's work. Like all relations, if viewed in the small it appears self-serving; if viewed on a grand scale, it may appear to make contributions to one's culture.

Social. The social reality, in combination with the sensory, forms the preeminent American reality. The social reality is based on values, not on the "stuff" of the sensory world. People holding a social worldview are concerned with the relations among the values held by themselves and others. A pure social viewpoint would lead to paralysis and the inability to decide among conflicting personal evaluations of alternatives. Social reality supports an interest in social philosophy, moral causes, and engagement with others for shared joy and anguish. The concept of social reality is in close agreement with the concept of social reality developed by Schutz (1945) and Berger and Luckmann (1966).

- *Concepts of change.* Change is fundamental to the social belief, for there is a continual need to establish values based on interpersonal relations. For a person holding a social world-view, change is essential in the natural course of life and death, in social movements, and in grand evolution.
- *Action modes.* The mode is interactive.
- *Criteria.* Is it fair? Does it support interdependence?
- *Responsibility.* The joint condition of free will and pluralism creates a recognition of a multitude of individuals with volitions of their own, each able to affect the world according to his or her power. Thus each is responsible for the other. This is the reality of moral responsibility.
- *Relation to others.* Common values are central to the social reality. Thus relations with others are the source of value. Engagement per se is valued, whether in harmony or in conflict.

Mythic. The mythic reality is monistic and free of predetermination. Its reality is the *symbols* that create relationship within the totality. While every word is a symbol, for example, we can see this reality more dramatically established in the symbolic impact of the race to the moon in the 1960s. The power of a symbol, its weight, is measured by the degree to which it captures (the whole of) existence. In the extreme view, the mythic belief produces solipsism—the belief that ''I am the only existing being'' and that ''I have total free will to create the world as I wish.'' In less extreme form, a mythic person might hold that ''I have unique power over a domain as large as the world or (alternatively) restricted to my immediate self.'' The basic attitude is "I can make anything happen—within the domain I control." We characterize one who operates in a mythic reality as unpredictable, creative, playful, self-centered, even demonic. The mythics of great power are the "creators" of the world, the artists and spiritual and political leaders. Creation in all domains—science, politics, religion—comes, in part, from a mythic view. Mythics are the symbol makers, giving meaning to experience.

- *Concepts of change.* Paradoxically, there is no change in the pure mythic world, for it is always the created world that is. The mythic creates in the moment the total existence— present, past, and future. In less extreme beliefs, change may be recognized but is of little importance if it applies beyond one's domain. To the observer, the mythic person may be involved in unending, unpredictable, and chaotic change. It is destructive, even life threatening, for the mythic to be forced to change within his or her own domain. Persons holding a mythic belief are the least likely to become "organization men."
- *Action mode.* The mythic's action mode is proactive and self-starting.
- *Criterion.* Does it make *my* world work?
- *Responsibility.* There is total personal responsibility for one's acts, and one is thus responsible for the whole world one accepts as real. The mythic reality incorporates no meaning for morality in the sense of taking care of the other, for there is no other. At one extreme, the mythic carries the burdens of the world; at the other, the mythic as viewed by others is totally independent of what goes on around him.
- *Relation to others.* Interrelations such as those seen by the social or sensory person are meaningless. The mythic creates the other as a character in his or her "dream." Conversely, by that act of creation, the other person is made present, reified, and given meaning. This ability to *create the other* (making one feel alive, larger, more potent) is the basis of the charismatic leader's power.

So simple a characterization cannot provide enough variety to show the difference in personalities that can arise out of the mythic (or any other) worldview. A mythic person may operate at a primitive level, apparently manipulating symbols to gain a "magical" outcome. Here the manipulative behavior, as in voodoo, leads to private advantage. Alternatively, a mythic person may encompass a spiritual worldview of such power as did Gandhi or the poet William Blake. Yet, at both levels, the person works from the assumption that the part can control the whole, for by symbolization the part becomes identical with the whole.

Unitary. The basic worldview of the unitary is of continuity, community, flow, immediacy. Like the mythic, the unitary reality provides an environment in which extremely diverse behavior arises. In the extreme belief in the perfect unity, we find deeply spiritual people who accept the totality of the world as it is, the most obvious instances being mystics of the various religious traditions; more common are the conservatives who maintain their provincial worlds against any surprises. This worldview provides the peace, freedom from choice, and unifying love of humanity that is most desirable and must be jealously guarded from being totally lost by the intrusion of doubt, a fear of disunity, or guilt from thinking heretical thoughts. When trust in the wholeness fails, when the slightest suspicion creeps in suggesting that there may be a dark side as well as a light one, the typical behavior becomes defensive and then aggressive toward anyone who supports diverse beliefs. Thus within this worldview we find the most beatific and the most violent of all expressions: "Onward Christian soldiers, marching as to war." Those who hold a generally monistic, if not perfectly unitary, position are of central concern for those interested in change, for the unitary worldview underlies the bureaucratic personality and the followership of the monistic leaders—and thus those most resistant to change.

- *Concepts of change.* There is no change in a unitary world. Everything that will be already is. That which others might

call change is here considered nothing but clarification, har-
monization, or the exposition of the utopia that is inherent
in the universe.

- *Action modes.* For the unitary, action is staying in tune with
  the flow of events.
- *Criterion.* There is no meaning for *criterion* within the pure
  unitary world. But to one who accepts the *possibility* of something, the criterion is "Are you one with us?" or "Does
  this belief lie within the dogma?"
- *Responsibility.* To remain at one and to support others in so
  doing is the basic responsibility of the unitary. There is no
  concept of wrong except that which violates the unity, that
  is, the heretical act.
- *Relation to others.* The unitary perceives an undifferentiated
  community based on fundamental sameness. Relations are
  nominal, simply conveniences in the daily rounds.

These descriptions of the four alternative realities are given
in terms of archetypes, people who view reality from nearly pure,
polar viewpoints. Most people do not come close to being extreme types, of course; rather, they make significant use of
elements of each reality. My observations, supported by the
Realities Inquiry (a paper-and-pencil instrument designed to
measure the relative strength of a person's beliefs), indicate that
most people in the United States operate to a significant degree
from two of these belief systems and a few work from three.
The resulting personalities and modes of engaging with the world
are thus incongruous combinations of the aspects of the different
realities. Which particular realities are called upon at any moment depends on the stimuli. It is hard to say whether behavior
arises from some combination of reality views or is a sequence
of acts chosen from one or another reality; the latter seems to
be the better explanation. Working alone, we may be easily
swayed by others around us to accept elements of their reality.
By collecting around us people of like beliefs, however, we can
maintain confidence in the "reality of our choice." Thus there
is a tendency in society for people of like reality to associate

together, reinforcing their beliefs—and causing one to suppress his own beliefs when they deviate from the norms of the group. Such concentrations of people with similar worldviews develop in organizations and communities as a result of movement into jobs and roles for which the individuals are temperamentally suited. Cultures, at every level, form concentrations by supporting one or another worldview, so people coming from other realities tend to suppress their differences, even losing the ability to appreciate the basics of their innate style. The greater the concentration of belief, the more a reality appears to be uniquely valid. Such concentrations have a deep impact, usually negative, on our ability to effect large-scale change.

The distribution of pockets of worldviews within the environment of a change effort is critical to the outcome of change iniatives because of the differences in the way the worldviews consider change. Perhaps the most striking implication of this view of large-scale change is that the kind of change we seek in QWL projects, in community redevelopment, and in organizational development is beyond the comprehension of most worldviews—particularly those dominated by the unitary, sensory, or mythic forms of thinking. Only those holding to the social reality are able to work consistently with the various forms of planned change. The "resistance to change" arises out of the most basic beliefs of the unitary, sensory, and mythic mind-sets. The person believing in the unitary reality sees no possibility of change, for the world is one, perfect, and perpetual, subject only to cleansing acts. The sensory believer, in the extreme, sees change as the result of lawful forces of nature, not susceptible to the choice of humans. The mythic person sees only that which is present to himself; indeed, the mythic believer can create anything in the moment without noting any change, as is frequently observed in the strongly charismatic or entrepreneurial person. Thus the attempt by a person holding a social reality to induce change is variously threatening for those maintaining the other realities.

This approach to purposeful change leads to a different consideration of the environment than do other change models (for example, Emery and Trist, 1973). Of all change processes, only those based on a sensory reality will take the environment as primary as does Paul Lawrence in Chapter Three in this volume. From a sensory worldview it is logical to begin an engagement with consideration of the environmental factors, including questions of the cause, or need, for change; in the extreme all change is simply the imperative response to the environment. From a mythic viewpoint, the environment is to be constructed or, more accurately, it comes into existence as it occurs in the minds of those involved. From the unitary viewpoint, as we often see in the Soviet treatment of both history and the present, the environment is posited to be in agreement with the dogma. The familiar paradox of multiple realities raises its horns, however, for in order to assess the situation the consultant must sense the world, at least, from a pluralistic worldview. So we, as agents of change, may begin by assessing (sensorially) the distribution of realities among the members and stakeholders in order to be in a position to recommend strategies that do not, themselves, depend on the sensory worldview. The reason behind a change effort is a function of the espoused reality of the fomenter of that change—the leader, the change agent, the revolutionary party, or whoever is choosing to act. The attribution of the ''cause'' of a change, even the language with which we discuss it, stems from the definition of the reality, which is, in turn, a choice of leadership or a constraint set by the society. The environment must be treated, in this meta-praxis, not as an external condition of the effort but as a construction that is introduced, for example, to bound the effort, to raise an army, or to judge the moral impact. The definition, even the existence, of the environment is a function of the meta-praxis and treated as external only as the strategy requires it.

The strategies, theories of change, or ''paths of resolution'' as I label them, are considered later. First, however, I want to introduce and characterize the modes of effecting change and the leadership styles that direct these changes.

Change and the Modes of Resolution

Since World War II ''change'' has become a major practice at the personal, organizational, and societal levels, in individual therapies, organizational development, and various forms of social action from Gandhi's nonviolence to Paulo Freire's pedagogy of the masses. Change is no longer simply the course of history but the result of intentional action by purposeful, sentient human beings. Change, in this sense, arises out of social and mythic realities, out of the premise that, individually and collectively, we create destiny.

These practices greatly enriched the range of change processes beyond the long-established and familiar modes based on the deterministic realities, the sensory and the unitary. Theories arising from a deterministic worldview perceive change as coming from an "imperative"—technological, historical, or theological—or as personal destiny. The achievement of an imperative does not produce change that is comparable to that attained from the social or mythic worldviews, however, so I argue that it is wrong to label the whole field "change." A more inclusive and neutral term is *resolution,* as in the resolution of tension or conflict or a disparity or simply becoming clear. Thus I reframe *large-scale change* as *resolution* (in large systems).

Purposive change is an anomaly for the scientific and for most religious worldviews. There is no explanation for change that does not violate the premises of positivistic scientific theory; there is no provision for it in the tenets of Western religions. Yet it is an unrecognized companion in the very acts by which we advance science and initiate religious dogma. Social scientists examine the occasions of change with the tools of empiricism and get confounding results which deny that any change has taken place while every person on the street is already experiencing the change. Purposive change is a paradox under the scientific paradigm. Just as Zeno pointed out the paradoxes of motion to the pre-Socratic Greeks, the recognition of multiple realities allows us to display the dilemmas of change under the paradigm of rationality. By making the dilemmas explicit we can build strategies to respond to them that do not require us to hide the horns under a blanket of social science jargon. This I believe will be a major accomplishment, though it just sets the stage for a full understanding. We should not be impatient. It was not until long after the invention of the calculus that Zeno's paradoxes were finally resolved. That took 2,000 years. We may have to wait for the much heralded ''new paradigm'' to have a worldview that sufficiently transcends the present paradoxes surrounding change.

This study of meta-praxis began with an exploration of resolution of complex issues—how we deal with the issues of family life, urban and environmental decay, technological change, living under the threat of nuclear warfare. An important step of that exploration was the identification of the modes of resolution, that is, the tools (of change) that we use when we respond to complex issues. No catalogue of modes had been developed because there has been no organizing device by which to characterize them. The alternative realities, however, appear to provide a foundation for establishing such a catalogue and identifying the tools.

Structuring the tools of change into four basic modes of resolution provides a basis for the practice of what we have been calling change. This structure identifies the premises, the modes of operation, the criteria, and the skills and conditions required to use each tool. A general mode of resolution derives from each of the four realities and, somewhat incompatibly, from combinations of elements of two or three realities. Figure 9.4 places each mode of resolution within the domain of one of the alternative realities. Two of these placements are familiar: In American society we are well trained in the *analytic* modes through which we construct solutions according to scientific or practical custom, and we have learned over the last few decades about the many *axiotic,* that is, value-based, methods used to induce changes in accordance with the social reality. What we call *design* is best viewed as operating within a combined unitary-sensory worldview. The other two modes, the *dialectic* and the *mythic,* are less well understood, though they are widely used in practice. Note that the use of mythic both as a reality and as a mode is intended. While it may be confusing to make dual usage of the term it captures the essential identity of the mythic existence and the mythic mode.

The modes cannot be fully described here. Each represents a grand tradition of work with a vast supporting literature. The following descriptions point to these bodies of ideas and practice,

Figure 9.4. Modes of Resolution and Change.

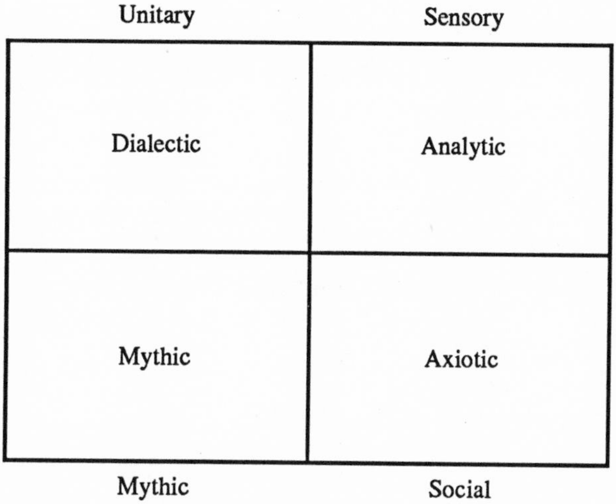

	Unitary	Sensory	
	Dialectic	Analytic	
	Mythic	Axiotic	
	Mythic	Social	

labeling aspects that may be novel and disturbing for some students of philosophy and praxis. Table 9.1 lists a variety of characteristics of the four modes.

The *analytic mode* is based on empirical thinking and depends on hypodeductive and inductive methods, using all logics, theories, and information available to the senses to identify possible solutions, predict implications, and evaluate outcomes. In this era it is primarily associated with the scientific and the quantitative methods. It provides no guides for the processes of change, but determines (or predicts) outcomes. Change is driven by the sense both of efficiency and of optimally organizing to produce that which can be produced. The drive for change is the technological imperative, though commonly in our society it will be explained by some motivation that has its foundation in the social reality.

The *dialectic mode* contains a variety of methods we might see as totally distinct and arising from contrary worldviews. It is not easy to see that the methods of war, of the law courts, and of theology and spiritual transcendence are all based on the unitary premises and are therefore closely related. Such com-

Table 9.1. Comparison of Modes of Resolving Complex Issues.

Quality	Dialectic Mode	Analytic Mode	Mythic Mode	Axiotic Mode
Reality Base	Unitary	Sensory	Mythic	Social
Onta	Relations	Objects	Symbols	Values
Criteria	Is it right?	Does it work?	Does my world work?	Is it fair?
Outcome	Unity	Products/plans	That which is	Transformations of values
Ideals	Utopia	Conformity to empirical observation	Confirmation of one's reality	Consciousness
Mode of change	Cleansing Selecting Revolution Synthesis	Constructing Reframing based on boundary shifting	Creating (no change, only what is at the moment)	Reframing based on value convergence
Methods	Redesign Legislation Elimination of the "other"	Using models with data to make decisions	Ritual sequences The creative cycle	Organization Development Open systems planning
Logic	Dialectic or Aristotelian	Scientific	Mythic	Value calculus
Morality	None (true/false)	None	Total responsibility (personal obligation)	The critical concern
Quality of resolvers	Loyalty	Rationality	Positiveness Assertiveness	Fairness, openness
Governance	Authority	Accepted professionals	Self (or leader)	Self-governing or facilitated by outside consultant
Required condition	Commitment to law or a cause	Stability of a measurement scheme	Charismatic leadership	Belief that there is a shared value set among stakeholders

plexity in the dialectic has been recognized since the Sophists developed the method in Plato's time. Simultaneously it is the mode of argument, of disputation among partisans of opposing views, of adversarial law courts, of politics, and of those who seek Holy Oneness, benevolent community, and the absolute control of the fascist state. All dialectic resolutions establish or preserve the Truth. All are methods of unification. Where there is an established Truth, resolution simply deals with questions of interpretation. "Change" serves to cleanse the system of error, correct a deviation, or protect the domain of the Truth. We can see such efforts in political and religious settings and to a lesser degree in all institutions, be they academic, industrial, or professional. Most of what is labeled organizational development has the purpose of cleansing its host of impure (inefficient) practice. When the "one Truth" is challenged, resolution is likely to be achieved through conflict. This conflict is between the supporters of established thesis and those of challenging antithesis. The resolution is likely to be achieved by the destruction of one position or by a synthesis in which a new Truth emerges out of the destruction of both theses. In the formation of a synthesis, the dialectic also produces *evolution*. Such evolution, as in the Marxist view, is not a process of change but a historically driven imperative that progressively cleanses the organization of impure functions.

Change that arises out of these two realities tends to be called structural, but, more accurately, they are changes *within structure*. Structural changes (changes within structure) do not affect the ideology of the organization. Most political revolutions, for example, are simply inversions of the social order, leaving the basic institutions (structures) intact. The methods labeled "design," "construction," and "progressive" are defined within the dialectic and analytic modes. An example of such a change at the General Electric Company is provided in Jay Galbraith's Chapter Four in this volume.

The *axiotic mode* (that is to say, value-based) is one of value exploration, of resolving issues by developing new, and shared, evaluations of events. It often works through the "recontexting" or transformation of images by which an issue is dissolved. It is the only mode concerned with issues of morality, fairness, and personal behavior. The tools are ancient but, beginning with Kurt Lewin in the United States, the methods of small-group communication, attitude change, participative decision making, purposive planning, and therapeutic and personal development began to be systematically studied and developed as the "behavioral science" approach to change—an unfortunate and wholly inaccurate label. The changes induced by value-based transformations may affect the ideology of a system and thus be profoundly disturbing to those of a unitary belief.

The *mythic mode* includes methods of symbolic creation. At the deepest level, mythic events create new meaning, literally producing something out of nothing. They produce resolution by transcending the existing structures and the meanings that are given to words, situations, objects, stories, and so on. The mythic inventions that are successful in creating large-scale change are those that are in tune with the needs of the system— that is, where the inventor senses what a culture needs, what will capture its energy. They are typically realized through acts of charismatic leadership that capture the will and the faith of the involved population, as grand an exercise as Gandhi's non-violent ouster of the British from India or as invisible as the direction Kareem Abdul Jabbar provides his professional basketball team. The basic methods of the mythic are those we associate with the creative endeavor, the use of intuition, and the strong adherence to premises of the mythic reality, particularly the belief that one can achieve whatever one intends to. Such an approach to the world is as difficult for those of a sensory belief as are the axiotic changes for those of a unitary belief.

In the popular usage, resolutions occurring through predominantly axiotic and mythic modes are called *process changes,* because they typically change the very premise of the organization. Neither mode respects the established ideology. The mythic is the source of ideology, however, so that a change initiated in the mythic mode may take on the character of a cause or movement, attracting a following of people with a unitary worldview. This is the path of all religious movements and of most political movements, both of the extreme right and left wings.

I have postulated here that the basic modes of resolution lie within distinct constructions of reality. It is a natural extension to suggest that people demonstrating belief in a particular reality will be most secure using the resolution modes of that reality. Further, they will take on the professions associated with that reality—for example, some people governed by a social reality will gravitate toward the human services; those dominated by the unitary will be lawyers or mathematicians and work well within bureaucracies; tradesmen and scientists share an appreciation for the sensory; mythics are likely to choose the arts or entrepreneurial games. Similarly, and more important for a theory of large-scale change, the leadership *style* closely follows the person's belief system. Thus the modes of resolution must not only relate to the dominant reality of the relevant population but also to the realities of the available leaders.

Leadership Style

Change and leadership are inextricable, so it is not surprising to find that the forms of leadership can also be associated with the map of realities. All the recognized forms of leadership correlate with the various combinations of realities. *Task leadership* is the natural style of someone holding a mixed unitary-sensory worldview; *participative leadership* is likely to operate from a sensory-social base. The "magic leader" of which Nadler and Tushman write in Chapter Six follows the characteristics of one with a strong mythic-sensory reality supported by a social sense in the Western countries and with a unitary sense in the Arabic world. Figure 9.5 and Tables 9.2 and 9.3 present the basic characteristics of ten styles of leadership, some of which have not been defined in the literature of leadership but are easily recognized in the ways of known leaders (Tannenbaum, Margulies, Massarik, and Associates, 1985).

This link of leadership style to resolution modes enables us to develop coherent change strategies not only in terms of various situational variables but also in response to the types of leaders available. There are many instances of industrial and political change efforts in which failure has been attributed to

Figure 9.5. Leadership Styles.

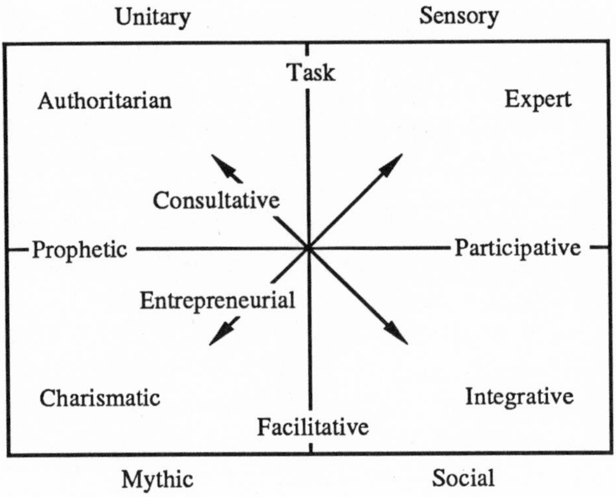

the lack of appropriate leadership. But more accurately the failure should be attributed to a failure to match the strategy with the established or available leadership.

Paths of Resolution and Change

The record of the past twenty years must certainly lead to the conclusion that there is no single formula for all large-scale change efforts. Certainly we cannot claim that the use of any particular formula has fully achieved the degree of change desired. Even if we recall those instances where there has been a modicum of success, it is most unlikely that anyone can identify a common path. Surveying the major change efforts with which I have been associated over the past ten years assures me that we will not find any simple strategy to be used in even a majority of these situations. Consider the following change situations:

- A sociotechnical redesign of a chemical plant at a site with twenty-six unions, some Marxist, and two management cultures

- Creating governance for two new cities in Saudi Arabia
- Transferring control from the founders of a conglomerate grossing $2 billion a year to their sons
- Redirecting a telephone company in response to deregulation and major technological changes in its environment
- Human resource management in a military aircraft company
- Resetting direction for a state (Montana) that is settling back into the nineteenth century
- Revitalizing an R&D laboratory in an old high-tech company
- Designing a process to initiate formal collaboration among the Caribbean island states

What change path do all these situations have in common? This question is as unanswerable as "How big is a box?" This question calls for questions in return. The diversity of situations, of "boxes," requires a logic of inquiry far more complex than this question; it requires a theory of practice to select an answer, as well as appropriate data, and the courage to go beyond the familiar tools of the trade.

The complexity of large-scale change is not only in the situational differences indicated in the examples just listed. There are also major complexities facing those attempting to change an organization, complexities that come from the distribution of realities within that organization. In most mature systems, the people holding different views of reality have collected into clusters of like views around the various roles in their organizations, as one might predict from theories of organization and culture. An example of such a distribution is the large, stabilized organization we often refer to as a bureaucracy. There we might find a distribution of dominant realities as depicted in Figure 9.6. This figure could be a map of a typical U.S. firm. We would find different configurations in an Arab organization, a new enterprise, or a "learning organization." Each domain on this map of realities will respond differently to change initiatives, suggesting that a change strategy must be as rich and environmentally responsive as a military strategy for a major campaign.

By whatever name, we need a theory to organize and structure the relations between the situations calling for large-scale

Table 9.2. Leadership Styles Based on a Single Reality.

Characteristic	Authoritarian	Charismatic	Expert	Integrative
Major purpose	Clarifying and conforming to values and rules of establishment	Creating belief in and commitment to leader's own belief systems	Discovering/testing scientific facts	Developing shared value systems
Objective	Directing efforts within belief system; maintaining status quo	Reifying one's ideas; system is not bounded and thus not optimal; sky's the limit	Obtaining clear evidence regarding the task	Providing conditions for flexible, adaptive movement toward group goals (not bounded)
Type of organization	Hierarchical: authority structure	"Star" form with flexible assignments for subordinates	Project; varying with task; small units only	Open systems, task and process structured
Goals in resolving conflict	Preventing divisiveness	Creating unity	Supporting a common worldview based on scientific principles and data	Resolving issues of fairness

	Unitary	Mythic	Sensory	Social
Means of dealing with internal conflict	Denying conflict—no open personal differences; destroy the enemy	Overcoming conflict via excitement and commitment	Rationally resolving conflict; systematic and logical	Exposing and organizing efforts to resolve interpersonal problems in a broad context
Future and planning	Utopian; short-term planning for an unchanging world	A device for creating hope and a sense of possibility; flexible; long range but highly unstable	Maximum adaptation via knowledge, anticipation, and clarification of alternatives; as long range as the data permit	Visioning toward possible futures, adaptive and long range, aims at openly creating a future
Supervision style	By the rules; paternalistic	Leader little involved except around issues of trust	Informing, measuring, evaluating	Encouraging, exploring, listening
Ideal follower behavior	Reliable, loyal, knowing the rules; imitative and supportive of supervisors	Trustworthy to leader, carrying out orders, uncritical, flexible; the "true believer"	Informed, skillful, capable of follow-through; can take delegation well; assured	Direct, confronting, informing, courageous, open, conscious
Reality base	Unitary	Mythic	Sensory	Social

Source: Tannenbaum, Margulies, Massarik and Associates (1985, p. 286).

Table 9.3. Leadership Styles Based on Two Realities.

Characteristic	Styles Based on Adjacent Realities			Styles Based on Opposing Realities		
	Task	Participative	Facilitative	Prophetic	Entrepreneurial	Consultative
Major purpose.	Carrying out established goals in relation to external	Proper allocation of human and physical resources	Bringing out energy and skills of participants	Bringing the word of authority to members	Realizing a personal image	Using subordinates to effect policy
Objective	Logically exercising power to achieve organizational goals	Managing optimally for resource use—short and long term	Optimal sharing of production of ideas and responding to members' values	Obtaining compliance with "the word"	Reifying one's ideas in the "real world"	Best ideas to achieve organization's goals
Type of organization	Hierarchical; task	Functional	Open system	Tribal	Charismatic, growing into hierarchy	Hierarchical; task
Goals in resolving conflict	Task accomplishment	Short- and long-run effectiveness of operation	Open communication and emotional support	Conformity to "the word"	Causing the issue to disappear	Shared perception of imposed policy
Means of dealing with internal conflict	Requiring conformity to policy	Negotiating to find shared values	Active counseling to involved parties	Establishing true word and rejecting heretics	Wiping out power base of the opposition	Clarification of issue with involved parties

Future and planning	Explicit temporal and resource allocations	Plans designed to optimize present and future achievement	Expansive exploration of possibilities	Strong bias toward assuring future performance	Same as charismatic, but steadier goal orientation	Informed movement toward established goal
Supervision style	Clarification of goals, technology, planning	Supportiveness in connecting people	Evocative facilitation	"Shepherding"	Hard-driving, achievement-oriented	Responsive and demanding, with danger of double bind
Ideal follower behavior	Technically competent; accepts organizational demands	Cooperative and analytical	Independent, open, inner-directed	Trustworthy, loyal; accepts rules and suspends judgment	Self-abnegating; flexible and responsible	Informed, open, accepting of authority
Reality base	Unitary-sensory	Sensory-social	Social-mythic	Mythic-unitary	Mythic-sensory	Social-unitary

Source: Tannenbaum, Margulies, Massarik and Associates (1985, p. 290).

Figure 9.6. Dominant Realities in Various Locations
of an Organizational Hierarchy.

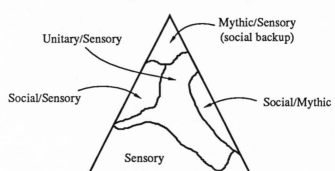

change efforts and the various practices that might be employed
to affect the change. That is, we need a means of relating the
various theories of change to the situations in which they might
be used. A fully developed meta-praxis will guide the selection
of the theories to be used in a change effort. In the interim, the
meta-praxis developed here can help us explore the range of
possibilities, chart courses, and identify effects in terms of the
characteristics of the approach taken. To suggest that we can
empirically establish the courses of optimal large-scale change
lands us back with the logical absurdities of designing change
efforts in a universe of multiple realities.

Figure 9.6 serves as a graphic base for identifying alternative paths of change. Some of the major paths used in contemporary work are represented in Figure 9.7. These paths indicate the realities through which the process must flow, and
thus the forms of leadership and the general modes of resolution that should be employed. Path 1 represents the sequence
called *organizational design,* which originates in a hypodeductive
mode (unitary-sensory realities) and is realized by construction
(sensory). Russell Ackoff's *Redesigning the Future* (1974) presents
an excellent exposition of this classic planning/change path.
Another version is the "exposition and propagation" theory that
rests on the assumption "that the men who possess 'truth' will
ultimately lead the world" (Bennis, 1966, p. 101). This path
is the style of sociologists, architects, sociotechnologists, city

Figure 9.7. Paths of Change.

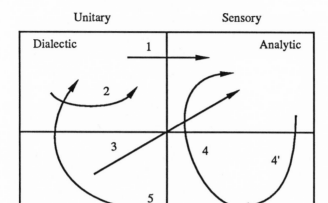

1. Design (specifically, organization design)
2. Cleansing, expiation (for example, changes in responsibilities)
3. Entrepreneurial
4. Participative
4'. Organizational development (collection of data precedes participative involvement)
5. Emergent

planners, and financial planners. It is a contingency model relating the environment to internal conditions of the organization.

Path 2 is a path of *clarification,* such as that required to establish a new interpretation of law or scripture. In societies with strong religious codes—for example, the Muslim countries—such cleansing or expiation is the proper form of change. Much of conventional organizational development serves this function; that is, its function is to bring behavior into line with the organization's principles by psychologically sensitive means. Path 3, the *entrepreneurial* path, is the reification of a creative initiative that appears in all manner of myth and story. We used to cite Horatio Alger and Thomas Edison but now, with entrepreneurialism in vogue, new characters appear daily in fact and fiction. This path is particularly notable for frequent deviation from the norms of the involved culture—as noted earlier, the mythic creation is done without regard for social values. Thus the entrepreneurial route may violate the society, express its values perfectly, or take it in a new direction.

The currently popular behavioral science interventions, based on communications, participation, and QWL schemes, may follow Path 4 (see Blake, Mouton, Barnes, and Griener, 1964). This path is curved to suggest the use of monistic methods in much of this work. Currently, those trained in organizational development typically begin their work with a survey of the situation that collects data in the sensory quadrant (Path 4'). A great many variations of this path have been developed in recent years, particularly under the general label of "normative planning." See, for example, Calvin Pava's "Normative Incrementalism" (1980). In the extreme, these OD interventions produce radical change, either by establishing new values, as in organizational transformation, or simply by reviving the value base that created the society.

Path 5 represents an effort that may begin in an unorganized community through the evocation of values—the outcome of protests, radical writing, or spontaneous demonstrations. Such events foment the organization of social change efforts. An example of such formative events is the frequent sit-ins, boycotts, and violations of segregation that occurred in the Deep South following World War II. These events culminated in the emergence of a charismatic leader, Martin Luther King, Jr., and the coalescence of the civil rights movement. The third stage of the change is the development of an organization to carry out the leader's vision, first during his tenure and, subsequently, to establish the movement, which is directed by a "priesthood" or a secular bureaucracy. This route is but one of many paths of self-creation that begin in an amorphous community.

Open-System Planning. A useful heuristic through which to search for effective paths of change is to extract paths of development from the myths, cosmogonies, and epic tales of the organization's culture (see Batista, 1988). Among the most durable epic forms in Western culture is that of the *eternal return,*

Figure 9.8. Open-System Planning Spiral.

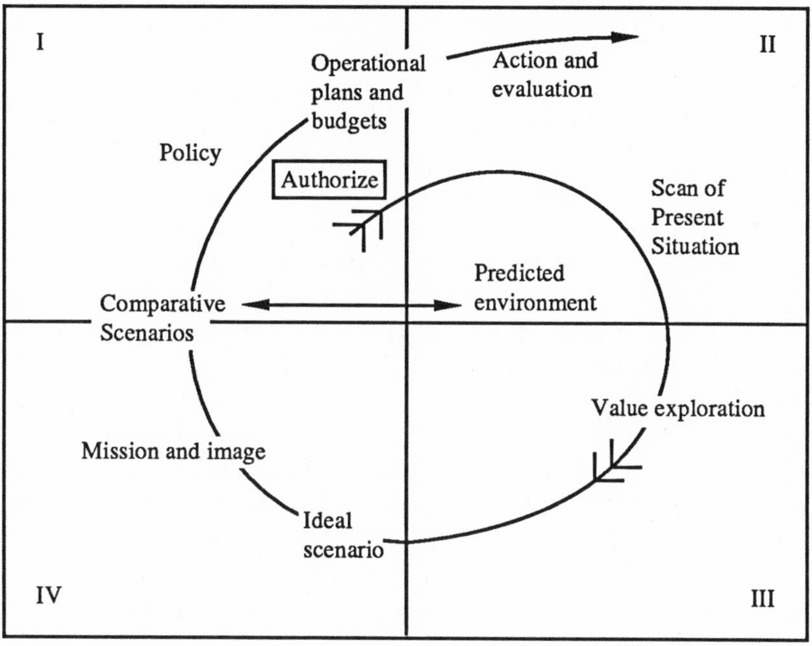

also called the night journey and the return for a better start, often symbolized as a spiral (see Figure 9.8). It is chronicled in the story of Jonah and the Whale, in Dante's *Inferno,* and in a thousand tales of transformation. It follows the basic sequence of retreat, reformulation, and reengagement that is commonly recognized in creative work and planning functions. The major elements of this path can be described as a sequence of steps.

The initiating step authorizes an "invasion" into the processes of the organization or person. Its purpose is to obtain an initial release from the dominant drives in order to reflect and then to redirect energy. It requires a political act of acceptance (surrender) allowing the boundaries of one's system to be opened in preparation for a return for a better start. It is Kurt Lewin's *unfreezing stage.* As shown in Figure 9.8, this authorization comes from within the unitary reality. Formally the authorization may come from a senior executive, but to be effective the invasion must be accepted by those just below who tend to be far more jealous of the established order than the top leadership. (In the postindustrial world, this surrender changes social planning from a monolithic process of governments and major powers to a process of pluralistic networks and social fields that parallel the participative structures being developed within organizations.)

The second step is carried out within the sensory reality. It might be done as an environmental scan and organizational audit. For the participants, this exploration grounds them in their present situation and helps them to see the present, past, and future as did Scrooge on Christmas Eve—but it is not meant to solve problems. The change agent's major use of this exploration is to determine the distribution of realities held by an organization's members and its stakeholders.

The regression in the service of the ego produces the decentralization of power, softening the boundaries in the service of individuation. It is a movement toward questioning the current structure of values and the established premises. It is achieved by reverting to a lower level of integration—by *decoupling,* that is, reestablishing the primacy of a lower level of organization, for example, subsidiaries of a corporation, the individuals in a group, or the pre-ego ''self'' in the individual. This transition from sensory to social reality is a move toward the choiceful *part*—to the awareness of the individual's subpersona or the elements of the organization involved in the change effort. It is done mostly by bringing into consciousness the values that individuals hold and the relation of these values to the operant values in the entire system. This work has by-products: personal and career development for those involved and a stronger participation in decisions and greater acceptance of change throughout the system.

Next comes a consideration of new possibilities, usually through creating scenarios to test values and the interactions among desired qualities. This phase ends in the adoption of an *ideal scenario* through which to experience the future (creating anticipation) and establish a normative ideal. Though the scenario is based on the social reality, the creative work itself is done with the tools of both the mythic and social modes.

Mission and image come next—a reconceptualization of the organization's goals or personal goals, expressed first as a *mission statement*. Second and more significant is the evocation of a *core process statement* that provides the path of transformation for the organization. Since the core process is a creation arising from the mythic reality, it does not contain the concept of motivation. It is a concept of pure action—the specific "becoming" of the organization. As pure action, it differs from the mission and goal statements, which are dualistic constructs deriving from a discrepancy between a present and a desired state.

With the creation of the core process the path turns back to relate to the world of action. The next phase is an exploration among alternative paths of action to find those which give the greatest comparative advantages. This stage does depend on sensory data about the environment. The exploration is done by developing various *comparative scenarios* based on the idea images already created and data-based assumptions about the future. Design thinking is done within the unitary-sensory worldview to test the images that originated in the mythic.

Next comes a specification of *policy*—that is, the selection from the various scenarios of the specific directions the organization is to take. The formulation of policy represents the recollection of power in the service of concerted action; it is the executive's reassertion of control and direction. This formulation is set in a unitary worldview, anticipating the plan's realization in the sensory world. Note that what is often called "strategy formulation" is no more than this statement of policies.

The selection of an *action plan* begins effecting the change. The plan may call for specific actions, but its effect is to create a sequence of actions that maintain the direction in accordance with the core process while responding to the exigencies of the moment.

As the change process is implemented, a new spiral may be begun by the *evaluation* of these actions against the operational plans, mission, and image that have been adopted. If such evaluations are done in reference to the newly established policy, the organization is self-stabilizing; if they are done as a reconsideration, or a revaluing, a spiral of change is reentered.

This modern form of an ancient spiral process has been used successfully since 1970 in creating the green-field factory sites and complete small organizations. In one variation or another, it is now widely used in the revitalization of organizations. A similar model, though lacking the stages of regression and individuation, is called the *search process*. It has been used effectively by Fred Emery and many of his colleagues in a number of community and regional and industry-wide change efforts (Emery, 1976). The spiral path has a strong record, yet like all strategies it is limited to situations in which the distribution of realities among the members and stakeholders is suitable—and when there are sufficient resources to survive the "little death" in the regression (or searching).

Other Great Paths. There are other great paths to resolution that have been little used in contemporary organizations for diverse reasons. The *Hegelian dialectic* has been used in problem solving (Adizes, 1978; Mason, 1969), but the impact of its application to organizational structures has been too threatening to the established stakeholders to be tolerated. Of course, we may view a history as a continual dialectical, but not as a consciously chosen path. A second grand path is the *hermetic transformation,* expressed in alchemical language (Jung, 1963). These two paths operate almost completely in the social and mythic realities, finding little support in the pragmatic cultures of American industry and politics. Another persistent myth is the search for the Holy Grail represented in the Arthurian legends, for which Luke Skywalker is the current incarnation. It exemplifies an ideal-seeking path based on the mythic and the unitary realities and typically produces organizations having a spiritual cause.

Clearly there is no single path that is appropriate for all large-scale change efforts, purposive or naturally determined. The complexity of contemporary society, exemplified in such efforts as those listed at the beginning of this section, requires a far more sophisticated strategic response than our usual training prepares us to carry out. In order to go beyond the various forms of incrementalism and ad hoc reactions that have been our first responses to the complexity of the latter half of the twentieth century we need some form of meta-praxis, one that will allow us to choose paths equal to the complexity and obstacles that will be encountered.

The Four Games of Chess

Meta-praxis is neither an easy theory nor an easy practice. It is a seminal construction based on concepts of reality that are not easily assimilated. By reformulating the theory into a metaphor, however, it can be absorbed directly, permitting the reader to make immediate applications without having to integrate the multiple realities and theoretical implications developed here. One suitable metaphor employs the familiar game of chess to explore organizational change. It can be viewed as a change model or as a planning model, for meta-praxis concerns induced change.

Consider the situation that leads up to making plays on a chess board—what goes into selecting the moves of your pieces. You must know the rules of chess: which moves are allowed and which are excluded. You must recognize that your opponent has the same basic information about the game that you have, is constrained by the same set of rules, and shares the same objective—that, in fact, you are both playing the same game. The choice of each move is based on a plan of what you will do generally, as well as in the next few moves. The plan of action, based on forecasts of what your opponent's responses will be, assumes that both of you have the same long-run objective to checkmate your opponent or force his withdrawal. Thus, planning is an *analytic* process. Such planning is directly analogous to the operational planning done within the firm in response to conditions expected within the firm and in its markets. In Figure 9.9, this mode of change is represented as play on the first board, identified with the common terms tactics and operations.

Now envision a chess game in which there is a second board. On this board the play of a piece will change the rules

Figure 9.9. Four Games of Change.

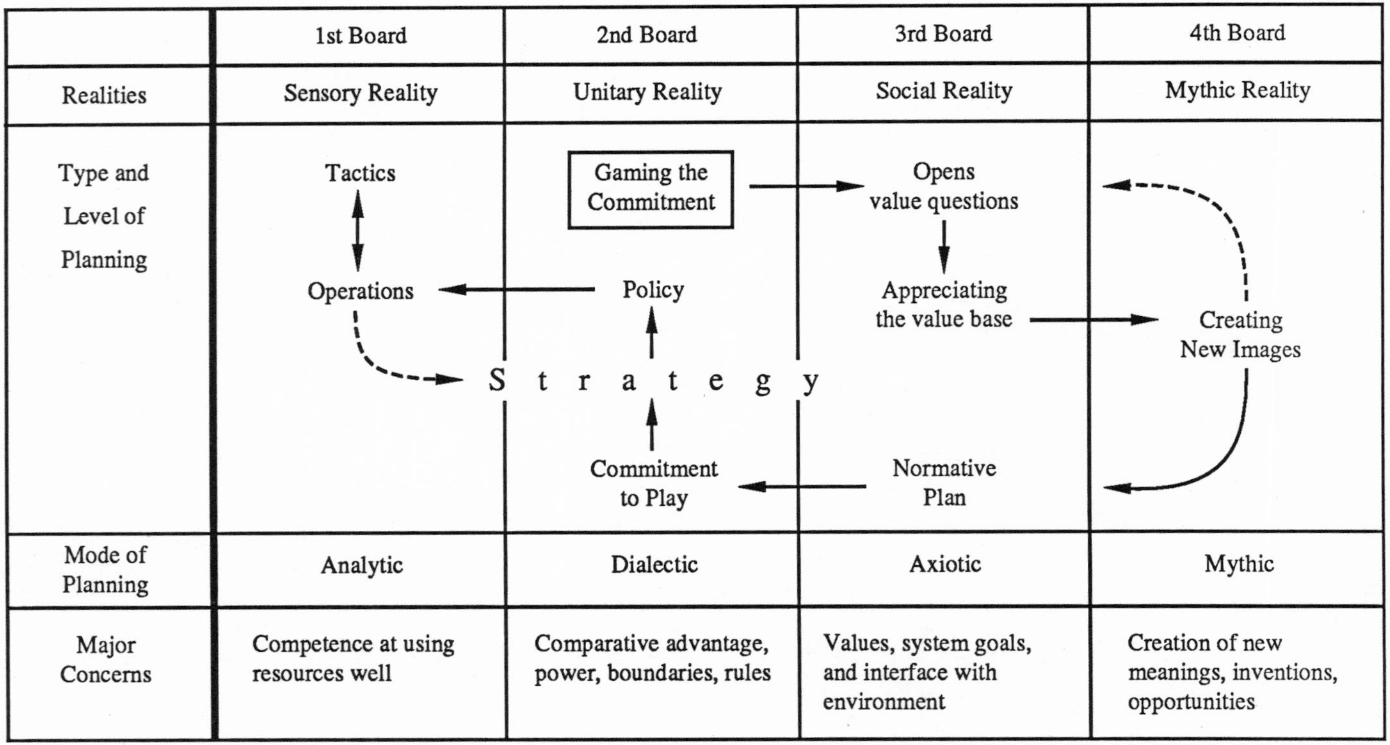

	1st Board	2nd Board	3rd Board	4th Board
Realities	Sensory Reality	Unitary Reality	Social Reality	Mythic Reality
Type and Level of Planning	Tactics ↔ Operations	Gaming the Commitment → Policy ← ← Commitment to Play	Opens value questions → Appreciating the value base → Normative Plan	Creating New Images
Mode of Planning	Analytic	Dialectic	Axiotic	Mythic
Major Concerns	Competence at using resources well	Comparative advantage, power, boundaries, rules	Values, system goals, and interface with environment	Creation of new meanings, inventions, opportunities

Strategy

by which the game is played on the first board. A move could add squares to the playing board, for example, or allow you to trade a piece captured from your opponent for your own lost piece. A recent dramatic example of such play in the business world is the development of the various forms of leveraged buyouts—for example, using ''junk bonds''—that have radically changed the rules by which executives manage a firm's assets. T. Boone Pickens has been the hero (or an Antichrist) of this extended game. Such changes in the rules of the game itself are imposed because the player believes the changes will provide strategic advantage. That is, he believes such changes will rig the game in his favor. Of course, in such games the opponent, too, can play on the second board, introducing more new rules. We have seen a great variety of devices emerge to counter the takeovers—for example, ''poison pills'' and bringing in ''white knights.'' Whereas the first game is the analyst's, this second game is one of *power*—the power to establish the rules by which the game will be played. It deals with control over territory, assets, and expectations. War over the rules of war is at the heart of the rigging that has been going on in the great political struggles between East and West over the past forty years. This is clearly a dialectic.

When the impact of the play on the second game has been absorbed and new rules accepted, attention returns to the first board and the analytic minds return to their operational gaming in accordance with the newly defined situation. Sometimes power plays to change the rules are made explicitly—for example, when legislation was passed to favor a particular contractor to run the California lottery. But most often rules are made subtly, appearing first as a normal move on the first board. Thus we frequently experience the play as if the two games are collapsed into one. A particular move may have both operational and strategic consequences.

Now envision a third chess board. On this board a play changes the *values* of the play—the purpose of a game, the definition of a win, and, more generally, the worth of any move. In a chess tournament, for example, the rule might be changed to define a winner as the one who created the most novel strategy.

This change in the objective calls on the player to demonstrate ingenuity to go beyond simple analytic power. Such a new criterion for winning might find favor among the experts as computers come to rank higher and higher against the human players. In the corporate world, the *purpose* of conducting business has recently become a concern. Whereas twenty years ago it was improper for a stock company to do anything but maximize profit, today executives occasionally look to a broader set of values in deciding how their business should perform. It has become the main role of leadership to set the direction and general tone of behavior (the organizational culture). General Motors, perhaps for the first time in half a century, is claiming that its efforts to design the new Saturn plant must fulfill a social (even a nationalistic) purpose. A variety of QWL and industrial democracy projects call for adding new values of human and social resource development to the technological and commercial objectives of traditional American management. And, as is often pointed out, the adoption of new objectives changes strategic play by freeing the company from third-party agreements, thereby attaining great cost advantages. Thus again a move on the third board can appear on a collapsed board, appearing as a play on the first and second boards as well as producing value changes. A move can simultaneously have normative, strategic, and operational utility.

Looking at trends in the environment at large, we recognize there is an opportunity to make far greater changes in the way we engage with the world than simply by changing the rules of our games and the value of play. We can create fundamentally new games with plays on a fourth board—games that, in their novelty, create whole new symbols, values, strategies, operations, and tactics, games that might not even be recognized as games. I am not sure there is an example of such a creation that goes beyond the consummate game of chess, but there are certainly deep creations occurring in the worlds of technology, commerce, and social practice, creations so encompassing as to form part of a grand paradigm shift in which the *meaning* of goods, work, and social organization is changing. The activity on the fourth board is really beyond games, for whole new forms of human activity may emerge. Creating an economics without the axiom of scarcity, for example, would lead to great societal rearrangements. A play on the fourth board is different from what is called ''planning,'' for it creates that which is to be.

In Figure 9.9, the open-system planning spiral is displayed on a chart of the four games. The change begins with a player becoming open to a radical change in the game—a political move on the second board. It continues with play on the third board to reevaluate the elements of the game and perhaps to create an entirely new game (on the fourth board). Once the image of the desired game is accepted, the play returns to the second board where strategic decisions must be made to define a game the others will play. The policy constitutes the rules of the game. Once the policy is established, play reverts to the first board, returning it to the experts who will run the changed game, organization, or society. Note that the major concerns for each board are listed at the bottom of Figure 9.9. These concerns relate to the skills that must be employed on each board for change to be accomplished. Since the open-system planning model is played on all four boards, it calls on leadership styles and skills requisite to play on each board. Other, less complex paths of change, such as those displayed in Figure 9.7, must be used if the full range of styles and skills is not available.

Conclusion

For all the words and charts, I have presented here just an abstract of a praxis—a map with some directional arrows to suggest possible routes to large-scale change. It is not yet a full theory, but rather a structuring of possibilities. Underlying it is a testable proposition: As individuals and cultures, we hold onto diverse concepts of reality that lead us to diverse concepts of change. The evidence collected to date supports both the diversity in realities and the association of each reality with different concepts of leadership and the notion that this diversity calls for different approaches to change. The practice that follows from this proposition is not so easily tested. There are the inherent paradoxes of evaluation across alternative realities, and there

are many other system characteristics external to this meta-praxis
that may determine the approaches to be used. But validation
is not the main issue. More important is its ability to create
awareness of alternative paths and ways to explore their use.
There is considerable value of even so rudimentary a meta-praxis
flowing from this service to change agents, helping us to com-
prehend the complex world we enter when we take on a large-
scale change effort.

References

Ackoff, R. *Redesigning the Future: A Systems Approach to Societal Problems.* New York: Wiley-Interscience, 1974.

Adizes, I. *Dialectic Conversion for the Management of Conflict.* Los
Angeles: University of California Press, 1978.

Batista, J. "How to Rebuild Spanish America." Unpublished
doctoral dissertation, Fielding Institute, Santa Barbara, 1988.

Bennis, W. G. *Changing Organizations.* New York: McGraw-Hill,
1966.

Berger, P. L., and Luckmann, T. *The Social Construction of Reality.*
Garden City, N.J.: Doubleday, 1966.

Blake, R. R., Mouton, J. S., Barnes, L. B., and Griener, L. E.
"A Managerial Grid Approach to Organization Develop-
ment: The Theory and Some Research Findings." *Harvard
Business Review,* 1964, *42,* 135–138.

Brown, D. L. "Planned Change in Underorganized Systems."
In T. G. Cummings (Ed.), *Systems Theory for Organization
Development.* New York: Wiley, 1980.

Cummings, T. G. *Systems Theory for Organization Development.* New
York: Wiley, 1980.

Emery, F. E., and Trist, E. L. *Towards a Social Ecology.* London:
Plenum Press, 1973.

Emery, M. *Searching.* Canberra: Center for Continuing Education, Australian National University, 1976.

Jung, C. G. *Mysterium Conjunctionis.* Bollingen Series XX. Princeton, N.J.: Princeton University Press, 1963.

LeShan, L. *Alternative Realities.* New York: Ballantine, 1976.

Levy, A., and Merry, U. *Organizational Transformation: Approaches,
Strategies and Theory.* New York: Praeger, 1986.

Mason, R. O. "A Dialectic Approach to Strategic Planning." *Management Science,* 1969, *15,* B403–414.

Miller, E. "The Ahmedabad Experiment Revisited: Work Organization in Weaving." In C. Crouch and F. A. Heller (Eds.), *International Yearbook of Organizational Democracy.* Vol. 1. New York: Wiley, 1983.

Pava, C. "Normative Incrementalism." Unpublished doctoral dissertation, Wharton School, University of Pennsylvania, 1980.

Schutz, A. "On Multiple Realities." *Philosophy and Phenomenological Research,* 1945, *5,* 533–576.

Tannenbaum, R., Margulies, N., Massarik, F., and Associates. *Human Systems Development.* San Francisco: Jossey-Bass, 1985.

Trist, E. L. "QWL and Community Development: Some Reflections on the Jamestown Experience." Unpublished manuscript, 1986.

10

A Completely Integrated Program for Organizational Change

Ralph H. Kilmann

The field of organizational development, as it first emerged in the 1950s, was envisioned as providing methods for system-wide planned change that would significantly improve the functioning of entire organizations. For the most part, this majestic vision has been lost and forgotten.

During the 1960s and 1970s, efforts at improving organizations became more and more specialized and, eventually, fragmented—focusing on the narrow use of specific techniques such as team building, survey feedback, and performance appraisal. Academics, following traditional guidelines for rigorous research, tended to study improvement methods primarily suited for tightly controlled, isolated parts of the organization—thereby ignoring a system-wide perspective. Executives found this research approach to be consistent with their own traditional prerogatives, since it did not require them to question either the corporate culture or the power structure of their organizations. Until now, there has been little incentive for either academics or practitioners to pursue improvement efforts on a large scale.

In the 1980s, however, as many organizations are coming to realize that "future shock" is upon them, the need for large-scale system change is being voiced frequently. Now entire organizations must be transformed into more market-driven, innovative, and adaptive systems if they are to survive and prosper in the highly competitive, global environment of the next decades. Thus there is a dire need to rejuvenate the vision and methods of organizational development (OD).

For the past fifteen years, my research program and consulting work gradually have moved from a narrow OD perspective to large-system change. Briefly, during the 1970s, I concentrated on one single action lever after another: reorganization, management training, team building, strategic planning, the design of reward systems, and, eventually, managing corporate culture. By the early 1980s, I began to appreciate the limitations of these single efforts at change: If organizations are truly complex and interconnected systems, then a more integrated and holistic approach to organizational change is mandatory.

After several successful projects using an integrated approach to planned change, I documented all my theories and models in one book, *Beyond the Quick Fix* (Kilmann, 1984). Since then, I have had the opportunity to apply my "complete" program to other organizations, thereby extending my understanding of large-system change, as reported in my new book, *Managing Beyond the Quick Fix* (Kilmann, 1989). This chapter describes the essence of my learning to date—my quest to broaden the concept of organizational development to embrace organization-wide transformations.

A Program of Planned Change

A change program can be considered complete only if it specifies all the controllable variables that affect organizational success and all the action steps by which managers and consultants can adjust these variables for organizational success. *Organizational success* means creating and maintaining high performance and morale over an extended period of time.

Regarding the first ingredient, a complete program must integrate a variety of approaches—ranging from those that recognize the emotional conflicts of individuals to those that act on the system-wide properties of organizations. This strategy enables managers and consultants to control all the leverage points in the organization—not just one or two. Specifically, when I wrote *Beyond the Quick Fix* in 1984 I believed that the full range of leverage points could be addressed by five carefully designed and integrated tracks: (1) the culture track, (2) the management skills track, (3) the team-building track, (4) the strategy-structure track, and (5) the reward system track. Today there is a "sixth" track—referred to as the "shadow" track—that runs parallel to the other five tracks (Kilmann, 1989). As I will explain a little later, the shadow track facilitates implementation by forming a steering committee representing all members in the organization and by making use of internal consultants throughout the implementation process.

Regarding the second ingredient, it is not enough to indicate what must be changed; a complete program must outline *how* change can be effectively managed in the organization. While a quick-fix approach blindly implements one single remedy after another, a *complete* program recognizes the intricate process of introducing and managing change, including the need for top management's support, the importance of defining problems before solutions are chosen, and the necessity to be flexible while implementing change in a living, breathing organization. Specifically, the five stages of planned change are (1) initiating the program, (2) diagnosing the problems, (3) scheduling the tracks, (4) implementing the tracks, and (5) evaluating the results. During these five stages, the full range of action levers will be discussed via the five tracks. A recent addition to these stages (particularly "scheduling the tracks") includes a discussion of which organizational unit should begin the change program (following a diagnosis of the whole organization) and how to spread change from one unit to the next. When I wrote *Beyond the Quick Fix* in 1984 I was primarily concerned with creating change in any unit of the organization. In the past few years, I have been involved with projects aimed at organization-wide transformation, where spreading change throughout the whole organization was a primary objective at the outset (Kilmann, 1989).

Figure 10.1 shows the five stages of planned change in the form of a model. To be successful, all programs for improving organizations must devote sufficient time and effort to complete each stage. Movement from one stage to the next, shown by the single arrows, should not take place until all the criteria for the earlier stages are satisfied. Otherwise, any glossed-over stages will come back to haunt the organization. Moreover, continual recycling through all five stages, without success, will eventually wear down the organization. It is desirable, therefore,

Figure 10.1. The Five Stages of Planned Change.

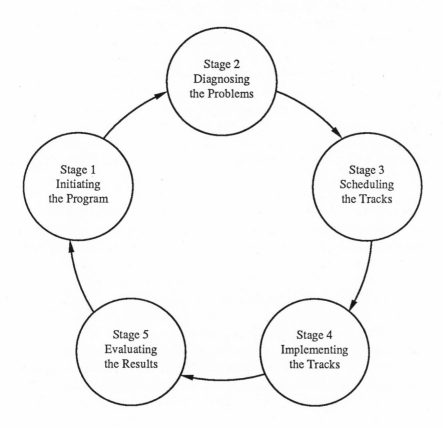

to halt the entire change program until a particular stage can be conducted properly; or, if it seems that the necessary commitment and learning are unlikely to develop, the entire program should be terminated. There is simply no reason for an organization to go through a long and difficult process if success is impossible.

The five stages of planned change should be approached as a collaborative effort among managers, members, and internal and external consultants; this is the best way I know to guarantee the success of the whole program. In many cases, however, top managers may prefer to manage the five stages on their own, just as they ordinarily make decisions and take action. But I do caution managers not to conduct single-handedly those aspects of the program that are clearly beyond their skills and experience. Managers must recognize their limitations. It helps, for example, to have external consultants for collecting sensitive information about management and organizational problems, revealing cultural norms, exposing outdated assumptions, confronting the organization's troublemakers, and helping managers hear honest feedback about their team's functioning. Therefore the diagnostic stage—and major portions of the culture, management skills, and team-building tracks—should be guided by external consultants. Implementing the strategy-structure and the reward system tracks can be done primarily by the managers, although even here consultants can help foster a more participative approach than managers can promote by themselves. The shadow track, incidentally, is conducted almost exclusively by members; the reason for using internal consultants is to enable the organization to learn the process for subsequent efforts at planned change.

Initiating the Program

The search for a way of initiating large-system change often proceeds in a rather informal political manner by a few key executives of the firm. Several times I have witnessed a pattern that begins when one enlightened executive is thrilled to learn that at least one other similarly minded person sees the growing problems facing the organization. After several informal discussions, they search out other executives who either share their perceptions or can be influenced to see things in the same way. Eventually, when such informal support is mobilized, the executives find a way to put the topic of planned change (or whatever they choose to call it) on a formal meeting agenda. A formal discussion then ensues whereby other executives learn about the issues and are able to voice their opinions. If the necessary commitment has not been developed, the agenda item is dropped and the topic goes back to an informal discussion among disgruntled executives. If the informal mobilization of commitment *has* been successful, however, the agenda item is translated into a task force or committee effort to explore the topic in much greater depth. Following a formal presentation of the committee's deliberations, one or more executives are charged with contacting the designated consultants.

The consultants should be most interested to learn if the organization is ready for change. Managers may voice their commitment, but the real test is subsequent action. At best, the consultants attempt to infer from several indicators the existence of true commitment. Do the managers openly acknowledge their role in the creation of the problem? Do they consider alternative perspectives and approaches? Do they seem receptive to a full diagnosis by the consultants? Do they realize the extensive and involving nature of the program? Or do they hope to find another quick fix? If the consultants do not believe that sufficient commitment exists for a complete program of change and do not think it is likely to develop, I recommend expressing this view to the top management group as the primary reason for terminating the project. Nobody needs a long-drawn-out failure.

If there does appear to be sufficient basis for continuing, the consultants meet with more managers (including the top management group) to discuss their objectives and expectations. Much like the formation of a personal relationship, the outside consultants and the organization see if there appears to be a fit. If this rapport does not develop, it may be due to an interpersonal quirk or to a true difference in style. In any case, I have never heard of a successful case of change in which the client and consultant did not get along. A difficult process of change must be rooted in a firm foundation of trust, liking, and mutual respect.

We must recognize, however, that some organizations seem to have the capacity to *anticipate* problems before a crisis is reached. This is the case when a number of senior executives recognize that it might be easier to conduct planned change while the organization is still in a relatively healthy state. Members might be more willing to participate in various programs to improve performance and morale when their jobs are not on the line and there are high expectations of long-term success.

I have found it useful to think of a "window of opportunity" for organizational change—somewhere between the point of not quite recognizing that certain problems will only become worse if they are not addressed soon and the point of crisis when members do not believe that the organization has the time and capacity to alter its gloomy prospects. In most cases, however, a change program is initiated amidst a crisis or great uncertainty. Too infrequently do consultants and managers come into partnership under anticipatory conditions. Most often it seems that the organization has to be *hurting* for some time before the call for a new approach is sounded and accepted.

Diagnosing the Problems

The diagnostic phase is very much guided by the external consultants, who have to be sure that the diagnosis is based on their assessments independent of the initial reasons that brought them into the organization. The consultants, with the aid of the managers, develop a plan to pinpoint all the problems in the entire organization. The objective is to sample each level in the hierarchy—and each division and department—so that a representative view of the organization can be obtained. I always insist on interviewing everyone in the top management group simply because their views, and especially their commitment to change, are so critical to the program.

It is essential to explicate the model that is used to ask questions and record responses during the interviews (for example, see Tichy, 1983). If the interviewers only see organizations as a network of interpersonal relationships, they will only ask questions and record responses with regard to interpersonal problems and experiences. The same holds true for seeing organizations as document-producing systems (formulating strategies, organization charts, or job descriptions), cultural phenomena, management styles, or group dynamics. Large-system change must be seen as a complex holographic image—a three-dimensional image created by reflecting beams of light at different angles—including the multitude of views about how organizations function and why. Any perceptual filters that limit the search for a full understanding of the organization's problems will limit the variety of action levers for change that are considered—which will automatically prevent large-system change from occurring.

Figure 10.2 shows organizational life as a holographic image. The image—model—is used for discovering an organization's full range of problems standing in the way of organiza-

Figure 10.2. Barriers to Success.

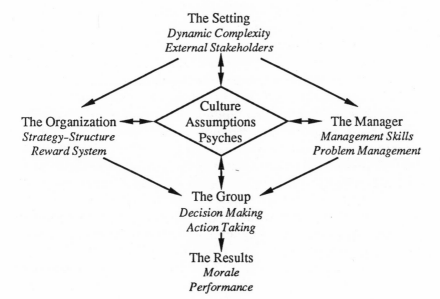

tional success: its barriers to success. The model consists of five broad categories representing the at-the-surface aspects of an organization plus, at center stage, three below-the-surface aspects that add the dimension of depth. The five broad categories are the setting, the organization, the manager, the group, and the results. The three holographic aspects are culture, assumptions, and psyches. The double arrows surrounding the ''holographic diamond'' signify the strong reciprocal influence between the three below-the-surface aspects and the other categories. Similarly, the single arrows show the primary (but not exclusive) impact one category has on another, particularly how several categories combine to determine decision making and action taking, as well as morale and performance.

At the top of the Barriers-to-Success model is the setting, the broadest category of all. It includes every possible event and force that can affect the success of the organization. Even if many of these events are generally irrelevant, they can become a significant factor for the organization to consider at any time. The term *dynamic complexity* summarizes the two qualities that are having increasing impact on all organizations: rapid change and interdependence in a global marketplace. *External stakeholders* are any individual, group, other organization, or community that has some stake in what the focal organization does—making dynamic complexity both unique and operational for an organization. Not only do the stakeholders vary tremendously depending on the organization being studied, but new stakeholders can enter into the organization's setting at any time—such as new competitors with improved products, new government agencies with new regulations, new research groups developing new production methods, and new consumers with different tastes. The setting provides the context in which the organization's internal properties and dynamics are understood, interpreted, and subsequently aligned.

On the left-hand side of the Barriers-to-Success model, the formal organization can be diagnosed according to strategy, structure, and reward systems. Strategy refers to all the documents that signify direction: statements of vision, mission, purpose, goals, and objectives. Structure refers to the way resources are marshaled in order to move the organization in the designated direction: organization charts, policy statements, job descriptions, formal rules and regulations. The reward system includes all documented methods to attract and retain employees, but particularly to motivate employees to high levels of performance—given the established strategy and structure of the firm. The essential issue is whether all these documented systems are barriers or channels to success.

On the right-hand side of the Barriers-to-Success model, the styles and skills of the managers can be diagnosed for how well they fit with the types of people and problems in the organization. Until recently, managers have been thought of primarily as decision makers—persons who must choose among a set of alternatives to arrive at an optimal solution. This is all well and good if the alternatives are already determined and the rules for choosing among them are clear-cut. With dynamic complexity, however, it is not even clear what the essential problem is, let alone what the alternative choices are. Today's managers have to be problem managers—sensing and defining problems—even more than decision makers selecting and implementing solutions.

At the center of the Barriers-to-Success model, the uniquely holographic, below-the-surface aspects of the organization can be diagnosed: culture, assumptions, and psyches. Each of these aspects functions at a different level of depth. Just below the surface, and thus easiest of the three to manage, is *culture:* the invisible force behind the tangibles and observables in an organization, a social energy that moves the membership into action. Culture is defined as *shared* values, beliefs, expectations, and norms. Norms, in particular, are easiest to define: They are the unwritten rules of the game. For example: Don't disagree with your boss; don't rock the boat; don't share information with other groups. These norms are seldom written down or discussed. Often work groups pressure each member to follow such dysfunctional norms out of habit. As a consequence culture—as manifested in norms of behavior—greatly affects how formal statements get interpreted and provides what written documents leave out. Of special concern is how culture often steers behavior in the exact opposite direction from what is "requested" by job descriptions and work procedures or "dictated" by supervisors and higher-level managers.

The second holographic aspect of organizations is at the next level of depth after culture. Simply put, *assumptions* are all the beliefs that have been taken for granted but may turn out to be false under closer analysis. Underlying any decision or action is a large set of generally unstated and untested assumptions. For example, managers may be assuming that the following unstated beliefs are unquestionably true: No new competitors will enter the industry; the economy will steadily improve; the government will continue to restrict foreign imports for the industry; the consumer will buy whatever the firm produces; the availability of capital will remain the same; employees will continue to accept the same compensation package and benefits plan; yesterday's structures are best for solving today's problems. In short, all previous decisions and actions may have been based more on fantasy and habit than on reality and choice.

The third holographic aspect of organizations is also the deepest: the innermost qualities of the human mind and spirit. While *psyches* cannot be changed in a short period of time, if at all, an accurate understanding of human nature is essential in order to design strategy, structure, reward systems, cultures, and the implementation of all business decisions. In essence, the assumptions that members make concerning human nature— what people want, fear, resist, support, and defend—underlie the eventual success or failure of all these systems and decisions.

The lower part of the model portrays the decisions and actions that follow from group efforts. While individuals do make decisions and take actions on their own, today's organization requires multiple contributions from members of one or more groups in order to manage complex problems. Groups can be nominal—existing in name only—as information is not even discussed among the members. Worst yet, in some groups (as in powerful cliques) information is kept secret. Alternatively groups can be teams—highly interactive, cohesive sets of individuals all working toward the same objectives. Generally, it is the team approach that will provide the most comprehensive source of expertise and information to solve complex problems, where synergism enables the team to contribute more than the sum of its members. Such team efforts will result in high-quality decisions *and* member commitment to implement these decisions effectively—the ideal model for organizational success under conditions of dynamic complexity and shifting stakeholders.

The holographic model illustrates why the team approach will fail in most organizations in which the barriers to success are still in place. If managers do not have the proper styles and skills to manage complex problems, group decisions will be made by majority rule or by the dictates of the manager himself. If the culture pressures members to withhold information so that each member can protect his own territory, again the quality of decisions will be adversely affected. If the strategy of the organization is rooted in false assumptions about the consumer and the firm's competitors, every group decision will be moving the organization in the wrong direction. If the structure of the organization makes it difficult for members in various departments to join together on decisions that affect them all, the expertise and information needed to make high-quality decisions will not even be present in the group. Furthermore, if the reward system encourages individual efforts instead of team efforts, members will not be motivated to commit to the group decision-making process in the first place. Indeed, only if an organization is composed of well-functioning teams with minimal barriers to success in every category does it have a chance to be the truly break-away company in a competitive, global marketplace.

These interrelated dynamics, as captured by the Barriers-to-Success model, illustrate the variety of issues that arise again and again while diagnosing organizations. Naturally there are differences from one organization to another; there are always unique circumstances or histories that moderate the extent and variety of these basic issues. Nevertheless, I wish to emphasize the almost uncanny pattern that has emerged in all the research and consulting I have done in organizations. Rarely do I find that the formal organization *alone* needs readjustment for organizational success. Rarely do I find that managers learning new skills about complex problems will *itself* solve the organization's performance and morale problems. I have never encountered a case in which only the culture had lagged behind and there was an effective formal organization already in place with managers applying up-to-date skills. The culture problem has always been associated with problems in the organization, the group, and the manager as well.

These general findings are not that surprising. Seeing the organization as a holographic image reveals an interrelated set of above-the-surface and below-the-surface dynamics and properties. Given such a filter, what is the likelihood that today's organizations can cope with dynamic complexity and shifting external stakeholders by adjusting only one category in the Barriers-to-Success model? It is very unlikely indeed. What about adjusting most but not all of the categories shown in Figure 10.2? That is just as unlikely, sorry to say. Rather, it seems that *all* the categories have to be considered and acted upon in all cases. This is the new rule of organizational change, not the exception. Management development, organizational design, and culture change, all with an enlightened view of the world and all its stakeholders, are necessary to revitalize our organizations. Otherwise, the extent and variety of complex problems will continue to impose troublesome barriers to organizational success and will continue to prevent large-system change from occurring.

When the top managers accept the general diagnosis provided by the consultants, as summarized by the Barriers-to-Success model, it then becomes desirable to convey these findings to the entire membership. It takes conviction for the top managers to be willing to share the diagnosis with others. But this willingness is critical for demonstrating commitment to the membership. The act of top managers acknowledging problems to themselves and to others, while painful, is an important event in the life of an organization.

Scheduling the Tracks

The Barriers-to-Success model, which guides the full diagnosis of the organization's problems and opportunities, contains two categories that are uncontrollable, at least in the short run. The *setting*, the broadest category, is more powerful than the organization itself while the *psyche*, the most personal category, is too deep-seated to change. Five categories in between these macro and micro aspects of the model are directly controllable by managers and consultants: culture, management skills, teams, strategy-structure, and reward systems. These action levers constitute the program of five tracks.

The third stage of planned change involves three elements: (1) selecting the first unit to participate in the program and planning the spread of change to the remaining organizational units; (2) selecting the techniques (methods for bringing about change) that will make up each of the five tracks in each unit—to address the specific problems identified during the diagnostic stage; and (3) scheduling the five tracks into a timed sequence of activity in order to promote effective learning and change in each organizational unit. Once a plan for action is formalized in this stage, managers, members, and consultants will work together to implement it in the following stage.

Scheduling the five tracks first requires a decision on which unit of the organization should begin the program (see Beckhard and Harris, 1987). Sometimes an autonomous business unit is chosen as a pilot project. Following an evaluation of the results (described in the last stage of planned change), one by one, other business units implement the program of planned change. This sequence proceeds until all business units desiring or requiring change have implemented some version of the five tracks. Alternatively, corporate headquarters might be the first unit to be scheduled for the program, followed in turn by the remaining units.

My experience in scheduling units in the organization for planned change suggests that the first unit scheduled should be a *primary* business unit. The criterion for such a choice is that of credibility: Which unit, if it undergoes the change program and is successful, would serve as the best example to the other units that such change is important, necessary, and possible? In most cases I have found that business units are chosen because they are, in fact, isolated from the core of the organization. Perhaps this represents a safe strategy: If the program is not successful, the whole organization is hardly affected. But if the program is in fact successful, the other business units will not regard the pilot project as a relevant example of what they should be doing. If the intent is to spread change throughout the organization, units should be chosen that are critical to the success of the whole enterprise, a strategy that involves greater risk: An unsuccessful program is damaging to the whole company while a successful effort is likely to spread to other units. This greater risk in picking the core business units to implement the program should be reason enough for the senior executives to do whatever it takes to make the program a success (see Beer, 1980).

A plan is then developed that specifies the ways in which the change can be spread. This plan includes not only the order in which the remaining units are scheduled for the change program, but also the supporting mechanisms and procedures. As the pilot project is under way (and as other units begin the process as well), for example, regular communications can be conveyed to the rest of the organization indicating what is taking place and why. Some managers or members from the pilot project might be temporarily transferred to the next unit to help facilitate the change process. Moreover, various organizational rewards and perks might be offered to those units as they participate in the program in order to convey the special nature of the project and the importance of successful results (see Walton, 1975).

While the choice of a pilot project to begin the program and the sequence and methods by which other business units participate certainly varies from company to company, what makes each application of a change program different is the particular techniques used in each of the five tracks. Just as the diagnosis varies for each organizational unit, so does the choice of technique to address each problem. In some cases the management skills track will cover leadership styles, conflict-handling modes, and ways of minimizing defensive communication. If the managers have already acquired these skills, management training moves directly to teaching methods for managing complex problems, including assumptional analysis. Clearly the consultants and the managers should be aware of the diversity of techniques that exist (or can be constructed) so they can choose the ones that best fit the problems in each organizational unit (Huse, 1980).

The one thing that most distinguishes the change program from the quick fix is the integrated nature of the five tracks. These tracks and their host of techniques are not scheduled in a random order, nor is a shotgun approach used in which all tracks are implemented haphazardly. The guiding principles in organizing and sequencing the five tracks include the capacity of members and their organization to change, what change is easiest and best to accomplish early, and what change should be left for later. Specifically, the first three tracks concentrate on the informal organization whereas the last two address the formal documents. My experience with planned change has shown repeatedly that if the informal organization is not properly prepared for change, modifications in the documents will be ignored at best and ridiculed at worst.

Here is a brief summary of the primary objectives of the five tracks:

1. The culture track: establishing trust, information sharing, and adaptiveness; being receptive to change and improvement
2. The management skills track: augmenting skills to cope with complexity; exposing and updating assumptions
3. The team-building track: infusing new cultural norms and assumptions into each work unit; fostering cooperative efforts
4. The strategy-structure track: aligning all work units and resources with new strategic directions
5. The reward system track: establishing a performance-based reward system; sustaining the whole improvement effort

The culture track is the ideal place to start the program. It is enlightening to discuss openly what was seldom written down or mentioned in any conversation. Members enjoy—even laugh at—the revelations that occur as the dysfunctional norms, the unwritten rules of the game, are brought to everyone's attention. It is also much easier to blame norms than to blame oneself or other people. So long as members take responsibility for change, it does not really matter if using norms as a scapegoat takes some of the pressure off their egos. But without an initial culture change, it is unlikely that the other four tracks can be successful. The members must believe that this program is for real and is entirely unlike all the other quick-fix programs that have failed in the past. The culture track consists of a five-step process: (1) surfacing actual norms, (2) establishing desired norms, (3) identifying culture-gaps, (4) closing culture-gaps, and (5) sustaining cultural change. Thus the culture track first exposes the old culture and then, if necessary, creates a new *adaptive* culture.

After the culture track has begun and made some progress, the management skills track can start. In most cases, the managers have contributed substantially to the organization's problems, even if unintentionally. The managers usually have not kept up with the environmental setting and its new types of problems. Traditionally managers pick the first available quick-fix solution before they even bother to define the root causes of the problem and then, to top it all off, they implement the quick-fix solution in a mechanistic manner; not surprisingly, the problem never gets resolved. But once managers are receptive to change—through the culture track—they can be taught the full set of skills needed to conduct a five-step process for effective problem management: (1) sensing problems, (2) defining problems, (3) deriving solutions, (4) implementing solutions, and (5) evaluating outcomes.

The management skills track also offers a systematic method for uncovering the underlying assumptions that drive all decisions into action. If these assumptions have remained unstated and therefore untested, managers may have continually made the wrong decisions. But given a new culture that encourages trust and openness, members now will be able to analyze their previously unstated assumptions before any critical decisions are made. No longer will the membership be held back by its own faulty assumptions.

As the culture track and the management skills track are providing some early successes (even if these are conducted primarily in a classroom setting away from the job), the next effort lies in directly transferring this learning into the mainstream of organizational life. Specifically, the team-building track does three things: It keeps the troublemakers in check so they will not disrupt cooperative efforts; it brings the new cultural norms and management skills into the day-to-day activities of each work group; and it enables cooperative decisions to take place across group boundaries, as in multiple team efforts. In this way, all available expertise and information will come forth to manage the complex technical and business problems that arise within and between work groups. As the culture opens up everyone's minds as well as their hearts, work groups can examine, maybe for the first time, the barriers that have held them back in the past. Through various team-building sessions, old warring cliques become effective teams.

Eventually it becomes time for the membership to take on one of the most difficult problems facing any organization in a dynamic and complex environment: aligning its formally documented systems. One might think that the mission of the firm and its corresponding strategic choices should have been the first topics addressed. Why should the organization proceed with changes in culture, management skills, and team efforts before the new directions are formalized? Is it not logical to know the directions *before* the rest of the system is put in place? Yes, that is logical. But there are other things operating in a complex organization besides logic. If we understand human nature and organizational culture, we recognize that it makes little sense to plan the future directions of the firm if members do not trust one another and will not share important information with one another, expose their tried-and-true assumptions, or commit to the new directions anyway because the culture will not allow it. If the prior tracks have not accomplished their purposes, the strategy-structure problem will be addressed through politics and vested interests, not through an open exchange of ideas and a cooperative effort to achieve organizational success.

The strategy-structure track is conducted in an eight-step process: (1) making strategic choices, (2) listing objectives to be achieved and tasks to be performed, (3) analyzing objective/task relationships, (4) calculating inefficiencies that stem from an out-of-date structure, (5) diagnosing structural problems, (6) designing a new structure, (7) implementing the new structure, and (8) evaluating the new structure. As a result of this process, the members remove a two-sided barrier to success: bureaucratic red tape that moves the organization in the wrong direction. In its place is a structure aligned with the firm's strategy.

Once the organization is moving in the right direction with the right structure and resources, the reward system track completes the change program by paying for performance. A seven-step process is used to design a performance-based reward system: (1) designing special task forces to study the problem, (2) reviewing the types of reward systems, (3) establishing several alternative reward systems, (4) debating the assumptions behind the different reward systems, (5) designing the new reward system, (6) implementing the new reward system, and (7) evaluating the new reward system. Only if the earlier tracks have accomplished their objectives will members believe that the reward system really works and that important rewards will depend on their performance. Such a reward system motivates excellence in contrast to mediocrity.

To help members improve their performance from one work cycle to the next, the reward system also considers how performance results and reward decisions are communicated to each member of the organization during face-to-face meetings with a superior. Two different types of meetings are established: a performance review to provide information for evaluative purposes and a counseling session to provide feedback for learning purposes. With a well-functioning reward system in place, all improvements derived from the change program will be ingrained in the everyday life of the organization.

The reward system track is futile, though, if all the other tracks have not been managed properly. Without a supportive culture, members will not believe that rewards are tied to performance—regardless of what the formal documents state. Instead, they will believe that it is useless to work hard and do well since rewards are based on favoritism and politics. Similarly, if managers do not have the skills to conduct performance appraisal, for example, any well-intentioned reward system will be thwarted; the arousal of defensiveness will inhibit each member's motivation to improve his performance. Without effective teams, managers and members will not openly share such information as the results of performance reviews and the distribution of rewards; in the absence of this information, imaginations will run wild since nobody will know for sure whether high performers receive significantly more rewards than low performers. Furthermore, if the strategy and structures are not designed properly, the reward system cannot measure performance objectively; only if each group is autonomous can its output be assessed as a separate quantity as close to the individual level as possible—a necessary condition to make the pay-for-performance link a reality in everyone's eyes.

What if people disregard the formal reward system and strive to excel for intrinsic rewards, such as personal satisfaction for a job well done? If the other tracks have not been managed properly, even the most dedicated efforts by the members will not lead to high performance for the organization. Instead, members' efforts will be blocked by all the barriers to success that are still in force: dysfunctional cultures, outdated management skills, poorly functioning work groups, unrealistic strategic choices, and misaligned structures. Alternatively, whatever improvements were realized as a result of the earlier tracks will not be sustained if the membership is not ultimately rewarded for high performance: The old dysfunctional cultures, assumptions, and behavior will creep back into the workplace. Thus the reward system is the last major barrier that must be transformed into a channel for success—the bottom line for the membership.

Figure 10.3 illustrates the scheduling of the five tracks for a major industrial organization. The horizontal line for each track signifies an ongoing cycle of off-site meetings (in a work-shop setting with consultants present) and informal meetings (organized at the workplace without consultants present) in order to pursue the topic in question (say, cultural change). As the figure shows, a track does not have to be completed before in-itiating the next track. The guiding principle is that the earlier track should have established the necessary conditions in order for the next track to succeed. After the culture track has estab-lished a basic foundation of trust with regard to the change pro-gram, for example, managers will now be receptive to learning new styles and skills and so the management skills workshops can begin. After the managers have learned new skills, the team-building track can begin to encourage managers to use these new skills back on the job. It is not as if the entire culture change must be intact and all new skills learned before the member-ship can make use of the new culture and skills in their various business and technical decisions. Similarly, those who will be involved throughout the strategy-structure and reward system tracks can begin their discussions on this topic before every manager and team has completed the whole program.

If the complete program takes too long, gradually the mem-bership will lose interest and become disillusioned because the promised benefits (say, the new reward system) are not forthcom-ing. Alternatively, if the program is too short, the foundation for the successful completion of each track will not have been set and the membership will experience disappointment or even fail-ure with the results of each track. Thus careful orchestration of planned change is essential with an understanding of human na-ture and the capacity of organizations to undergo massive change.

Implementing the Tracks

The shadow track has been developed to facilitate the im-plementation of the five tracks by placing primary responsibility for the program on the shoulders of one group (the shadow group). This group of approximately ten to fifteen members, representing every level and division in the organization, meets

Figure 10.3. Scheduling the Five Tracks.

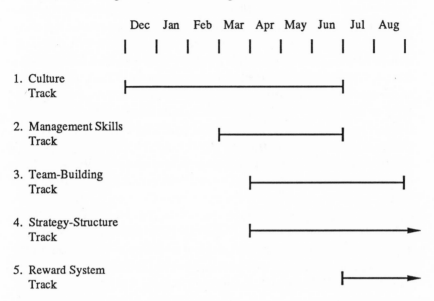

regularly to monitor the program and discover ways to improve the whole process of implementation. For example, this group might monitor every written document distributed by the executive office to ensure that a consistent message (signal) is being given. If a memorandum on a new policy is about to be sent to the membership, the shadow group would review it and suggest how it could be reworded to accord with the intentions behind the program of planned change in general and the culture change in particular.

The shadow track also seeks to increase members' involvement in the program by having the outside consultants work with inside consultants (say, human resource professionals or organizational development experts). This collaborative effort might include the training of inside consultants by outside consultants or entail some sort of pairing method. (An outside consultant might conduct each track with the aid of one or more inside consultants.) In these ways, the organization not only uses its internal resources as a partial substitute for excessive reliance

on outside expertise but also builds its own base of expertise
to implement change in the future.

In whatever way the shadow track is designed and conducted, it is one thing to schedule the five tracks but quite
another to adjust the schedule as it is implemented. Obviously,
the plan *never* takes place exactly as intended. There are always
surprises. Human nature and human systems, being what they
are, do not lend themselves to a predictable path. Besides, if
people feel they are being programmed in any way, it is not
unlike them to do something illogical, irrational, or unexpected
just to show how free and independent they really are. Implementing the five tracks is just another example of the dynamic
and complex world we live in.

The key issue during implementation, therefore, is flexibility. Is is important not to get locked into any plan; this makes
it very difficult to back off and change to a new one. The schedule
of five tracks is helpful as a starting point, since without it there
would be confusion and misguided efforts. As the schedule is
implemented, however, the consultants must look for cues, take
suggestions, and, in short, adapt.

Special requests are made for counseling sessions, feedback sessions for staff meetings, additional culture sessions, more
management skills training, and so forth. In each case, consultants and managers must consider the request and respond
according to their objectives and their sense of what will work.
Sometimes requests are turned down, but the reasons are always
presented and discussed. At other times, requests are acted
upon—but in a fashion different from that first suggested. Often
it is the managers themselves who initiate additional activity,
adjusting to what they perceive is needed—to nudge this person or that group or to support any effort that turned out to
be more difficult than first thought.

A shared expectation, which should develop as the program is initiated, is that the consultants have the freedom to
schedule whatever activities are necessary to move the change
effort forward. I have come across a number of organizations
that at first failed to appreciate the importance of this option.
I remember a few cases in which the managers expected the con-

sultants to know exactly what activities would take place and when. Since the members' needs and demands are constantly changing, however, frequent adjustment is essential to any improvement effort. Today's organization also needs the same approach relative to the needs and demands of its external environment. The former is merely a microcosm of the latter.

The most enjoyable part of the implementation stage is seeing changes and improvements take hold. Initially everyone is a little leery of what to expect and unsure whether the organization has the ability to change. As early successes are won, however, confidence develops, which inspires an even greater effort at improvement. This is not to suggest that the road is smooth and without obstacles; on a week-by-week basis, some things get a lot worse before they get better. In some cases, the organization expects the change to develop quickly and with little pain, regardless of what the managers or consultants have stated. When an event seems to reinforce the old ways or attitudes of the past, it is easy to be discouraged and feel that nothing has changed. But if one looks at month-by-month trends, instead of examining week-by-week fluctuations, the process shows a definite pattern of improvement.

These fluctuations in perceived accomplishments and moods illustrate the importance of setting realistic expectations in the beginning and making sure that impatience for change does not raise members' expectations to unattainable levels. Disappointment and frustration result when these expectations are out of line with reality, which subsequently affects both the individual's and the organization's confidence to continue. The managers and consultants have to nurture expectations very carefully during implementation.

After a number of months go by, it becomes more and more apparent that the membership has internalized the overt behavior that one is observing. Each person does not have to apply new skills and enact new cultural norms deliberately; rather, the new ways are enacted quite automatically. The new skills and behaviors become more natural and easier. At a certain point (which is very difficult to specify in advance), the hump is crossed and the old gives way to the new. The best way I can describe this transition is to say that the members and the managers would not return to the old ways even if they could because the new ways are so obviously better and more useful for their personal satisfaction and for accomplishing the organization's mission. Strangely, it is even hard for these members to recall how different things were just six months or a year ago. The past is really put aside in their behavior, attitudes, and memories.

The implementation stage is complete when the external consultants and managers both believe that the organization can manage its problems on its own. During the last few months of implementation, the outside consultants become less involved in scheduling and implementing activities; the managers and the inside consultants now decide on their own what team building or skills training is needed and then proceed to fill the gap—sometimes with outside help, sometimes not. The organization thus moves into "independence." The membership has solved, and can continue to solve, the problems for which the program was initiated in the beginning.

One difficult question is always asked: "How long will the whole change program take?" And it is asked repeatedly, not just once. My response is: "I can't say exactly; I can only suggest some rough guidelines from my experience." These guidelines consider the size and age of the organization, the number of organizational units involved, the complexity of the problems that were uncovered in each unit, the severity of the problems, the time available for conducting the five tracks, and the desire on the part of both managers and members to learn and change. Since the organization cannot shut down its operations just to engage in a change program, the five tracks have to be conducted as other work gets done—even during crises and peak seasons.

In general, one can expect most change programs to take anywhere from one to five years. Less than one year might work for a small division in which the formally documented systems need only a fine tuning. But a program taking more than five years might be necessary for a mega-organization involving major breaks from the past in every way. If the program were to take more than ten years, I would assume that insufficient commitment over this time period was at fault.

Evaluating the Results

There are essentially three purposes for evaluating the results of the program: collecting information from the pilot project (or any earlier application) in order to improve the implementation process for the remaining organizational units; collecting information from any unit that implemented the program in order to learn what barriers to success still remain in that unit so that additional activities can be conducted to remove them; and determining the impact of the whole program on organizational success.

The first purpose for evaluation recognizes that something is learned every time the program of five tracks is implemented. A principal task is monitoring the pilot project to learn what to modify as other units begin the program. The shadow track or some independent group should keep a close watch on the process so that any new insights or methods are adopted as one unit after another embarks on the journey of planned change.

The second purpose for evaluation recognizes that the "complete" program for large-system change is never complete—it is ongoing and forever. Thus each unit's results are evaluated to uncover problems (barriers) that sill need attention in that unit. An evaluation might reveal, for example, the need for additional work to close the culture gaps in a few of the more troublesome work groups. Or, as a result of new managers entering the organizational unit after most of the program has taken place, additional skill-training sessions can be conducted to bring the new managers up to speed with the rest of the membership. Continuing with the five stages a second or third time, however, is generally less involving than the first pass. Typically, subsequent cycles entail more of a fine tuning (incremental change) than organizational transformation (revolutionary change).

Both the first and second purposes for evaluation (information collected in one unit in order to benefit other units or information collected to enhance the change process for the focal unit in continuing cycles of planned change) can be approached by engaging in another round of interviews. If diagnostic interviews are the most effective way to learn about the organization's barriers at the start, this same methodology can be applied again to assess what could have been done differently and what still needs to be done in order to remove any additional barriers to success. I find it useful to have the internal consultants conduct these interviews at the evaluation stage rather than the external consultants who conducted the first round of interviews during the diagnostic stage. At this point in the process, I have found that the internal consultants are often more objective than the external consultants. Alternatively, a number of trained professionals independent of the consultants might be the best solution to maintaining objectivity.

The third purpose for evaluation questions whether the program has improved organizational success. From the point of view of any stakeholders—consumers, stockholders, suppliers, federal agencies, the community—one usually can suggest some definitive outcome measures: return on investment, earnings per share, profit, sales, number of clients served, market share, budget increases, number of patents and new products, new contracts and orders, productivity gains, and many other performance measures. Making a before-and-after comparison on any of these measures (before and after the change program) should provide a solid basis for assessing the program's impact. If the change effort was successful, the differences in these measures should be evident—or so the argument goes.

While these bottom-line measures certainly can be convincing, one has to recognize their limitations. Improvements in the quality of decisions and actions, for instance, do not translate to one-for-one increments in performance and morale. Normally, a whole series of decisions and actions is combined in complex ways before their effects are noticed.

One should also remember there is a time lag between decisions and actions on the one hand and performance on the other. Some bottom-line measures will not be affected until months or years after a key decision has been made—improved decision making that results in new approaches to product development will not be felt in the organization's setting for years, for instance. If the before-and-after comparisons are made right after the change program has concluded, one cannot expect outside stakeholders to take note of any observable differences in outcomes. Ironically, if such before-and-after comparisons were to suggest significant improvements (or declines), they probably would be spurious or artifactual. Only if the bottom-line measurements are made over a period in which true effects can be expected can one take the results of such an evaluation seriously.

Conclusion

The complete program for large-system change is certainly complex, but so are the problems this program is designed to resolve. Quick fixes cannot solve complex problems. It is time that both managers and consultants accept this fact of organizational life. Any serious improvement effort must be able to affect every controllable variable in the organization, not just one or two. At the same time, if the whole program is not initiated properly with top management's support, and if the problems of the organization are neither diagnosed correctly nor accepted by top management, the complete program cannot provide its potential benefits. Moreover, the program must be implemented in an integrated manner, with flexibility and adaptability. Attempting to quick-fix a complete program would do the field of organizational development—and the organization—a great disservice. Large-system change is long-term, organization-wide, and involves every controllable variable between the human mind and the global marketplace.

References

Beckhard, R., and Harris, R. T. *Organizational Transitions: Managing Complex Change.* (2nd ed.) Reading, Mass.: Addison-Wesley, 1987.

Beer, M. *Organization Change and Development: A Systems View.* Glenview, Ill.: Scott, Foresman, 1980.

Huse, E. F. *Organization Development and Change.* (2nd ed.) St. Paul, Minn.: West, 1980.

Kilmann, R. H. *Beyond the Quick Fix: Managing Five Tracks to Organizational Success.* San Francisco: Jossey-Bass, 1984.

Kilmann, R. H. *Managing Beyond the Quick Fix: A Completely Integrated Program for Creating and Maintaining Organizational Success.* San Francisco: Jossey-Bass, 1989.

Tichy, N. M. *Managing Strategic Change: Technical, Political, and Cultural Dynamics.* New York: Wiley, 1983.

Walton, R. E. "The Diffusion of New Work Structures: Explaining Why Success Didn't Take." *Organizational Dynamics,* Winter 1975, 3–22.

11

Large-Scale Change
and the
Quality Revolution

Robert E. Cole

This chapter focuses on large-scale organizational change associated with dramatic upgrading of quality performance.[1] By large-scale organizational change I refer to major organizational transformations involving practices, norms, and values. This focus on large-scale change is intended to shed light on two analytic issues important to students of organizational change. The first is the basic question of why organizations change. Paul Lawrence in Chapter Three points out that change specialists focus too much on the questions of how and what to change without pursuing the prior question of why organizations change. Second, I will be concerned with how organizational transformations occur. In particular, I focus on the question, raised by Jay Galbraith in Chapter Four (drawing from James Brian Quinn) of whether large-scale change occurs through a process of implementing a well-laid plan or through a process of logical incrementalism (see also Kanter, 1983). In the latter model, the organization responds to unanticipated consequences moving incrementally and opportunistically as events unfold. Outcomes are a function of the relationships between planned and unplanned events. Strategy emerges as part of an iterative process as organizational leaders engage in repeated interactions with the organizational environment and internal interests within the organization. I contend that such contrasting formulations do not do justice to the empirical complexity.

Sustained improvement of quality has come to be identified in the last decade as one of the key competitive challenges facing American industry. It is a challenge that has come primarily from Japan, a nation long regarded as a producer of shoddy goods. As Joseph Juran, the well-known quality specialist and long-term observer of Japan notes, Japan's new reputation as a quality producer is the most spectacular quality success story of our time and deserves careful study by all students of national quality control efforts (Juran, Gryna, and Bingham, 1974, chap. 48, p. 6).

Quality Leaders

In my treatment of this subject, I have chosen to examine national experiences through the teaching of leading quality specialists in Japan and the United States and discover how these teachings interact with corporate activities. Some readers will focus on the correctness and falseness of the respective teachings. The intent, however, is not to focus on the teachings of the quality gurus per se but to reflect on the national seedbed out of which such ideas developed. Moreover, we can learn about management cultures in the two nations and the nature of environmental and organizational constraints from the receptivity that management in each country has shown to certain ideas regarding organizational change.

Closely associated with the rise to quality success in Japan is the name of Kaoru Ishikawa, former Tokyo University professor of engineering and among the founders of the Japanese Union of Scientists and Engineers (JUSE) in 1949. JUSE was the major organizational instrument for diffusing quality improvement activities among Japanese firms. It played an active role in synthesizing best practices, and Ishikawa came to serve as its president. To follow Ishikawa's ideas is to get a good idea of the emergent Japanese views on the organizational changes involved in achieving sustained quality improvement. There are divergent views among Japanese experts, to be sure, but there has emerged a strong consensus about the requirements of quality improvement. One nevertheless must be careful for there is the same tendency in Japan as elsewhere to rewrite history to make the process appear more orderly (and therefore more planned) than it was (see Kanter, 1983).

I rely heavily on Ishikawa's recently translated book, *What Is Total Quality Control?* to capture his views, and to a lesser extent on *Keiei to Hinshitsu Kanri* (Management and Quality Control), a JUSE publication written by Tatsuo Sugimoto and directed at corporate managers. One last caveat: To say that Ishikawa's views are representative and that he provided leadership is not to say that he was a prime mover in bringing about the organizational transformations associated with the quality revolution in Japan. There were many leaders, though certainly Ishikawa was among the most prominent.

Some Americans would claim that W. Edwards Deming was the prime mover in bringing about the quality revolution in Japan. Such views popularized by journalists and TV producers bear little resemblance to reality (see Cole, 1987). Even Japanese leaders have paid obeisance to Deming in their public statements, but this reflects more the cultural pressures for modesty than it does the true extent of his contributions. To be sure, Deming was important in exposing the Japanese to the statistics of mass production, which in turn rested on the ideas of Walter Shewhart developed in the 1920s. Similarly, other Americans like Juran and Feigenbaum taught important principles to the Japanese. Yet the Japanese were by no means so backward as the prewar image of "producers of shoddy toys" would suggest. Consider the following American evaluation of the Nakajima Ki-84 "Hayate" fighter plane used in World War II:

> The captured Frank fighter S-17 was test flown against the best U.S. and allied fighters.[2] During these tests, it was found that the Frank would outclimb all allied aircraft including the P-51D Mustang. It was more maneuverable in turns and even

outperformed the Spitfire which had a high reputation in this field. . . . [In a later evaluation pro-
gram] the Frank was [found to be] comparable to
the P-51 Mustang and P-47 Thunderbolt. Although
the P-51H and P-47N had a slightly higher top
speed, the Frank climbed to altitude faster. The
Frank was more maneuverable in turns and will
turn inside either the P-51H or P-47N. The control forces were also lighter than those of most American aircraft. The range of the Frank was found
to be about the same as that of the P-51H. . . . In
evaluating the Frank with the Zeke 52 it was found
that in addition to having a higher top speed, the
Frank had less vibration at comparable velocities.
*It is interesting to note that in all the long hours the Frank
fighter was flown, under all conditions, no serious faults
were experienced with the airplane* [italics added] [Aero-
nautical Staff of AERO Publishers, 1965].

This hardly suggests that the ideas spread by Americans in the
postwar period fell upon an uncultivated field. Indeed, many
of the postwar leaders of the Japanese quality movement, not
surprisingly, did come from the aircraft industry. At another
level, while the Japanese did borrow many basic principles from
their American teachers, they showed extraordinary ingenuity
in adapting American ideas and combining them with indigenous resources.

     In the United States there is no clear leader who can speak
for the quality movement. The names most commonly listed
among the gurus of quality are Joseph Juran, W. Edwards Deming, Philip Crosby, and A. V. Feigenbaum. I focus on Crosby
because he represents the clearest contrast with Ishikawa. Since
he is less influenced by the Japanese experience than the others,
Crosby represents a purer American approach though he is by
no means representative of all American thinking on the subject. Nevertheless, as former president of the American Society
for Quality Control, vice-president and director of quality for
the ITT Corporation for fourteen years, and quality manager of

Martin Marietta, Orlando, for eight years prior to that, he has been a highly visible figure on the quality scene. As originator of the concept of zero defects at Martin Marietta and author of the best-seller *Quality Is Free* (1979) and *Quality Without Tears* (1984), Crosby has achieved a considerable reputation. *Quality Is Free* has sold particularly well to professionals outside the field. For these managers, this may well be the only book on quality they will ever read (Groocock, 1986, p. 22). Therefore, it is extremely important to assess the utility of his formulations.

Crosby founded Philip Crosby Associates (PCA) in 1979; General Motors bought a 10 percent share in 1986 and is one of a number of major corporate clients.[3] These include major firms noted for their quality reputation, such as IBM, as well as those who have suffered in the past from a reputation for poor quality, such as Westinghouse Corporation. Featured prominently in Crosby's promotional literature is the decision of the Japanese Management Association to license his materials for use in Japan.[4] The clear message to executives is that this is one firm in which American ideas dominate, and indeed it is the Japanese who are learning from our "born-in-America" materials. This interpretation is reinforced by an examination of his written materials, which contain little discussion of the Japanese experience. Thus, for that not inconsiderable number of American executives who are afflicted with a Japanese allergy—the "not invented here" syndrome—the Crosby materials have considerable appeal. Since the promotional materials of Philip Crosby Associates make clear that his two books contain the basic concepts of PCA, I rely primarily on them for clarifying the organizational aspects of his approach. In so doing, I hope to capture some of the dilemmas of American management in seeking to achieve sustained quality improvement.

There are a number of similarities in the thinking of the quality leaders in the respective countries. Crosby and Ishikawa take a similar position on such basic issues as the importance of top management's providing continuous support and leadership and serving as a role model for all employees in their commitment to quality, the belief in setting quality standards and measuring performance along these dimensions, management's primary responsibility for poor quality (not workers'), a commitment to continuous learning, and the view that quality improvement will lead to cost reduction. Yet there is reason to believe that our understanding will be significantly advanced through an understanding of where they differ in the context of what they tell us about management cultures in the two nations.

Let me turn now to the basic question of why organizations change. I would like to broaden the why question, however, not only to cover why top management decides to change but also why all employees come to see change as necessary. Too often the literature focuses only on the matter of top management and ignores the fact that for large-scale organizational change to occur, most employees must come to see that change as desirable. In so doing, of course, we blur the difference between why and how organizations change, since the issue of why employees other than top managers change is usually seen as part of the how question. I believe that such dichotomous thinking does a disservice to understanding large-scale organizational change.

Japanese Developments

In the case of Japan the matter is deceptively simple. Westerners tend to have an image of the Japanese as always working with well-thought-out plans for the long term. In its extreme version, this view sees a conspiratorial strategy to eliminate Western competitors.

After World War II, Japanese industry was devastated. In order to regain and improve their living standards, it was deemed necessary to improve their economic performance. Indeed, in retrospect, we can see that with the military option closed, a century-long preoccupation with catching up to the West focused national energies on economic achievement in the postwar period. In the early postwar period, with living standards falling well below prewar levels, there was a sense of crisis that led to a single-minded focus on improving economic performance.

The decision to stress quality performance must be seen in this broader context. Particularly in the postwar period, improvement in product quality was seen as essential to ensuring that the nation would be able to export sufficient products to restore their national strength. In a nation with few natural resources, the value-added contributed by its human resources was seen as providing the critical margin to ensure competitive strength. In this context, quality and productivity improvement were plausible strategies.

To be sure, there was much thrashing about, and it was well into the late 1950s before the outlines of a coherent quality improvement strategy began to emerge. There was, for example, an early overreliance on statistics as guaranteeing superior quality outcomes, and only when that failed to produce the desired outcomes was there a recognition that good management decisions were critical too.[5]

A national consensus gradually came to be forged in Japanese industry around the theme of quality improvement, spearheaded by JUSE and leading companies and reinforced by a variety of governmental actions including the passage of the Export Inspection Law in 1958 and the establishment of November as Quality Month in 1960. JUSE was a fledgling organization that provided an opportunity for academics and managers to exchange ideas; it had the strong support of Keidanren, the leading business organization in the country. Keidanren provided legitimacy for JUSE activities, an outcome no doubt facilitated by the fact that Kaoru Ishikawa's father was the head of the Keidanren in this early critical period. JUSE's activities preempted the role of private consultants. Their large training programs served as critical resources to companies in the initial stages of quality improvement. In the early postwar years, these activities were primarily reactive strategies designed to get the ship of industry turned around and pointed in the right direction. It was only later that the full potentialities of a quality focus came to be realized.

Japanese inferiority in quality was publicly recognized, and a strategy of catch-up was formulated. As a latecomer to industrialization, no particular shame was associated with such an admission. Gradually, Japanese management developed and perfected the central insight of their postwar quality drive; it was that higher quality could be used as a driver to reduce costs, especially in the mass production industries. This principle was well embedded in the thinking of American theorists like Joe Juran and A. V. Feigenbaum. It grew out of prewar and early postwar thinking in industrial engineering that if one concentrated on basic work elements and tasks, one could reduce costs by identifying what tasks could be reduced or eliminated if things were done right the first time. While such conceptualizations were part of the thinking of American scholars, few American firms had acted to operationalize these principles, nor were the American scholars particularly adept in translating their ideas to practical action.

Central to the Japanese implementation strategy, and directly counter to Western experience and advice, was the notion that all employees and departments (total quality control—TQC) had to take responsibility for quality improvement if their efforts were to succeed.

Neither of these notions was present at the start of the quality movement; both represented a later proactive stage. The strategies for implementing them gradually evolved in the 1970s and became accepted over time. Still later, sometime in the late 1970s, Japanese leaders came to recognize that they could use quality to change the very rules of the game. They learned that they could use quality as a marketing strategy, creating high-quality expectations among consumers that they were then in a unique position to satisfy.

We can see the unplanned character of events in the evolution of today's quality control circles. An examination of the first issue of *The Workshop and QC* published in April 1962 by JUSE—just at the time that circle activity was crystallizing—reveals a conception of workshop activity relating to quality that was still quite removed from the actual operation of quality circles today. The focus was on training foremen how to get their employees to accept and maintain work standards so that quality objectives would be met. Getting workers more involved in taking responsibility for setting and revising work standards was the strategy advocated (JUSE, 1962). The circles developed as a rather spontaneous adaptive process as management sought to encourage joint study between foreman and workers. Gradually, these ideas growing out of the quality movement merged with the ideas of decentralization of authority and group decision making. Once management came to understand the potentialities of these small-group activities, spontaneity gave way to active management involvement in forming and maintaining circle activity.

This account clearly demonstrates that the strategy of worker responsibility for problem solving was an emergent process. In the early stages of quality circle development, JUSE was struggling to assume its leadership position much like the Charlie Chaplin character of a revolutionary leader rushing to the head of demonstrating workers to show that he is really leading the process.

What we see here is a process of logical incrementalism that proceeded in stages of awareness and understanding. Gradually, quality came to be seen as a driver for all sorts of other desirable organizational changes and outcomes. The evolution of cost-reduction strategies and the just-in-time delivery system, to take two prominent examples, both benefited from a strong quality consciousness and in turn reinforced the quality emphasis. They developed simultaneously. What we see is the gradual evolution of a quality philosophy based on the sophisticated integration of quality, cost, and production scheduling. For example, they have carefully analyzed how to improve the quality of the production scheduling process (see Sugimoto, 1981). This goes far beyond the typical stand-alone quality philosophy pursued by many U.S. companies. To make pious statements as Crosby and many others do that quality must be as important as cost and scheduling appears simplistic next to the worked-out integration achieved by the Japanese.

Again, Japanese managers hardly perceived these relationships at the onset of Japanese industry's commitment to quality improvement in the late 1950s and early 1960s. Plans were constantly modified to take the new circumstances into consideration. We see an example of large-scale organizational change in which serendipity and ability to capitalize on unanticipated consequences play a major role. As understandings of the new opportunities developed, however, thorough planning to ensure effective implementation and maximal payoffs was characteristic of Japanese management behavior.

This discussion suggests that the Japanese operated somewhere between achieving change through well-laid plans and a process of logical incrementalism. There was constant planning for change, but they were ever alert to new unanticipated opportunities so that we could say they planned for opportunism. It is like a boxer "in training" waiting for a weakness to develop in his opponent—the opponent, in this case, being poor quality and inefficiency. As a result, when new opportunities appeared they were quick to seize upon them and engage in thorough planning to ensure the most effective implementation.

U.S. Developments

In the United States, product quality has long been regarded as a characteristic of American industry. In fact, however, in many of the consumer goods industries quality improvement had stagnated in the postwar period. Firms in large, growing industries seldom competed over quality. Some exceptions might include the food, drug, and cosmetic industries where a large number of competitors emerged and did tend to compete over quality.

Companies with high quality were often seen as the premier firms in the industry with high quality being associated with extra costs. In the private sector, the Cadillac probably symbolized that connection more than any other product. In the public sector, NASA was the symbol of American high-tech and quality until the Challenger tragedy, and quality here was achieved through the building of redundant systems, overdesign, intense inspection, and other such strategies. With fewer cost constraints than the consumer goods industries, it was easy to see how high costs and high quality came to be associated with one another in the minds of corporate managers.

The Japanese onslaught of high-quality consumer products in the late 1960s and 1970s began to challenge existing assumptions in those industries directly experiencing Japanese competition. Yet even in such industries, American managers focused on the Japanese advantage achieved through low costs; they saw this as being achieved through unfair competitive practices such as government subsidies and exploitative labor practices. In short, many managers refused to recognize the quality component in Japanese success.

In the case of the auto industry, incredibly, as late as 1980 American auto executives were still publicly denying a Japanese quality advantage or stating that it was only a matter of "fit and finish." It was believed that to publicly recognize the American disadvantage would contribute further to the competitive advantage of the Japanese. By this time, however, most management officials conceded in private that they had a serious problem. One difficulty of this approach is that until managers were prepared to recognize the problem publicly, it was difficult for them to approach their own employees, impress upon them the seriousness of the problem, and elicit their support in improving quality. What we see here is a characteristic response of denial where organizations fail to recognize the need for dramatic large-scale change and thus are incapable of responding.

Even after the public recognition, the public posture of companies such as General Motors was that the gap would be quickly closed and quality would be a noncompetitive issue by the late 1980s. Yet the going has been slower than many companies anticipated, and the Japanese themselves present a moving target. In one major plant of a large Japanese automaker I visited, they had reduced the cost of quality (cost of quality equals cost of quality failure plus cost of appraisal plus cost of prevention as a percentage of sales) from 2.38 percent in September 1984 to 1.55 percent in September 1986, a gain of 34 percent in less than two years. It is remarkable that such large gains are still being achieved when the cost of quality has already been reduced to such a low level and under conditions in which new car models were being introduced, as was the case in this example. A U.S. auto manufacturer or supplier plant would consider itself to be doing very well if its quality costs were only 8 percent of sales, and most are estimated to have quality costs in excess of 10 percent (see Groocock, 1986, pp. 58–61).

Motivational Factors

What do our national experts have to say on the why of quality improvement? In the case of Crosby, we find little discussion of managerial motivation, much less worker motivation, for quality improvement arising from international competition. Since he puts little stress on learning from the Japanese, it is not surprising perhaps that he does not stress competition from the Japanese as a motivating factor. He does stress the well-established methodology of firms assessing their costs of quality as a means of getting managers to recognize that they have a quality problem. Once managers are aware of the high costs of poor quality, they are presumed to be motivated to undertake quality improvement. Parenthetically, it may be noted that despite persistent urging, quality experts have had great difficulty persuading American managers to initiate and sustain systematic cost-of-quality monitoring activities. Even when they do undertake such measurements, the results are often used to reward and punish employees rather than for problem-solving purposes.

The Japanese have eschewed cost-of-quality programs preferring to concentrate instead on measuring life-cycle costs to the consumer. The focus is on the benefits companies receive from knowing more about the customers' use of the product—a market orientation—than the in-house costs of quality. Quite unlike even those American companies that do conduct cost-of-quality activities, Japanese companies typically publicize quality-performance information widely throughout the firm so that each employee experiences quality through competitive benchmarks. Implicit in such action is an assumption that employees are by and large positively oriented to contribute to organizational goals of improvement. By contrast, Paul Lawrence argues that American managers tend to underutilize the social psychology of competition as a motivator of productive organizational behavior. Perhaps this is because management does not assume that employees are positively disposed toward organizational goals.

Most important, while Crosby stresses the significance of showing *managers* the costs of poor quality as a motivational strategy, the Japanese stress the motivation of all employees through the regular sharing of quality-performance information. In this fashion, the why of organizational change gets widely communicated throughout the organization. This latter strategy seems much more conducive to producing the large-scale organizational change required for sustained quality improvement. A spin-off effect of such a strategy is that when workers and managers are seeing the same data on quality performance (or any other performance measure for that matter) it is likely to substantially raise the level of trust among the various parties.

Central Concepts

If one were to identify the single theme that is central to Ishikawa's vision of quality improvement and the single theme that is central to Crosby's vision of quality improvement, what would it be in each case? Kaoru Ishikawa places primary importance on the role of the customer; it dominates almost every facet of his discussion. Indeed, it is the theme that dominates almost all Japanese discussions of quality improvement. Tatsuo Sugimoto talks about management for consumers in the following terms: "to establish a system which intimately incorporates the consumers by producing and selling attractive merchandise which consumers are willing to buy, by providing customer service, and by directly connecting to retail stores."

We see the stress is on "intimately incorporating" the customer into the management of the firm. This emphasis is extended through the slogan "Make the next process downstream your customer." It was Ishikawa himself who began to use this phrase after visiting a steel plant in 1950. When examining scratch defects on steel sheets, he discovered strong sectionalism was preventing employees in connecting proces-ses from cooperating to eliminate defects. In trying to explain the need for cooperation, he developed a key idea: "You must imagine that the next process is your customer" (JUSE, 1983, p. 76).

This is not simply a matter of slogans. Of particular importance here is the development of quality function deployment systems (QFDS). This involves the development of checking systems (forms to be filled out) for ensuring that employees from different departments, initially marketing and R&D with design, will work together to collect data that match up customer wants and needs on specific dimensions with engineer specifications. These matrices ensure this outcome by requiring data collection to measure the fit between the two areas. When deviations occur, the relevant personnel from the different departments must work out ways to eliminate them. Data are also collected on the performance of competitors, and their fit is compared to one's own performance. This same process is next applied to measuring the fit between engineering specifications and manufacturing processes. Again, responsible personnel must work together to resolve any deviations.

From an organizational point of view, this system integrates different departmental activities through the common task requirements associated with implementing the quality function deployment matrix. All this is done to minimize deviation from customer wants throughout the product design and production cycle. Put differently, the purpose is to pursue ismorphism between customer wants and organizational performance throughout all organizational processing activities. It is interesting to compare QFDS to matrix forms of organization in American corporations. American firms have often tried to achieve departmental and specialist cooperation through matrix organization designs, but such efforts frequently fail because of their artificial nature (see Galbraith and Kazanjian, 1986). Quality function deployment systems achieve the desired ends through their common and permanent task requirements.

What comes through most clearly in Ishikawa's thinking and Japanese company applications is the system character of their efforts and the way in which "how to accomplish" controls are structured into operations. By contrast, Crosby is more oriented to motivation and to tracking performance without building in systems for correction. He confuses labeling a problem with providing a solution. As a consequence, students of his programs often come back to work and can do little more than urge employees to "make it to print."

What about Crosby's central concept? It is the "cost of nonconformance." Thus the primary focus is on setting agreed-upon requirements for each process and ensuring that employees adhere to them. He qualifies this statement to the effect that these requirements must be consistent with customer requirements or they should be changed. This is mentioned, however, almost in passing; it is not a central theme. There is no guide explaining how employees should go about getting requirements changed.

Implicit here is a view that changing requirements is an engineering responsibility. This is consistent with Crosby's overall emphasis on employees turning over their complaints and suggestions to engineers. It goes back to a view that engineers create work standards and specifications and workers are merely supposed to follow. While there are occasional pious statements about the workers as experts, the overall thrust is profoundly elitist. When he says "everyone must be involved," the usual reference is to getting all departments involved. When he talks about the team approach to problem elimination in his training materials, the reference to participant selection states that one should choose only those persons with knowledge and experience relevant to solving the problem.

There is no discussion to suggest that historically American managers have defined the holders of expertise far too narrowly so as to exclude most shop and office floor employees. Nor is there room for union involvement in Crosby's vision of quality improvement. In both books there is only one reference to unions and there he recommends that the union representative serve on the quality improvement team as an individual. Many firms using Crosby's approach have in fact involved unions in their quality improvement efforts. It has been tough sledding in many companies, however, with union leaders being instinctively hostile to their perceived lack of place in the Crosby framework.

By contrast, Ishikawa places front and center the adjustment of standards and specifications to rapidly changing customer standards and consumer taste. He stresses that standards and regulations are imperfect. They must be reviewed and revised constantly. The employees actually doing the task take major responsibility for these efforts. If newly established standards and regulations are not revised in six months, Ishikawa says, it is proof that no one is seriously using them. His emphasis is on determining the best method and making it publicly available to all those with similar responsibilities; this is the real meaning of standardization according to Ishikawa.

Ishikawa is also very alert to the differences between "true quality characteristics (what the customer expects) and the proxies we create to mimic them." This creation process is often extremely difficult and has major consequences, for it is these proxies that eventually become the standards organizations use. In summary, while Ishikawa agrees with Crosby on the virtues of conformance to standards, he shows an understanding of the subtleties and dynamic nature of the concept that seems quite beyond Crosby.

Elitism Versus All-Employee Involvement

Clearly, all-employee involvement has been a central feature of Ishikawa's thinking. His association with the development of the quality circle movement typifies that commitment. Moreover, he has been extremely active in the Japanese movement for simplification of statistical methods so that all employees with a basic education can benefit from these methods and make a contribution toward quality improvement. He developed the cause and effect diagram as a diagnostic tool that all employees could use during World War II. When the definitive history of the postwar Japanese quality movement is written, it will include a strong emphasis on the role played by the "democratization of statistical methods"—democratization in the specific sense of mass participation. These developments made it possible for ordinary employees to understand the why and how of organizational change.

We can contrast these developments, which began in the early 1960s, to the popularity of Kepner–Tregoe problem-solving methods for managers that were much in vogue in the United States at the same time. Many of the problem-solving methods that Kepner–Tregoe were teaching to managers were being taught to ordinary blue-collar workers in Japan. It was not until their 1987 workshop schedule that Kepner–Tregoe announced that their new materials included "a totally new approach to statistical process control which permits this powerful tool to be used not only by managers but other key shop floor workers and specifically develops trouble-shooting skills enabling them to participate in quality improvement opportunities." In other words, prior to this time it was assumed that key shop and office floor employees were incapable of absorbing the Kepner–Tregoe problem-solving methodology or did not have a contribution to make. Other formulators of problem-solving methodologies have yet to adapt their materials to shop and office floor employees.

While Ishikawa is keen on all-employee involvement, he shows no greater interest in unions playing a role in quality improvement efforts than does Crosby. The difference, however, is that unions in America in large manufacturing firms have a much greater potential to obstruct development of quality improvement than they do in Japan. This is true by virtue of their active shop floor presence compared to Japanese unions.

Implications of the Two Emphases

There are a variety of implications for the different emphases contained in the two approaches discussed here. Above all, through a stress on meeting customer needs, Ishikawa provides managers and workers with a powerful motivational mechanism for undertaking sustained quality improvement. Employees can more easily see the link between meeting customer needs and company success. It is then another small step for individual employees to see this linkage as central to meeting their own needs for job security and material benefits. Moreover, Japanese management works hard at educating *all* employees to understand customer needs and complaints. With regard to lower-level production and office workers, failed parts and examples of poor service are often brought into the workshop and office so that all employees can understand customer experiences. Wherever possible, areas of failure are traced back to specific work stations.

This approach contrasts with the stress on the costs of non-conformance. While strict adherence to correct standards is indeed critical to quality success, by itself it provides little in the way of managerial and overall employee motivation. Too often, employees do not know why they are being forced to maintain certain standards. Nor are they always given the proper tools to do so. In this connection, it is noteworthy that until recently Crosby ignored the use of statistics in assuming adherence to standards.

One of the major lessons of behavior science research on work is that workers are likely to be more committed to their work and less alienated when they understand how it fits into a coherent whole. Conformance to standards by itself does not serve this purpose. Meeting customer needs does—and in so doing it contributes to a heightened commitment to sustained quality improvement. H. Ross Perot, that recent gadfly of General Motors, remarked: "In a lot of these big companies, what it takes to be successful has nothing to do with making better products or serving the customer or what I call the rules of the marketplace. It has to do with following procedures" (*Detroit Free Press*, 1986). Stressing conformance to specifications perpetuates this bureaucratic mind-set and tends to be interpreted by employees as just another set of arbitrary rules. It harks back to Tayloristic admonitions to blue-collar workers simply to follow orders. By contrast, through educating employees in how such rules influence customer acceptance, the firm can increase the probability that employees will be motivated to take conformance to standards as a serious personal goal.

Reward Systems

One additional note on the why of organizational change is in order. Crosby writes about quality improvement objectives as though managers—and all employees for that matter—only need to have the importance of quality demonstrated to them in order for them to support quality objectives. We are given no sense of competing priorities. Crosby assumes that if employees just understood the costs of doing things badly and are given some help, they would want to correct their actions. Consider this quote from *Quality Is Free:* "Let me see if I have this clear. We are going under the assumption that the people of this company have never had it made clear to them that we expect every job to be done right every time. Therefore, we are going to tell them that slowly so that they don't get too shocked. Then we are going to help them perform to that standard by fixing the problems they tell us they have. All this is going to eliminate errors. Correct? Yes, says Kate, I've never heard it stated so clearly."

In practice, of course, a great many things get in the way of accomplishing quality improvement objectives, or any new objective for that matter. People may not be properly trained to do the job, equipment may be inadequate, employees may not be motivated to improve quality because they are rewarded for other things, and so on. Note that Crosby's focus in this quote is on "we" are going to fix "their" problems.

Of particular interest is this matter of reward systems. Crosby says that awarding money for quality improvement is demeaning. There is in short no serious discussion of reward systems (monetary or nonmonetary) as a strategy for changing employee priorities at all levels of the organization. Yet if there is one sure-fire predictor of organizational behavior, it is that you know a whole lot about what to expect if you know what people are rewarded for and what they are punished for. Running through all serious scholarly work on large-scale organizational change is the notion that you have to change old reward systems to support new practices (see Kanter, 1983, p. 300).

Crosby is strong on recognition as a motivational factor and stresses what I call the "trinket approach" to managing employees. By offering employees special pins and certificates, management thinks they will meet employee needs for recognition and thereby provide motivation for quality. While recognition as a motivator is indeed critical to employee performance and often underutilized, it is naive to think that it can serve as a long-term substitute for material rewards. The self-serving nature of such management views and behavior is quite visible to employees over the long haul. In any case, such an approach hardly puts the full potential weight of the reward system, both monetary and nonmonetary, behind the new values and practices concerning quality that one is seeking to institutionalize.

In the case of Ishikawa as well there is little discussion of reward systems. But this is a reflection of where Japanese organizations stand in the life cycle of quality improvement efforts. I have asked Japanese managers how poor quality performance would be treated on performance appraisals and when promotion decisions were being made. The typical answer was that, first, investigations would take place to ensure that the poor quality performance was not due to poor training, poor instructions, or equipment failures. If this turned out not to be the case, and it was a matter of a manager ignoring quality to achieve other objectives, it is inconceivable that they would be given a strong performance rating or a promotion. Almost in the next breath my respondents said that such an event would be a rare occurrence today. In other words, quality as a priority has become strongly institutionalized into the web of company activities.

Quality Is Free?

Crosby is quoted as saying that quality improvement requires a long-term effort and cannot be achieved overnight. The titles of his books, however, *Quality Is Free* and *Quality Without Tears,* as well as much of the content, suggest that achieving sustained quality improvement is an easy task. It is for this reason that he has had strong appeal among top managers looking for an easy way to quality success. His suggestion that rewarding quality with cash is demeaning further strengthens his appeal with many top managers. One CEO of a major electronics firm said to me recently, "See, Crosby taught us that *all* [emphasis mine] we need to do is to expect more from our people and we will have quality improvement." I had occasion to discuss the title of Crosby's books with the engine plant manager at the Honda Suzuka factory, and he said to me: "You know, I could agree with the idea that quality is free these last three years or so." Then he paused and said, "But there were a whole lot of tears for the first twenty years." What he has in mind is twenty years of learning, knowledge that had to be fought for and creatively applied. That does not sound like the free lunch Crosby is implicitly advertising.

One of the issues raised by this discussion is that the materials which U.S. consultants provide are often geared to the company "gatekeepers" who must approve their use for purchase. Crosby's message is particularly attractive to top managers. His presentation is studded with examples (management by vignette) from golf course experiences and morality plays. All this sells well with top management but lacks the operational content that middle managers require to produce the organizational transformation critical to sustained quality improvement.

Ishikawa's presentation by contrast has a subtlety and dynamism together with a clear focus on meeting customer needs. It is unambiguous in its message that management requires a long-term commitment if it is to succeed. Above all, it is based on a systemic organizational design that works to continually reduce deviation from target goals. Finally, Ishikawa's perspective is supported by a vast array of materials from JUSE that provide the operational how-to-do-it directions necessary for middle management.

By comparison, while we have quality leaders like Crosby, Juran, and Deming, we lack the organizational infrastructure provided by JUSE in Japan for diffusion of the information and training necessary for implementation. JUSE is supported directly by corporate members and engages in an extraordinary range of educational and training activities. The American Society for Quality Control is made up primarily of individual members and relies heavily on individually contributed volunteer labor; its contributions are modest compared to JUSE's professional activities.

Insofar as the two gurus themselves capture a significant segment of managerial thinking about how to think about quality improvement, it is no wonder that the Japanese are far ahead.

It is somewhat reassuring that successful American managers increasingly seek to synthesize the insights of Crosby with the contributions of Juran and Deming and to absorb the Japanese lessons directly. Just like any other modern technology, quality technology is increasingly developed and conducted worldwide, and any attempt to rely on a single home-grown version is likely to be hopelessly out of date.

With the first adopter, the innovator, of a complex new organizational system, the balance between reliance on planned versus unplanned developments is likely to shift heavily toward unplanned activity as there are no clear models to follow. Strategic plans must constantly be modified to accommodate unanticipated interactions. This was the case with Japan in the early postwar period as it charted a new course on quality.

Followers, however, are in a position to shift the balance somewhat more toward planned activities as they can draw on existing models of development to guide their activities. This is the position that many U.S. firms now find themselves in as they play catch-up on the new quality technology. Yet even for the follower, the balance cannot shift entirely to planned strategic activities because in the very process of coming to know past developments, firms invariably try to benefit from that knowledge by skipping stages and shortening the developmental process. They may also misunderstand what they are seeing. Finally, the "not invented here" syndrome distorts the learning process despite the presence of models. Under some combination of these conditions, new unanticipated outcomes occur, thus requiring the continual formation of new strategies.

Cultural Aspects of Japanese Approaches

A final word about the role of culture is in order. Is there anything about the Japanese experience that suggests a distinctive national or organizational culture in their achievements? At the national level, their attitude toward borrowing comes to mind. There was no hesitation about recognizing backwardness in quality performance, but rather than accept that status, the Japanese displayed a fierce determination to overcome obstacles, borrowing whatever from wherever was necessary. What they borrowed from abroad typically was combined with indigenous ideas and practices to produce something new. The "new things" were often organizational inventions such as quality circles or more generally the idea that every employee, regardless of status, and every department (TQC) have a contribution to make to quality improvement. This attitude toward borrowing is rooted in a 125-year history of playing catch-up with the West. This catch-up mentality in turn is firmly rooted in a strong sense of national pride.

The cultural element in this borrowing process arises from Japan's experience as an island nation seeing itself surrounded by superior cultures throughout much of its history—first the Chinese and then the West. Out of those interactions developed an almost instinctive tendency to look abroad for solutions almost as easily as one searched for domestic resolutions. One cannot help but contrast that to the insularity of American management, its slowness in recognizing the quality challenge, and its slowness in responding through intense study of the Japanese experience. While there was a vogue of studying the Japanese in the early 1980s, it was soon followed by a reaction of "I can't bear to hear anything more about the Japanese." The Japanese by contrast have been studying America, its institutions, and practices for almost 125 years. While there have been moments of xenophobia, they seem not to have tired of the effort, even now when they are acknowledged leaders in many areas.

A related aspect of the relentless Japanese focus on catching up with the West and borrowing whatever is necessary to achieve this goal is the sense among Japanese employees of the *normality* of change. This belief in the normality of change strongly aided the quality improvement effort. It is easy to underestimate the import of such a factor, but we saw clear evidence of its impact when we compared the dynamic approach to standards explicitly advocated by Ishikawa versus the rather static approach implicitly pursued by Crosby.

What about the central focus of Ishikawa on knowing and responding to customer needs? Is there a cultural component to that emphasis? I think not. It is rather the strong orientation to economic success in postwar Japan that has led them to stress customer satisfaction.

What about the focus on all-employee participation in achieving quality improvement? At one level, the notion of cooperation and participation of all employees in achieving organizational goals does have cultural roots. Yet it is also true that the prewar Japanese organizations were noted for their autocratic style. Defeat in World War II discredited those prewar and wartime autocratic leaders and opened the way to new talent and a stress on all-employee participation.

While many Westerners seem to want to stress cultural aspects of Japanese economic success, the Japanese involved in forging the new postwar organizational systems are likely to stress the enormous efforts involved in transforming organizational practices and culture. Company histories are full of melodramatic scenes of crisis as the protagonists seek to turn around their organizations against all odds. Many of the practices that we call culturally distinctive in large, Japanese, private-sector firms—such as lifetime employment—can be seen as impediments to change. These impediments are seen as being overcome by the same strong dose of top management commitment and vision and follow-through that students of Western organizations stress. Group activity may have a long history in Japan, but there is nothing in that cultural tradition which guarantees a task orientation to quality improvement. Strong managerial direction was necessary to move it in that direction.

Japanese managers in the postwar period have shown a strong ability to respond to employee needs for participation without losing their sense of organizational purpose. The focus has been on decentralization of responsibility more than democratization in the Western sense of sharing power. Ultimately, these choices and the ability to make them stick rest on powerful cultural constraints rooted in traditional authority systems.

Notes

1. I am indebted to the students in the Graduate School of Business Administration of the University of Michigan in my

course "Organizing for Quality Excellence" for their stimulation on this subject. Members of the East Asia Business Program's Faculty Seminar on East Asia and Corporate Strategy at the University of Michigan were generous with their comments on the first draft. I am also grateful to R. Eugene Goodson and William Golomski for their thoughtful suggestions. None of those referred to above, of course, bears any responsibility for the use I have made of their advice.

2. The "Frank" was the Allied code name for the captured Japanese fighter plane.

3. As of December 1986, GM alone had sent 4,000 employees, mostly executives, to the GM Quality Institute, which is licensed to teach Crosby materials. Moreover, many other GM executives experienced the Crosby program at his Winter Park, Florida, facility. GM, dissatisfied with its progress, has since shifted to more inclusive approaches in order to accelerate its quality improvement activities. The 1987 hiring of William Scherkenbach, a Deming disciple, marked this shift.

4. In fact, Crosby's materials have limited use in Japan; they are used by the Japanese Management Association primarily where U.S. companies have a joint venture with a Japanese company.

5. We see some of that same overreliance on statistics in the United States today with the belief many firms display that the installation of statistical process control will solve their quality problems. This is a manifestation of the well-known technological fix mentality, all too prominent among American management personnel.

6. The concept of TQC was developed by A. V. Feigenbaum, and in its original form it focused on improving the quality of the product with attention to those units directly contributing to that quality and with strong responsibility lodged among quality control specialists. The Japanese broadened the

concept to include all departments in the company and stressed all-employee responsibility. Although they have used the term TQC to designate this approach, they decided in 1968 to use the term *company-wide quality control* (CWQC) to distinguish their efforts from those of Feigenbaum (see Ishikawa, 1985, pp. 90–91). Feigenbaum has since adopted the broad Japanese definition in the new edition of his classic book, *Total Quality Control* (Feigenbaum, 1983, p.6).

References

Aeronautical Staff of AERO Publishers. *Nakajima Ki-84.* Fallbrook, Calif.: Aero Publishers, 1965.

Cole, R. E. "What Was Deming's Real Influence?" *Across the Board,* 1987, *24,* 49–51.

Crosby, P. *Quality Is Free.* New York: New American Library, 1979.

Crosby, P. *Quality Without Tears.* New York: New American Library, 1984.

Detroit Free Press. "The Man Who Speaks His Mind on GM." November 25, 1986, Business Section, p. 1.

Feigenbaum, A. *Total Quality Control.* (3rd ed.) New York: McGraw-Hill, 1983.

Galbraith, J., and Kazanjian, R. "Organizing to Implement Strategies of Diversity and Globalization: The Role of Matrix Designs." *Human Resource Management,* 1986, *25* (1), 37–54.

Groocock, J. *The Chain of Quality.* New York: Wiley, 1986.

Ishikawa, K. *What Is Total Quality Control?* Englewood Cliffs, N.J.: Prentice-Hall, 1985.

Juran, J. M., Gryna, F. M., and Bingham, R. S., Jr. *Quality Control Handbook.* (3rd ed.) New York: McGraw-Hill, 1974.

JUSE. *Genba to QC* [The Workshop and Quality Control], April 1962, *1.*

JUSE. *JUSE Quality Control Course for Top Management: CWQC.* Tokyo: Nihon Kagaku Gijutsu Renmei, 1983.

Kanter, R. M. *The Changemasters: Innovation and Entrepreneurship in the American Corporation.* New York: Simon & Schuster, 1983.

Sugimoto, T. *Keiei to Hinshitsu Kanri* [Management and quality control]. Tokyo: Nikagiren, 1981.

12

Strategic Choices for
Changing Organizations

Edward E. Lawler III

The design of an organizational change process involves a number of strategic decisions. Many of these decisions involve picking either one option or another; there is no middle ground. Sometimes the evidence from the organizational change literature is quite clear about how change should be carried out. But, not surprisingly in a field as young and underresearched as organizational change, this is not true with respect to many key strategic choices. At times the literature seems to suggest dramatically different design decisions. With regard to the choices considered in this chapter, arguments can be made on both sides of the issue. These arguments will be reviewed and, where possible, I will indicate which approach is most likely to produce successful organizational change.

Conceptual Approach

Before we consider specific strategic choices, a few words need to be said about the overall framework that will be used in analyzing them. Let us accept the view that organizations are complex, open social systems that take input from the environment and subject it to various transformation processes which result in an output. As systems, they are composed of multiple interdependent parts. Changes in one element of the

255

system result in changes in other parts. In addition, organizations have the property of equilibrium—that is, the system will generate energy to move toward a state of balance in which the different parts of the system are congruent with each other. Finally, as open systems, organizations need to maintain favorable transactions with the environment—that is, they need to use the inputs from the envioronment effectively in developing their outputs or they will cease to exist.

A number of congruence models build upon this view of the organization as an open system. (See, for example, Galbraith, 1973; Nadler and Tushman, 1977.) In these frameworks, the organization is made up of systems such as tasks, formal structures, informal cultures, individuals, and various subsystems. Many of the critical questions concern the congruence among the internal components of an organization. Are the demands of the organizational task consistent with the skills of the individuals? Are the rewards well suited to the needs and desires of the individuals and calculated to motivate the kind of behavior that is needed for organizational effectiveness? The basic hypothesis of these models is that organizations will be most effective when their major components are congruent. Problems of effectiveness due to management and structure are believed to stem from lack of congruence among the key organizational components.

Finally, contingency thinking is important to the analysis of organizational effectiveness. There is no one right way to manage, select individuals, and develop strategies. What is effective differs greatly from organization to organization and from environment to environment. It all depends on the kind of transactions the organization wants to have with the environment—and, of course, the characteristics of the environment. In order to produce certain products and offer certain services, an organization needs to be structured one way; while for producing others it may need to be designed entirely differently. What is common, however, is the assumption that congruence among its various parts is critical to the organization's effectiveness.

With these general points in mind, we can turn to a consideration of the key choices involved in designing an organizational change process. First, we will examine the issue of whether organizational change is facilitated or hindered by taking an experimental project approach.

Using Experiments

There are a number of reasons why, on the surface, it appears to make sense to take an experimental approach to organizational change. (See, for example, Lawler, Nadler, and Cammann, 1980.) In essence, the major argument says that trying a new design on an experimental basis allows an organization to find out whether the new approach works and gives it a chance to learn how to use it effectively. Moreover, it frees people to try things; in effect, it gives them the right to fail. Organizations can often be encouraged to try things they would never try if they could not run "experiments." Overall, the arguments in favor of experimenting are rather impressive, and at first glance it is hard to argue with the idea. Indeed, it is based in the very scientific model that most organizational researchers subscribe to. It also generally fits the learning model that says we try, learn, and improve.

Before we conclude that experiments are a good way to start a change process, however, we need to look at some of the down-side impacts of experimentation. An interesting one is suggested by the systems model and the congruence argument. Experimenting usually means trying something in a small part of the total organization or changing only one of its components to operate in a new way. This, it is argued, gives a sense of how a more comprehensive change will affect the organization. Yet this kind of experimentation might give a completely false impression of how effective a new practice or a new design will be if it is installed in the total organization.

Having a small group within the organization operate in a new manner is both qualitatively and quantitatively different from having the whole organization operate in a new way. The experimental group's environment is radically different from that of a group operating in the same manner as the rest of the organization. Similarly, changing just one system in an organization to see how it works before changing other systems (changing job design, for example, but not the pay, selection, and training systems) can provide very misleading results. In essence, the experiment often amounts to sticking a foreign body in an organization and judging how it survives in an incongruent and sometimes hostile environment. Because of the pressures toward equilibrium, new approaches often fail to survive. Thus experimentation can produce interesting data, but it may not tell how effective a new approach will be if it is installed throughout the organization.

It is true that experimentation gives individuals and organizations a chance to fail, but this is a dangerous feature of any change. In many cases, successful organizational change depends on a high level of commitment. If people know that they are involved in an experiment and that things can revert to the status quo if it fails, they may not make the same kind of commitment to the change as they would if they felt they had to make it work. Thus although the idea of experimentation sounds good, it may in fact lead to a lower probability of success than would a full-scale, permanent, highly committed installation of the innovation.

Finally, experimentation often inhibits the spread of successful ideas to the rest of the organization. Much of the research on organizational change suggests that one key to getting implementation is to get the adopters involved in designing the change (Beckhard and Harris, 1977). Once a practice has been subjected to an experiment, it is very difficult to get the rest of the organization to feel they had a role in developing it. Instead, they often feel that even though someone else has proved it successful, it does not fit in their part of the organization. This "not invented here" phenomenon is particularly likely to occur where the innovation concerns human resource management, although it can also appear in areas such as accounting, production, and marketing.

Overall, there seem to be some strong pluses for experimentation, but also some very strong minuses. What, then, is the right strategic choice? Unfortunately, there is no straightforward answer to this question. Rather, we need a contingency approach to thinking about whether or not to try an experiment.

In situations where nothing else is possible and structures can be put in place to insulate the experimental group and avoid the "not invented here" phenomenon, it probably makes sense to go ahead with an experiment. But if it is possible to implement a system-wide change, it makes sense to do so—though it is important to maintain a learning perspective that includes studying, evaluating, and improving the practice. Rather than doing this on a small-unit basis or as an experiment, it should be done on an organization-wide basis.

It is important here to distinguish between two different change situations. The first is where a large-scale organizational transformation is being attempted. In this kind of change, a number of systems need to be changed for the organization to be more effective. The second is where just one or two subsystems need to be changed to bring the whole organization into congruence. The congruence approach suggests that experimentation is not advisable in the first type of change. In the first type, incongruence will be produced and the pressure will be great to eliminate the divergent practice or group. In the second case, however, where subsystems are being changed to bring them into congruence, the pressures toward congruence will work toward adopting the new practice and spreading it to the rest of the organization.

There is one compromise between the experiment and a full-scale adoption of change: the pilot approach. The pilot project approach has definite advantages over an experiment. Pilots can be defined as learning experiences for the whole organization, thereby reducing some of the disadvantages of experiments. This is particularly true if management declares at the outset that the pilot project is intended for wide-scale adoption and that the issue is not one of trying it out to see if it works, but trying it out to see how it can be implemented, improved, and adapted. The "not invented here" phenomenon can be reduced if task forces from the rest of the organization have some say in developing and improving the practice after the pilot is complete. Pilot projects are particularly useful where major changes are being installed in large organizations. It is often impossible in these situations to change the whole organization all at once. It simply requires too much in the way of resources and can create too much disruption. Running a series of pilots can create more manageable and practical change efforts.

In summary, then, despite its advantages, it is often unwise to use an experimental approach. Frequently either a total system installation or the use of a pilot model is preferable.

Intervention and End-State Congruence

The process used to introduce a new practice may or may not match the way the innovation will operate in practice. Numerous arguments favor the use of the same process for installing and operating the innovation (for example, see Argyris, 1970)—especially with respect to employee involvement practices. In essence, it is argued that they should always be installed in a participative way; to do otherwise would be telling people to do what we say, rather than what we do. In addition, by installing the new practice in a way that mirrors the desired end state, the organization has a chance to learn how to operate in the new way. There is no question that these arguments are compelling, and in many cases it may make good sense to ensure that the installation process is congruent with the desired end state.

But before we conclude that the installation process should always look like the desired end state, we should take a closer look at the issue of how to install participative management systems in organizations. There are so many things working against the successful introduction of participative practices in a traditionally managed organization that it may well be impossible to do so in a participative way. Not only are all the systems and structures in the organization tuned to another way of managing, many of the key power figures are used to responding to top-down authority relationships. Indeed, they have prospered in the traditional system. To expect many of them to decide democratically to abandon the system under which they have gained power and rewards may be, at best, naive. Moreover, many simply lack the skills and imagination to carry out the design and implementation of new, more participative organizational practices. Finally, many have also learned that the only changes which matter are those which come down from the top. As a result, they respond to power, clear direction, and little else.

What often is needed to change a traditional organization is a clear indication from the top that the organization is going to change to a more participative system and the lower-level managers are expected to cooperate. Some room can be left for employees and managers to design certain details of the approach, but strong direction from the top—and changes in the reward and career systems that say this is the way the organization is going to be managed in the future—are vital. In other words, there is no choice in whether or not the organization will be participatively managed; there is only choice in how some of the systems will operate.

Although on the surface it seems reasonable that the installation process should match the desired end state, we must conclude that this may not be the best way to install certain changes. Indeed, it seems to violate the earlier congruence principle with respect to how organizations work: In order to be effective, all the systems in an organization have to be congruent. If the change effort is based on a different notion of power, it may easily be blunted by the other systems in the organization. In order to change, it is necessary to start with an approach that is congruent with the dominant practices in the organization. If these practices are traditional and top-down, then a move to participative management, for example, may require initial moves that are congruent with most of the organization's policies and practices. Doing otherwise will fail to capture the attention and energy of its members.

Lead-Lag Strategy

Particularly in the case of major changes in management style, organizations face a heavy agenda for change. As indicated earlier, if an organization truly wants to change the way it manages, it may need to change all or most of its major systems. This can be an incredibly difficult, complex, and time-consuming task. Just changing one system, like the pay system, is a major change effort. If the organization is also trying to change the way work is designed, the way it moves information, the way it trains employees, and so on, the change agenda can be overwhelming. Thus it is common to think in terms of a lead-lag approach in which certain key features of the change are introduced first to be followed by others.

In some ways, the lead-lag approach is a variant of the experimental approach, but it is noticeably different. It does not operate from a "try it and see what happens" approach; it operates from a "single system at a time" model of how to accomplish organizational change. The arguments in favor of it are rather impressive. It gives the organization time to install each change that is planned, and it does not overload the organization with new ways to be learned. It can also be argued that if the sequence of change is correct, it is possible to start with high-leverage changes that produce good initial results (Lawler, 1981). These can then be followed by other changes that support and add to the original ones. Ultimately, after a period of years, the total change will be in place, and because the change effort at any given time is limited, there will not be a major disruption in the organization's performance. The lead-lag idea of change is inherent in the transition strategy outlined in much of the writing on organizational change. (See, for example, Beckhard and Harris, 1977.)

The problems with lead-lag strategies stem from the systems nature of organizations. Changing a single system may be more disruptive than constructive. All it is likely to do is put that system out of congruence with the rest of the organization and, as a result, cause the organization to function less effectively. Further, even with the greatest planning and forethought, it is often difficult to figure out which changes to implement first. There are no carefully prescribed road maps that say one should start with job design, compensation, or any other system. Therefore there is a real risk that the wrong change lever will be pulled first and, as a result, the whole change effort will fail. Indeed, if the congruence argument is correct, there may be no right change lever to pull—no matter which one you pull, it inevitably puts the system out of balance. What is needed according to the congruence argument is a simultaneous pulling of all the change levers in the organization.

Few mature organizations have simultaneously changed all their parts in order to move to a dramatically different way of operating. There are, however, many examples of new organizations, particularly new plants, that have successfully started up with radically different employee involvement approaches to management (Lawler, 1978). Interestingly, the evidence seems to indicate that starting these plants is a highly successful way for a traditional organization to become more participatively managed. This success suggests that more organizations need to look at a simultaneous all-systems change approach, rather than a lead-lag model.

How feasible is it to think of a virtually simultaneous total systems change effort in an organization? It is one thing to start an organization with participative practices. It is quite another to take an existing organization and, almost overnight, change all its practices so that they are congruent with a new approach to management. Most organizations are unwilling to try this approach unless they are in severe financial straits and desperately searching for a new, more effective approach to management.

Under the right set of conditions, however, it is possible to imagine an almost simultaneous change of all the structures, policies, and practices of an organization. Clearly, considerable work would need to be done to develop a new model, and quite a bit of training would have to be done in the details of the new approach. There would also have to be some symbolic gestures to highlight that the old has been completely abandoned. Changing the organization's name, physically rearranging space, bringing in new technologies, and even a symbolic burial ceremony of the old organization could highlight the end of the old and create a "cultural cliff" that the organization could walk off as a way of freeing itself from the obsolete. Another idea is to hold a kind of constitutional convention in which the organization would shut down until it could come up with a new total design that was ratified by its members. Obviously, total change is an extreme approach, but it may be preferable to incremental change that moves system by system and condemns the organization to slow and ineffective movement toward a new way of operating.

Rejecting the Old

Much of the literature on organizational change emphasizes the importance of motivating people to change. Observers often point out that change is possible only when there is significant dissatisfaction with the current state of affairs. Such practices as highlighting difficulties in the current approach and benchmarking the organization against competitors are often recommended as ways to expose the dysfunctional features of the current system. It is also important, the argument goes, to highlight the advantages associated with the new way of operating. Thus change is viewed as requiring a combination of dissatisfaction with the present state and a well-articulated, attractive new way of operating.

It is hard to argue with the view that change needs to be motivated. Giving up habitual practices can be difficult, particularly when people are asked to accept unfamiliar practices that can have a negative impact on their careers and work lives. Concentrating too much energy on identifying the problems with the present situation may, however, be counterproductive with respect to organizational change. One of the things that causes organizational change to fail is people's resistance. This resistance may come from fear and hesitancy to give up the old, but it may also come from a need to defend the past. Any change effort that criticizes the way things have been done in the past will produce defensiveness. Usually the people who have created the past practices and policies are still in the organization, and it is impossible for them to separate criticism of their systems from criticism of themselves. If they feel criticized, of course, they are quite likely to spend considerable energy explaining why things are done the way they are, rather than concentrating on the implementation of better policies and practices.

Perhaps the best way to motivate change, then, is to avoid focusing on the problems associated with the old way and to concentrate instead on the advantages of the new. Can change be motivated simply by focusing on the advantages of the new practices? Expectancy theory suggests that it should be possible if the new state is seen as attractive enough (Lawler, 1981; Vroom, 1964). The key is to outline the rewards associated with the new state carefully and give people enough personal security so that they do not feel threatened by the move to the new state.

Certain types of dissatisfaction with the old should sometimes be highlighted. In particular, problems having to do with environmental change should be discussed because they will not produce as much defensiveness. It can be argued, for example, that the practices or policies are no longer effective because the environment has changed, not because they were wrong at the beginning. This strategy should reduce defensiveness and make it easier for people to give up the past because they do not have to admit failure; they simply have to accept that external forces are creating the need for change. Indeed, in this context, it may even be possible to make people feel good about the old. On the surface, this attitude might seem counterproductive to change, but it sometimes reduces people's need to defend the past. The key is to show that what was done in the past was in fact appropriate, but times have changed and so it is no longer appropriate. In essence, the reason for the change is attributed to the outside world in order to produce less defensiveness and help people accept the new.

Programmatic Approaches

A number of arguments can be made in favor of prepackaged approaches to organizational change. There is clearly a great deal of efficiency in capitalizing on what has been learned in other organizations and implementing well-developed change programs. Quality circles, point factor job evaluation systems, profit sharing plans, gain sharing plans, and many other personnel practices can be easily adopted and installed by using an off-the-shelf program. This is easily done because many of the implementation materials and processes are readily available—for example, policy manuals, training programs, and trainers are easily obtained.

The problem with trying to produce change through the use of standardized programmatic materials is that they allow little room for invention and reinvention. In some cases this may not be a serious issue, but it can be crucial if the change effort is directed toward introducing an employee-involvement approach to management. Here the argument can be made that employee involvement needs to be at least partially reinvented in every part of the organization. If this is not done, then it runs the great risk of remaining a program rather than becoming part of the fabric of the organization. In the accounting system, for example, it may not matter whether people have a strong emotional commitment to the *type* of system that is used; it is only necessary that they comply with its mechanics. In an employee-involvement program, however, this is not the case. In fact, effective implementation often demands an emotional and value-oriented commitment to change. If managers simply comply with the wish that they be more participative in their management style, employees quickly recognize that the managers' behavior is not based on a strong personal commitment. Management's approach then becomes seen as insincere. When stress or controversy develops in the organization, the program is easily abandoned and managers revert back to their traditional way of operating (Perkins, Nieva, and Lawler, 1983).

Despite the problems associated with programmatic approaches, it is hard to argue that an organization should go to the extreme of allowing every unit to invent its own approach. Doing this means failing to capitalize on the things that have been learned elsewhere. Perhaps the best strategy here is to have each part of the organization do its own investigation and then come to an informed choice about what is best for it. This might be called guided or educated reinvention of the idea. In a sense, people are given a conceptual box within which they can design their system. They also are given information about some of the design alternatives, but it is up to them to develop a system that is within the box and that they are committed to. Obviously, the intent here is to reduce resistance to change and to create a model that is sensitive to local conditions and avoids the "not invented here" phenomenon.

Bottom-Up/Top-Down Change

Closely related to the issues of "not invented here" and the kind of process used to introduce a change is the "bottom-up/top-down" issue. One line of argument says that the only viable approach to introducing participative management is bottom-up. The bottom-up approach is congruent with the desired end state of participative decision making, and it allows people to invent their own version of participative management. Thus, the argument goes, they should be highly committed to whatever kind of participative management results. This is an intriguing argument, but there is also much to be said for the top-down approach. As indicated earlier, to get a traditionally managed organization moving toward an employee-involvement strategy it is often necessary to use the power that already exists in the hierarchy—and that power, of course, is at the top. Indeed, it is possible to argue that without top-down support, little change will ever occur in a large, traditionally managed organization. Since a major change involves the key systems of an organization, it is hard to see how change can go very far without support at the top.

But does this mean that bottom-up change is impossible? There is no easy answer. If it proves impossible to change the top, it may make sense to attempt some bottom-up change to show what can be done when new approaches are tried. Demonstrations of this type are limited in their impact and usefulness, however, because what occurs in a single unit of the organization is not a good test and has a high chance of failure. In essence, bottom-up change all too often turns into guerrilla warfare. In the political arena guerrilla warfare occasionally succeeds, but in most cases the guerrillas are captured and executed or banished from the country. In large organizations, guerrilla leaders are fired, not executed. This is just what happened in the well-publicized case of the Topeka Gaines dogfood plant.

On the other hand, it is hard to imagine, given what has already been said about resistance, that a purely top-down approach could ever work. As noted earlier, the right answer is a combination of top-down and bottom-up change. The top certainly needs to support the change and fund it, but many of the details must come in a bottom-up manner. To a degree, the agricultural model may be appropriate here. (No, not the one about keeping people in the dark and throwing manure on them—that is the mushroom model.) In agriculture, farmers throw out a number of seeds and do everything they can to see that they grow into satisfactory products.

In the case of organizational change, the top can plant the seeds and then do everything possible to see that the seeds grow. This effort can include providing funding, rewarding managers who are willing to take risks and start change efforts, and asking people throughout the organization to present plans for implementing their own change efforts. Given what has been said here about the importance of multiple system change, it is clear that all change efforts must at some point engage the top in a serious examination of what they need to do to alter the way the organization operates. On the other hand, a pure top-down change is destined to fail if it is used to install participative management.

Informed Consent

Often organizational changes are influenced by consultants whose primary role is to persuade the organization to change and then to help it implement the change. As I have stressed, major change often involves tremendous investments of time and effort and there is no guarantee of success. Indeed it is often hard for participants in the change process to imagine what is involved in a change until they are well into it. This raises a particularly difficult issue for the consultant: How openly and thoroughly should the consultant explain just how difficult the change will be to implement?

The arguments against fully informing the organization about the difficulties are self-evident. Full information may well scare the client off. Even when clients are told, it is often impossible for them to understand what is involved in the change process and, indeed, how much they will gain from the change.

Thus, the argument goes, it is best to ask them to trust the consultant and then, gradually, make them aware of the dimensions of the change process. This can be done incrementally and the organization can be given the chance to stop the process if they think it demands too much commitment.

The arguments in favor of full and informed consent essentially center around two issues: ethics and level of commitment. The ethics issue is probably the clearest. Many would argue that people should not be asked to undertake a change process without being fully informed of what is involved—just as anyone who is about to undergo a major experience at the hands of a professional researcher, doctor, or lawyer should be told all the facts. The argument holds that the person should have full information and freedom to decline the procedure (Argyris, 1970).

The commitment issue is different but nonetheless important. Many would argue that once people have committed themselves to the totality of a change effort, they are more likely to stick with it from beginning to end because they have made an informed decision. Obviously the validity of this point depends on the consultant's ability to communicate to the organization and its members just what is involved in the change effort. Informed consent means little if the organization cannot appreciate what is involved in the change effort, even though they have full information.

Despite the problems of acquainting somebody with what is involved in a change effort and the possibility of frightening people off, full disclosure is the only ethical approach. When somebody is acting in the role of consultant, they must inform the client of all that is involved in their consulting activities. "Hooking them" by presenting limited or false information simply is not a valid way to relate to an organization that is paying for the services of a professional. The point that full and informed agreement is likely to lead to a longer and stronger commitment may be valid, but it is not compelling. There are numerous cases on record where people's commitment to change has grown even though they did not know how much commitment would be required at the beginning.

Strategic Overview

Designing a change process for an organization is clearly a complex process. Few principles of change management are universally valid. As we have seen, every change effort needs to consider how organizations operate, as well as the kind of change being implemented. Because of its complex nature, organizational change does not lend itself to many simple prescriptions. The process does, however, suggest that change efforts should include the following design features:

- A combination of bottom-up and top-down change
- Encouraging limited reinvention of the change
- Organization-wide introduction or starting with a pilot project
- Moving as rapidly as feasible to install the total change
- Motivating change primarily by emphasizing the positive outcomes that can be expected
- Informed consent
- Using an intervention process that accounts for the way the organization is currently managed

References

Argyris, C. *Intervention Theory and Method.* Reading, Mass.: Addison-Wesley, 1970.

Beckhard, R., and Harris, R. *Organizational Transitions.* Reading, Mass.: Addison-Wesley, 1977.

Galbraith, J. *Designing Complex Organizations.* Reading, Mass.: Addison-Wesley, 1973.

Lawler, E. E. "The New Plant Revolution." *Organizational Dynamics,* 1978, *6* (3), 2–12.

Lawler, E. E. *Pay and Organization Development.* Reading, Mass.: Addison-Wesley, 1981.

Lawler, E. E. *High-Involvement Management.* San Francisco: Jossey-Bass, 1986.

Lawler, E. E. "Transformation from Control to Involvement." In R. H. Kilmann, T. J. Covin, and Associates (Eds.), *Corporate Transformation:* San Francisco: Jossey-Bass, 1987.

Lawler, E. E., Nadler, D., and Cammann, C. *Organizational Assessment: Perspectives on the Measurement of Organizational Behavior and the Quality of Work Life.* New York: Wiley, 1980.

Nadler, D. A., and Tushman, M. L. "A Diagnostic Model for Organizational Behavior." In J. R. Hackman, E. E. Lawler, and L. W. Porter (Eds.), *Perspectives on Behavior in Organizations.* New York: McGraw-Hill, 1977.

Perkins, D., Nieva, V., and Lawler, E. E. *Managing Creation: The Challenge of Building a New Organization.* New York: Wiley, 1983.

Vroom, V. H. *Work and Motivation.* New York: Wiley, 1964.

13

Changing
the Organization
Through Time:
A New Paradigm

Allan M. Mohrman, Jr.
Susan Albers Mohrman

The major organizational challenge of the postindustrial society is coping with the uncertainty of the new environment. That uncertainty is characterized by increasing complexity and interconnectedness and by an unrelenting rate of change. From a design perspective, organizations must develop the structures and processes that enable effective performance in such an environment. From a change perspective, organizations must learn how to change from their current design, developed in a less turbulent time, to a design suited for today's environment. They must then be capable of changing their design as they go, since a characteristic of their new environment is that it will continue to change at a rapid pace.

In response to this challenge, a new organizational paradigm is slowly emerging, one that goes beyond the capabilities of the traditional bureaucratic organization. The traditional organization fosters efficient, predictable behavior and top-down control. It assumes that work can be analytically broken into parts, or jobs, and that procedures and goals can be written for each job. The environment is stable enough that there can be a clear division of labor between the technical core of the organization, whose job is to reduce technical uncertainty, and the institutional leadership of the organization, whose job is to scan the environment for opportunity and introduce strategic change through the top-down redefinition of goals, structures, and responsibilities. Middle management exists to ''control'' the organization by ensuring that technical uncertainty is indeed kept to a minimum and that directives from above are implemented.

This model of organizing works well when the technology of the organization is easily understood, the organization is small enough that the various parts know what each other are doing, the environment changes slowly enough that top-down change is sufficiently responsive, the organization can take good enough care of its people to compensate for the demotivating aspects of top-down control and narrowly defined jobs, and the marketplace is sufficiently benevolent to enable the organization to pass on the costs of inefficiency to customers.

In today's environment these conditions are seldom present. Since the general economic environment is changing, we will talk about changing organizational requirements as though all organizations are affected. Although some organizations have been able to buffer themselves from the rapid forces of change and are well served by a very traditional model of organizing, our discussion will deal with the sizable number of organizations that find themselves having to change in a fundamental way in order to adjust to the shifting environment.

Emerging Organizational Attributes

An effective organization in today's environment is characterized by certain attributes that seem to constitute an emerging paradigm. In this chapter we rely heavily on the paradigm as a heuristic device that helps us understand the complex of issues involved in large-scale organizational change. We turn now to these attributes and their implications.

Change is an ongoing organizational process, not something that is periodically done to an organization. This is probably the most fundamental reorientation of the traditional mind-set that must occur. There is no indication that the pace of environmental change is slowing. Economists can tell us the broad outlines of the new economic world order that is emerging—for instance, national economies and financial markets are becoming more closely linked into a global economy; Third World nations are emerging as significant competitors; the United States is no longer the single dominant economy of the world; the life cycle of products is declining; significant political challenges to the free market are demanding new ways of doing business; and there will be a shortage of key technical skills.

These forces present general challenges rather than specific direction for organizations. At least in the short term, they do not know exactly what they are adapting to. How will the global economy shake out? What must a truly global competitor look like? What will be the role of national political bodies and trade policy? What does a firm look like that maximizes its use of an ever developing cybernetic technology? How will organizations change as more of their business is conducted in joint ventures and other strategic partnerships? What constraints will be placed on an organization by an increasingly diverse work force in a context of short supply of critical skills and an economy that can no longer guarantee an ever increasing standard of living? Organizations are already feeling the impact of all these forces, but the form of the new organizations that emerge will depend on organizational responses, societal responses, and many environmental factors well beyond the control of any one organization. Even after many years, organizations may only know that change will be the key characteristic of the environment to which they must adapt.

Organizations have responded in a number of ways to this demand for ongoing change. One approach has been the continual restructuring with which employees in many large organizations are by now very familiar. This top-down approach generally involves changing the organization's structure by regrouping functions and product lines, slashing the company's size, and eliminating layers. Selling off some units and closing others is a variant of restructuring. These efforts change little in the internal operating principles of the organization, however, unless they are accompanied by a redesign of other organizational features. By themselves, they do not make the organization better able to change through time.

Organizations have also tried to implement designs and practices that foster innovation (Pinchot, 1985; Kanter, 1983). Quality circles, quality improvement processes, and continuous improvement processes are various names for programs that parallel the ongoing organization and utilize small groups of employees to analyze work and suggest changes to improve quality and productivity. Other forms of the parallel organization including task teams and various temporary structures have been used to make changes at a more inclusive organizational level. The assumption behind the use of the parallel organization has been that since the organization is structured to foster efficient functioning and the status quo, the way to change the organization is to get outside it and use a structure that operates according to a different mandate and logic (Zaltman and Duncan, 1977).

Examination of parallel structure efforts, however, indicates that unless the organization's management style and its design both change significantly, the work of the parallel organization is often disregarded, the bureaucracy is impervious to efforts to change it, and the parallel structure itself withers away (Mohrman and Lawler, 1988). It seems that the processes of ongoing change and innovation must be woven more tightly into the fabric of the organization. This leads us to the next aspect of the emerging organizational paradigm.

Designs are temporary—and, by implication, so are all aspects of the organization: jobs, structures, human resource systems, measurement systems, and goals. In an environment where market, competitors, technology, financial and legal constraints, and labor market all are changing, organization designs must be fluid. As product life cycles grow shorter, organizations must be able to move rapidly through phases of design, development, and production, reconfiguring their resources as the emphasis shifts. This means that practices which lock in predictability, measurability, comparability, equality of treatment, and control may be constraints on the organization's ability to change as rapidly as its environment. Organizations must be able to change their own design easily. To do so, they must increase the employees' stake in the strength of the business and reduce their stake in the status quo.

Learning is built into the organization. Organizations must develop the capacity to change their own designs, to introduce an ever developing array of new technologies, and to understand and compete in a new economic order. Individuals must learn how to lead and participate in these changes, and they must master the new skills and knowledge required to contribute to organizational performance. Such learning will become a condition of continued employment for people in most jobs, not just in technical fields.

Lateral relationships are increasingly important, tempering the traditional focus on hierarchy. Organizational performance is defined by quality and service—as defined by customer requirements—rather than by predictability and efficiency alone. Control is at least in part a lateral phenomenon. Increasingly, white-collar, service, and technical work are subjected to measures of quality, service, and efficiency similar to those that have been utilized in production systems. More and more, quality and service are seen as systemic phenomena requiring ongoing cross-functional relations and teamwork rather than the analytical subdividing of the task into individual responsibilities. As we will see, this lateral emphasis extends beyond the single organization.

Organizations develop many linkages and close relationships with customers, suppliers, community groups, and competitors. Partnerships, joint ventures, consortia, sole supplier relations, and community action coalitions continue to emerge as organizations find that the challenges they face require concerted effort and resources transcending organizational lines, as well as coordination with other organizations that have special abilities and strengths that complement their own. Organizational boundaries are permeable, enabling employees of one organization to operate within a host of other allied organizations. Decisions are increasingly made by networks of allied organizations, rather than by single organizations.

Decision making depends on lateral influence and mutually satisfactory arrangements. The ability to achieve consensus among multiple stakeholders—diverse organizations, employee groups, financial institutions, community and government groups—is a vital part of managing an organization. As joint ventures, global companies with multiple products, and complex multifunctional projects become the order of the day, more and more decisions must occur without the comfort of relying on the hierarchy to integrate various perspectives, take final responsibility, and break the tie. No single hierarchy controls all the key stakeholders. As time pressures increase, organizations can no longer afford for the bureaucracy to entangle major decisions even within an organization. Pertinent information and skills, accountability, and responsibility for goal attainment are moved lower in the organization.

People management practices are involvement-oriented rather than control-oriented. Human resource practices are designed to attain high performance standards in a rapidly changing environment. They are geared to the performance needs of each organization and link the interests of employees with those of the firm. Static job evaluation systems may be replaced by skill-based systems. Yearly merit pay increases based on individual performance may be replaced by contracting systems with bonus potential based on short- and long-term organization results or by team rewards based on team and organizational performance. Career paths based on movement through predictable functional hierarchies are supplemented by career paths based on increasing one's value to the organization through multiple skills, perspectives, and experiences. Organizational designs move accountability and responsibility to the work unit rather than establishing layers of middle management to exercise control. This restructuring reduces the cadre of career middle managers. People are required to take responsibility for keeping their skills current in a changing arena, and organizations increasingly are called upon to provide development opportunities that enable the work force to keep up with changing needs.

As organizations move away from designs that foster security and predictability, its members shoulder increasing responsibility for managing their own careers and assume more risk than they did in traditional organizations when the environment was more benevolent. Effectively managing in such a setting requires that employees are given a stake in their organization's success and are empowered to make a difference. High-involvement management practices that foster the downward movement of information, knowledge, power, and rewards are particularly suitable in such a setting.

The role of management changes from control to leadership. Organizational leaders will increasingly be called upon to create a vision of where the organization is going, a set of values that link employees to the success of the organization, a set of criteria to enable good decision making throughout the organization, and an environment that fosters and rewards performance.

Managers' roles will change from personal control to handling complexity, thinking strategically, and promoting change and development. They must ensure that systems and processes change as rapidly as they need to—by continually challenging assumptions of past ways of operating and by facilitating innovation from within. Increasingly, managers will be part of decision-making processes that transcend work areas, departments, and organizations.

Taken together, all these emerging organizational characteristics constitute a scenario in which organizations will be fundamentally different in the future. The change process is under way in many organizations, although few have realized the extent to which their organization is irreversibly becoming a very different place in which to work. Permeable boundaries, lateral linkages, and interorganization and multistakeholder decision making limit the ability of an organization or unit to determine its destiny unilaterally. The temporary nature of organizational designs, alliances with other organizations, and the jobs themselves change the nature of the organization for its employees and the relationship it must establish with them. Creating change and existing flexibly in its shifting environment will be the key requirements if organizations are to survive and prosper.

Implications for Methodology

The question for those interested in managing large-scale organizational change is how to achieve the transition to this organizational paradigm. Can organizations avoid becoming casualties of "too-slow" change and ensure that they will be a strong part of the new order that is emerging?

Large-scale change is not simply the application of established change approaches in a new context. Change processes must be capable of stimulating a magnitude of change sufficient to bring about a new organizational paradigm. Novel forms of organization will emerge. Large-scale change is not change within the organization; it is the process of changing the organization itself. Furthermore, change processes themselves must be part of the emerging organizational paradigm. Rather than designing the organization for predictability, the organization must be designed for unpredictability and, consequently, for ongoing change. A change in organizational paradigm requires a change in organizational change methodology as well.

The tight coupling of change methodology and organizational paradigm constitutes a dilemma; from another perspective it constitutes a circularity; and from yet another view it is simply the nature of large-scale organizational change. The traditional organizational paradigm of control, hierarchy, and predictability counteracts efforts to change it. All its features are designed to foster stability, and the self-interest of the most powerful people in the organization is closely linked to the status quo. Hence the dilemma: Large-scale organizational change can only be accomplished by changing an organization that is built not to be changed. Change within the organization uses the very nature of the organization—for example, its hierarchy—thus perpetuating the nature of the organization. The nature of large-scale organizational change is consequently to change the organizational features to those that enable change to occur—to rebuild the organization. Change needs to occur by changing the way we change. This reasoning may seem circular, yet it simply defines the phenomenon and helps us to determine the features of a suitable change process. The new methodology of change is tied very closely to the new organizational paradigm.

Chapter One outlined the qualities that make up a paradigm: a way of looking at the world, a way of doing things, and a social matrix that thinks and acts in these ways. In the next section, we use the notion of paradigm shift to illuminate the changes that are necessary in the methodology of organizational change.

Paradigm Shift

There are three stages to paradigm shifts (Kuhn, 1970): a period of normalcy under the reigning paradigm; a period in which anomalies begin to accumulate that put the first paradigm at risk and create a growing state of crisis; and finally a period in which the first paradigm collapses and is replaced by a new paradigm. Once replacement occurs, a new period of normalcy begins.

Normalcy. In a period of normalcy, the prevailing paradigm is used to solve problems. Often normal change is characterized as organizational development or as the adoption of innovations. Innovations—which may be described as ideas, practices, or material artifacts that are perceived to be new by the organization (Zaltman and Duncan, 1977)—may in fact end up changing the nature of the organization. Office automation, for example, is an innovation that not only eliminates certain jobs and redistributes work but also changes the nature of work. Nevertheless, adoption of the innovation is viewed as something that can be done by the organization, and much of the literature concentrates on packaging the innovation so as to minimize organizational disruption. It has been argued by some, however, that the organization itself must be fundamentally changed to fully utilize new technologies (Adler, 1989).

Organizational development has also been applied within the prevailing organizational paradigm. Recent attempts to "change the culture of the organization" have acknowledged the depth of the change that is required, but even these efforts have in many cases failed to recognize the need to operate at the systemic level by redesigning the organization. Organizational development techniques have built on the traditional aspects of hierarchy, predictability, and control. Such strategies as programmatic change, top-down cascading change, and the general manager as client are reflections of the traditional nature of the organization. Problem-solving approaches such as team development and quality circles help units become more effective within (or parallel to) the organization as it exists. Such approaches frequently leave untouched the features of the organization that freeze its behavioral patterns. Thus the organization tends to revert to previous patterns after the intervention is over. Indeed, the very concept of intervention implies a change within the organization.

Change techniques within the traditional paradigm rely on existing knowledge—knowledge that has been gained by studying traditional organizations and changes within them. The formalization of this knowledge—and consequently the formalization of the traditional mode of operation—has been the approach of large consulting firms, many of which develop algorithms of packaged approaches to organizational change. The traditional approach to change relies heavily on experts—those who are schooled in certain interventions and knowledge bases.

Anomalies and Crises. Paradigms begin to break down when anomalies crop up that cannot be handled by the existing paradigm. Organizational anomalies include the traditional organization's inability to process all the information required to handle the uncertainty presented by the rapidly changing environment and the quick pace of doing business. The breakdown of the psychological contract in a business environment that precludes long-term promises of an ever increasing standard of living, upward mobility, and job security for managers creates an anomaly not easily handled by traditional notions of career and loyalty.

These and other organizational shortcomings are mirrored in anomalies that cannot be dealt with given the traditional notion of organizational development and innovation. Cascading team building, team development, the use of problem-solving groups, and the incremental introduction of innovations are simply too slow in today's organizational environment. Change programs that require five or ten years will not help an organization that can be forced out of the marketplace far earlier than that. Team development is frequently undone as organizations shed levels and layers and downsize; teams are reconstituted monthly. Efforts to establish teamwork and a high-trust environment can be undone by selling off a unit, retiring reluctant employees, or making an acquisition that involves sharing positions, power, and decision making with managers in the acquired unit.

The major anomaly, the fundamental crisis, has to do with the difference between making changes within the context of the existing organization and changing the organization itself. Often we hear frustrated managers say, "Once we finish this downsizing we can get back to normal and start to build a team." But it does not happen; normalcy does not return. More downsizing occurs, acquisitions change the shape of the organization, manufacturing goes to an offshore subsidiary, and so forth. The real questions are: What organizational features and change strategies are suitable in such an environment, and how can an organization assume them?

Paradigm Destruction and Replacement. The paradigm of organizational change is part of the paradigm of organization. The destruction and replacement of the change paradigm will only take place concurrent with the destruction and replacement of the organizational paradigm. The magnitude of the anomalies being faced by today's organizations requires new organizations; the change process must therefore be one of paradigm shift and redesign rather than development and innovation. Not only the features but the very nature of the organization must change.

The emerging paradigm will not totally dismiss the value of the old but will supersede it. The traditional organizational form will continue to be appropriate for organizations that live in tranquillity and predictability or those that can be buffered from the anomalies that are rendering it obsolete. Organizational development techniques such as team development, process consultation, and planned change will continue to be useful tools, but within the context of a larger change methodology of redesign.

Earlier in this chapter we summarized the emerging characteristics of organizations. These characteristics give us some hints about the emergent change paradigm. The change paradigm must result in the redesign of the organization and be suitable for addressing the ongoing organizational need for change and transformation. For example, shifting stakeholders and fuzzy organizational boundaries will not only need to be accommodated by the new change paradigm, but fostered by it. Such aspects of the organization invite a tension that continually creates the need for more redesign. The change process must not only result in a changed managerial role; it must foster ongoing change in that role and must enable managers to facilitate redesign of the organization through the years.

Characteristics of the New Change Process

If we accept that the emerging change paradigm involves the redesign of the organization and that the broad characteristics of the new organizational form are approximated by the eight qualities specified earlier in this chapter, we can begin to describe the characteristics of the new change process.

Reactive versus Anticipatory Changes. Change stems ultimately from the environment. Organizations can choose either to react to these environmental forces or to anticipate them by initiating changes before they occur. The former option is generally held to be bad management signified by lack of control. The latter is a goal of many good managers who seek a leg up on their competitors. Anticipatory change, in order to be successful, must be based on accurate anticipations as well as appropriate changes. Complete and accurate forecasts of the future are increasingly unlikely, however, as environments become more turbulent. Furthermore, with anticipatory change there is no crisis that can provide the energy and motivation to follow through with the change. Even those who espouse anticipatory change admit that it usually does not occur until the environment turns sour in some way—profits fall, for instance, or new competitors emerge. In these cases what is really being anticipated is not the environmental event but its continuation. The characteristics of the "future" organization cited earlier in this chapter, for example, are based on trends that are already under way.

Reactive change has another unsavory aspect related to lack of control. It implies the absence of proaction and a certain passivity as the organization jumps to the environment's tune. This need not be the case. Organizations can react to environmental forces by seeking to change them. In the turbulent new environments that organizations face—indeed that they help create by their proactive responses to them—reactive change may be the only reality. Successful reactive change depends on the timeliness with which the organization can accomplish it. It needs to be as "real time" as possible. It is energized by the very environment the organization is changing to fit.

Knowledge versus Inquiry. Whether we believe we need a new paradigm or can use traditional change methodologies determines the way we handle knowledge. Traditional change is guided by current theory. The task is to educate organizational members so that the knowledge is transferred. Diagnosis is done by experts because they know what to look at and how to interpret the results. Change is planned by experts because they know the contingency issues and the results of past change efforts. Change is implemented by experts because they know how to train and educate people and deploy materials and equipment.

Under the assumption of a new paradigm, knowledge is generated rather than simply applied. There is only partial knowledge to begin with. There is no all-encompassing theory from which to build. We do not know enough about the new paradigm to know how to get there; consequently, knowledge has to be created by the participants in the change. Diagnosis, planning, and implementation are all processes of joint inquiry and experiential learning.

Controlling Change versus Unleashing Change. Perhaps the most fundamental concept of organizational theory and present models of deliberate change is that of *control*. It permeates our organizational and change practices. On the organizational theory side, we worry about how we manage organizations, about how to ensure that organizations achieve their goals, about setting strategic direction, and about directing employees. For us a tension exists between, on the one hand, wanting to understand large-scale organizational change as a way of getting more control over how to do it and being able to make it happen and, on the other, realizing from our experiences that there is something inherently out of control in large-scale organizational change.

Control-oriented change strategies are planned, staged, programmatic, and top-down; they have a general manager as client. Strategies that have a tendency to unleash change are opportunistic, deal simultaneously with the entire organization, allow self-invention, are bottom-up, and multidirectional; they allow an evolving set of stakeholders as clients, accept free will, and assume that current behavior is subject to diverse and often conflicting sources. In the following paragraphs we review some of the differences in a change strategy that aims at control and one that enhances adaptation.

Lead-Lag versus Simultaneity. Edward Lawler crystallized this issue in Chapter Twelve of this volume. The lead-lag strategy entails a choice as to which organizational features should be changed first (lead variables) and which can be changed later (lag variables). It is control-oriented in two ways: First, the strategy reduces the number of variables or organizational subsystems that need to be dealt with at a single time; second, it assumes that changing certain parts of the organization (the lead parts) will set up forces that will eventuate in the change of others.

A strategy of simultaneity changes all organizational systems at once. It is a process of constant interactive adjustment among the parts, the results of which cannot be controlled or predicted. This change strategy consists of opening up the interfaces among the parts and facilitating the adjustment processes that take place. Changes in human resource management, for example, have to be closely coordinated with efforts to change the operational aspects of the organization.

Programmatic Change versus Self-Invention. Programmed change is based on control. The organization knows in advance (or thinks it knows) what will be required to effect the change, and success is believed to depend on following the program. Yet it is clear that change programs are constantly being derailed by individuals, groups, and entire organizations that refuse to ''get with the program.'' If change is to occur in these cases it needs to be invented at the local level. Self-invention strategies are examples of the new paradigm of change. They are frequently rejected by managers and change agents because of the lack of control and ambiguity that accompanies them. Nevertheless some reinvention usually occurs in every case of programmatic change. Even though it may be rejected a priori, most change situations that result in large-scale organizational change end up having to deal with reinvention.

Top-Down versus Bottom-Up. The top-down approach tries to ensure control over the change process by getting the top of the organizational hierarchy committed to the change and then using its authority to direct the progress of the change throughout the rest of the organization. As the entire organization becomes involved, however, the change will become bigger than the top group and the top group will likely be faced with a bottom-up redefinition of the original change effort. Thus the top too will have to change. Bottom-up change is not control-oriented but seeks to establish change by allowing or facilitating it throughout the organization. By definition, it leads to diversity, local design, and a sense that the system is out of control. With this approach, change occurs when a critical mass of organizational members embrace it. The key challenge is to establish enough interfaces among the various change efforts to ensure a common focus.

Education versus Discovery. Education, as we use the term here, is a control-oriented approach because it assumes the existence of knowledge. Its aim is to impart that knowledge to others through teaching or training. The knowledge gained through a process of inquiry or discovery cannot be controlled. Inquirers draw their own conclusions and lessons from their experiences. Organizational change that assumes a new paradigm will be based on a joint inquiry process that eventually will involve all the organization's members. The challenge is to ensure exploration and the sharing of information learned through inquiry to enable groups to learn from one another and from change efforts that have occurred elsewhere.

General Manager as Client versus All Stakeholders as Clients. This issue is a variant of the tension between top-down and bottom-up change. Starting with the general manager enables the change to be controlled from the location in the organization that has responsibility and accountability for the total organizational functioning and can guide the change from that unique position. The new paradigm would open up change efforts to include all stakeholders. The general manager would become a leader of change but not a controller of change. This means a constantly shifting political scene and high uncertainty. The challenge is to draw in all relevant stakeholders and acknowledge their legitimate interest in organizational design. In order for organizational members to become interested in being agents of change, their stake in the change must exceed their stake in the status quo. This implies human resource strategies that involve people psychologically and financially in the success of their organization.

Existing Organization versus New Boundaries. Focusing on the existing organization constrains the change and bounds the situation so that the organization can have at least the illusion of control over its own destiny. Involving all stakeholders often includes those beyond the formal boundaries of the organization and requires establishing processes that enable mutual influence between parties that cannot be controlled from the same power point. The increasing fluidity of organizational boundaries and novel linkages between organizations often requires that the change process occur at an interorganizational level—including relationships among more than one formal organization. Within an organization, the same notion is applicable to a change effort that requires opening up one unit to joint design with other units.

In summary, then, the characteristics of the change process must reflect the characteristics of the new organizational paradigm. Just as the organization must be able to make ongoing changes in its own design, the change effort must be an ongoing process of redesign. Change must be designed into the organization rather than done to the organization. People must have a stake in the change process and be involved in designing the change. Change is a learning process, and specific designs are temporary. Lateral relationships—between parties inside and outside the organization—must be built to enable interdependent stakeholders to find a mutually agreeable path of action.

Implications for Change Agents

Much of the change occurring today in organizations is not being guided by theory. Rather, it is both a creative and a pragmatic response of insightful individuals to the challenges and opportunities they perceive in the changing environment. This is not to say that many of these changes have not been predicted. On the contrary, astute analysts have predicted a good many of the emerging trends. (See Weick, 1977; Hedberg, Nystrom, and Starbuck, 1976; Lawler, 1986; Walton, 1985.) The weight of theory alone, however, is insufficient to create change. Actual change requires understanding of organizations and their environments, expertise in organizational functioning, design skills, and the ability to establish change dynamics.

In today's environment, a change agent must combine these four competencies: theory, practice, design, and change methodologies. Many of these agents will reside in the organization. As organizations are called upon to change themselves, more and more of their employees will become knowledgeable about the process. All these skills are unlikely to lie in the same person, but all of them must be included in the teams who are redesigning their organization.

The change agent must provide the systems perspective—and groups of change agents constitute a system—helping the organization to link together all the aspects of the organization and its environment. These individuals and groups must be able to learn just a little bit faster than the organization being changed and must be able to help organizational members focus their learning and design processes. Thus the job of the change agent is to help organizational members build a social system that is self-renewing—a learning community capable of self-designing (Mohrman and Cummings, 1989). This role goes beyond the role of expert and transcends the role of organization developer. It encompasses parts of both roles and, in addition, includes a bit of the artist—the designer of novel forms—and the doer. The change agent's value to the organization reflects the new paradigm. It is based on a broad array of skills and experience that establish the systemic perspective behind all large-scale organizational change.

Summary

We have argued that today's environment demands a new form of organization and that the notion of paradigm shift is useful in understanding the nature of change. The emerging organizational form is characterized by ongoing change, temporary designs, learning, reduced emphasis on hierarchy, and greater emphasis on lateral relations, multistakeholder decision making, and human resource practices that emphasize involvement.

Large-scale organizational change is needed to help organizations transform themselves from their traditional form. The methodologies of organizational innovation and development, however, are insufficient to accomplish this change. The appropriate change methodology is one of organizational design. It is in large part reactive—the design must fit the emerging characteristics of a changing environment. It relies on unleashing change dynamics that cannot be fully controlled in the traditional sense of organizational control. Many features of the organization must change simultaneously through a process of discovery, self-invention, and bottom-up change that involves all stakeholders.

Change agents who are effective in large-scale organizational change combine theoretical, practical, and creative abilities. As organizations are required to change more and more frequently, change agents will develop, enhancing the organization's ability to change itself continuously.

References

Adler, P. "Managing High Tech Processes: The Challenge of CAD/CAM." In M. A. Von Glinow and S. A. Mohrman (Eds.), *High Technology Management.* New York: Oxford University Press, 1989.

Hedberg, B.L.T., Nystrom, P. C., and Starbuck, W. H., "Camping on Seesaws: Prescriptions for a Self-Designing Organization." *Administrative Science Quarterly,* 1976, *21,* 41–65.

Kanter, R. M. *The Change Masters: Innovation for Productivity in the American Corporation.* New York: Simon & Schuster, 1983.

Kuhn, T. S. *The Structure of Scientific Revolutions.* Chicago: University of Chicago Press, 1970.

Lawler, E. E., III, Mohrman, S. A., Ledford, G. E., Jr., and Mohrman, A. M., Jr. "Quality of Worklife and Employee Involvement." In C. L. Cooper and I. T. Robertson (Eds.), *International Review of Industrial and Organizational Psychology 1986.* New York: Wiley, 1986.

Mitroff, I. I. *Business Not As Usual.* San Francisco: Jossey-Bass, 1987.

Mohrman, S. A., and Cummings, T. G. *The Self-Designing Organization.* Reading, Mass.: Addison-Wesley, 1989.

Mohrman, S. A., and Lawler, E. E., III. "Parallel Participation Structures." Publication G-88-3 (116). Los Angeles: Center for Effective Organizations, University of Southern California, 1988.

Pinchot, G. *Intrapreneuring*. New York: Harper & Row, 1985.

Walton, R. "From Control to Commitment in the Workplace." *Harvard Business Review*, 1985, *63*, 76–84.

Weick, K. E. "Organization Design: Organizations as Self-Designing Systems." *Organizational Dynamics*, 1977, *6* (2), 30–46.

Zaltman, G., and Duncan, R. *Strategies for Planned Change*. New York: Wiley-Interscience, 1977.

Conclusion:
What We Have Learned
About Large-Scale
Organizational Change

Susan Albers Mohrman
Gerald E. Ledford, Jr.
Allan M. Mohrman, Jr.

The chapters in this volume are quite diverse: They differ in focus and emphasis, theoretical orientation, and implications for practice. Several contributors argue that the genesis of large-scale organizational change lies in externally imposed crisis. Galbraith, on the other hand, sees possibilities (as at General Electric) for change in the absence of immediate external pressures of crisis magnitude; Nadler and Tushman talk about the possibility of anticipatory change; and McWhinney and Maccoby focus on a drive to improve the quality of life and relationships at work.

Several authors concentrate on the organizational level of analysis, while others (most notably Cole) focus on the societal level. Maccoby and McWhinney consider how individual character types and worldviews interact with change strategy. Lawrence examines contingencies that lead different types of organizations to develop different types of change, while others such as McWhinney and Kilmann are concerned with processes that may be common to all organizations. Intellectual roots range through such diverse fields as psychoanalysis (Maccoby), psychology (Lawler), sociology (Cole), and business (Lawrence and Galbraith).

In this chapter, we look back at the preceding chapters with an eye toward what we have learned and what remains unresolved about large-scale organizational change. We are concerned with the nature of large-scale organizational change, its causes, the process by which it unfolds, and how to create it. We begin by reconsidering the meaning of the term *large-scale organizational change*. Then we will consider what we have learned about each of its three dimensions identified in Chapter One—namely, depth, pervasiveness, and organizational size.

Definition

We began the book by proposing to define large-scale organizational change as a lasting change in the character of an organization that significantly alters its performance. Perhaps surprisingly, few of the other authors in this volume propose any explicit definition of large-scale organizational change or attempt to distinguish it from other types of organizational change. Definitions aside, however, there are clear parallels in the way the term is used. These parallels support the notion that LSOC involves changes that are both deep and pervasive.

Extremely large systems are the focus of much of the discussion in these chapters—including such giant corporations as USX (Lawrence), General Electric (Galbraith), and AT&T (Maccoby). Institutions at a higher level of analysis—such as the state of Montana and an Arab country (McWhinney)—are also considered by some as the focus for change. In one case (Cole), the primary focus is on societal attitudes affecting the behavior of organizations in the United States compared to Japan. At times, however, various authors move easily into discussions of change at lower levels of analysis, such as the plant or division, using the same terminology and perspectives used to discuss change in entire corporations.

There is general agreement with Galbraith's suggestion that LSOC goes beyond the routine changes that occur continually in all organizations. Organizational transformation is a term used frequently to contrast LSOC with routine change, although the term is rarely defined explicitly. McWhinney describes his study as developing a framework of methods "to produce large-scale sustainable change in the institutions of industry, commerce, education, political administration . . . that support the transformation of humankind." His primary concern is with the change of institutions to foster quality of life. Others focus on the transformation of organizations in order to increase the system's health and effectiveness in a changing environment. Although this difference of focus reveals significant value differences among the contributors, all are talking about change that is both deep and pervasive.

Helpful conceptual distinctions are proposed by Nadler and Tushman, who distinguish between strategic versus incremental changes and between anticipatory versus reactive changes. Using their terminology, the subject matter of LSOC is reorientation (strategic/anticipatory change) and re-creation (strategic/reactive change). Although most of the contributors would agree that LSOC is strategic, it is also argued, most persuasively by Cole, that strategic change emerges from an iterative series of changes as organizations address issues in their environment. Each change might be viewed as incremental, but all of them add up to strategic redirection.

Depth of Change

Virtually every author considers the dimension of depth in one way or another, although their terminology and frames of reference vary widely. Some of the major themes relating to this dimension are described in the following paragraphs.

Large-scale organizational change involves learning and understanding—either as a necessary part of the change process or as the fundamental source of all change. An implication of this idea also appears to be generally accepted—namely, since the change requires learning and understanding, the change process needs to be one of shared inquiry. The role of the change agent in the inquiry process is described in some detail by Kilmann, who regards the consultant as actively structuring the learning process and ensuring that adequate diagnosis and learning occur. Maccoby stresses the need to set up a dialogue between stakeholders to make sure joint inquiry occurs. McWhinney's open-system approach can be interpreted as a consultant-led process of joint inquiry.

Change must address multiple realities. Among the contributors, all of whom are researchers and specialists in organizational change, there are a variety of perspectives, ways of defining and understanding change, and ways of practicing the change agent's role. These differences relate to important value differences. They are vivid reminders that change means different things to different people.

Extrapolating from the differences we observe among ourselves, we can surmise that many people will resist a large-scale organizational change effort because it threatens crucial orientations, values, and beliefs. Indeed, this very point underpins many of the chapters. McWhinney, for example, identifies four modes of reality, and change assumes a different meaning in each of them. The kinds of change sought by organizational development, which assumes a social view of reality whereby change occurs through social interaction between people who together determine a direction, is incomprehensible to those in three of the four realities. In fact, for those who adhere to the unitary reality, the world is one already and cannot change. Maccoby describes different social character types. People of different types will see different threats and opportunities in each change situation. For example, the Company Men in the Bell System felt unfairly devalued by the new Gamesmen who were leading the company toward greater openness to the environment. For both McWhinney and Maccoby, understanding the "psychostructure" of the organization (that is, the distribution of types) is essential to determining a change strategy, since at least some organizational members are going to be threatened by a change effort or at least find themselves unable to relate to it.

Change must address the deep aspects of an organization. Kilmann argues that a change process must include diagnosis and change in the deep aspects of an organization, including the shared values, beliefs, expectations, and norms that constitute culture, the taken-for-granted assumptions, and the innermost qualities of the human mind and spirit—the psyche. Diagnosis must reflect the system's holographic image by looking at the organization from many angles in order to reflect all the different perspectives. McWhinney suggests going back to the grand myths and archetypal stories and reworking them as a means of gaining access to new myths and courses not yet run.

Cole and Lawrence, however, both depict aspects of culture as part of the context within which large-scale organizational change occurs and which determines how an organization will respond to a situation and what approaches to change will be effective. Cole points out, for example, that the Japanese were not afraid to borrow ideas from the West because they had been doing this for centuries as a strategy to catch and surpass their rivals. It is culturally less comfortable for American managers to borrow concepts from the Japanese. Lawrence suggests that U.S. organization may be underutilizing a key American value, competitiveness, in trying to motivate employees to change.

Leadership is a key element in large-scale organizational change. Galbraith in his cases and Nadler and Tushman in their framework deal expressly with the role of executive leadership in providing a vision, energizing the organization, and enabling change to occur. Nadler and Tushman discuss the importance of this "magic leader" in view of the need for change to be anticipated and the sense of urgency communicated in a compelling way to organizational members. They distinguish between this executive leadership role and the instrumental leadership role of implementing and controlling change. For Kilmann these roles fuse somewhat: One role of the leader is to display commitment and provide leadership in the five-track change process.

Maccoby too sees the need for far-sighted and committed leadership that can communicate a compelling business strategy, provide a vision of a new way of operating, and model a new way of relating. He also sees the possibility of leadership coming from within the organization—from innovative gamesmen and team-builders who are interested in trying out new approaches. Cole's chapter implies that top management is not always the party most interested in change that threatens the status quo; through democratization of information and conceptual tools, employees throughout the organization can be agents of change. He points out a certain elitism in the apparent American assumption that getting employees' energy behind change is viewed as part of the "how" of change rather than the "why."

The possibility that appropriate leadership is contingent on the type of change is raised by Galbraith, who observes that rarely are the same individuals able to lead organizational recoveries and organizational development. A different view of contingency comes from McWhinney, for whom four different kinds of leadership are called for by the four different realities. He also sees a need to match the change strategy to the kinds of leadership available and believes that different realities may assume prominence in the different stages of a change process, resulting in changing patterns of leadership as well.

Change requires a combination of top-down and bottom-up direction. Most agree that the top leadership must provide the strategic direction for change. Nadler and Tushman also put responsibility for providing the vision and the energy on top management. Others focus more on change stemming from political processes that empower other groups. Maccoby, for instance, talks about the fundamental change that occurs when the union is taken as a legitimate partner in planning change and discusses the dialogue required to resolve conflicting interests and values and establish a new direction. Lawler concedes that the power of the hierarchy may be necessary to energize change, but he notes that it may conflict with the ultimate change objective. The fundamental distinction is between those who see stakeholders' involvement as a way for a leader to implement change (in Cole's words, as a "how" of change) and those who think leadership is required to empower various stakeholders to influence the direction of change (stakeholders' input as a "why" of change). For many but not all of the contributors, the empowerment of various stakeholders is an explicit part of the changed order.

The change process requires resolution of conflict. Some conflict stems from different values that relate to the different modes of reality and character types discussed by McWhinney and Maccoby. Conflict also results from different interests in the status quo, an issue expressly addressed by Galbraith. Part of the leadership role is to promote dialogue on these differences and model constructive resolution of these issues (Maccoby) and to provide a vision that enables people to understand the need for change and to see how their own interests are represented by the change. Change is not simply an individual process but involves cultural, economic, and political processes as well. Resolution of conflict is required at each of these levels.

Pervasiveness of Change

There is extensive agreement about the pervasiveness dimension. Indeed, there are a number of points of consensus:

- Large-scale organizational change involves every level in the organization.
- It also involves the organization in relation to its environment.
- It is driven by a need for congruency between the organization and its environment and among its various subsystems.
- It is driven by the internal and external stakeholders of the organization.
- It concerns more than just behavior in organizations; it also involves technology, financial and legal considerations, and many other factors.

A number of points about the process of large-scale organizational change follow from its pervasive nature.

The change process must match in complexity whatever it is changing. Change that involves multiple levels and multiple subsystems in the organization must use multiple action levers. Galbraith emphasizes that Jack Welch at GE uses every conceivable action lever, and Cole points out that the Japanese transition to high-quality manufacturing entailed a change in every aspect of the organization that affects quality.

Change strategies must pay particular attention to sensing the environment and indeed might actively involve the environment. Lawrence, for example, suggests that change agents move to new arenas and levels of involvement in facilitating such efforts as the development of new ground rules for the relationship between business and government, the establishment of joint R&D ventures between competitors, and the negotiation of temporary government assistance to an organization in exchange for holistic programs of organizational renewal. Cole points out the key role played by customers in providing direction for Japanese quality improvement efforts and the role of a societal organization, JUSE, in providing tools and assistance. Maccoby's description of union/management cooperation at AT&T and McWhinney's discussion of change at levels such as states and nations obviously transcend the individual organization.

Change cannot be driven by peripheral or staff groups but must involve the fundamental stakeholders of the organization, including line management and core employees. None of the contributors describe a change process led by staff groups; all discuss change in which the general management level, often the chief executive, was intimately involved in the change process. Only at this level is there sufficient breadth of responsibility to energize pervasive change. Kilmann goes so far as to say that peripheral and staff groups should not be chosen as the pilot arena for a change process. Successful change in such groups will not be as compelling to others in the organization as will successful change in a central, influential group.

Change strategies must go beyond behavioral methods and involve knowledge from beyond behavioral science. Large-scale change involves an organization's technical, economic, financial, political, and legal aspects as well as individual, group, and organizational behavior. The changes at AT&T, for example, required that understanding of technical issues become more widespread in the organization. Managing change at the societal level, as proposed by Lawrence, would require in-depth knowledge of the law and understanding of political science. McWhinney's approaches require a solid grounding in cultural issues such as literature and mythology. Both the unleashing of these creative forces and the application of engineering approaches are required for organizational redesigns.

Size of Change

We indicated in Chapter One that organizational size is the most neglected dimension of large-scale change. This bias is reflected in the limited attention paid here to issues of size. McWhinney views his meta-praxis as applicable at levels of organization ranging from plants to nation-states. In some cases, large-scale organizational change is treated as simply a larger and more complex version of change at the plant level, as in Kilmann's discussion of changing a division or other organizational subunit versus changing an entire corporation. The recipe for change is the same, but it takes the chef longer to cook up bigger portions. (Kilmann proposes one year for some subunits versus five years or more for larger corporations.) Similarly, Maccoby indicates that AT&T and the Communications Workers of America based their model of change on a program developed at a manufacturing plant (the Bolivar, Tennessee, plant of Harman International Industries) where he was consultant. Maccoby points out that the larger the organization, the greater the opportunity for individual managers to hold out and interfere with the transition; consequently, it becomes more important for top management to communicate urgency and lead the process.

Differences in the nature of change for very large organizations versus small ones, or between very large organizations and subunits, can be surmised from some of the chapters. Galbraith's analysis applies primarily to entire organizations; subunits may lack the strategic control over their fate necessary to make acquisitions and divestitures, for example. He points out that in some respects very large corporations such as GE, TRW, Westinghouse, and GM have an overlapping, restricted set of options for development due to their size. If acquisitions are made to improve corporate performance, only a huge acquisition will have such an impact. Certain acquisitions are more desirable than others for all giant public corporations—for example, conglomerate acquisitions are treated negatively by the stock market. Conversely, all of these corporations are trying to enter service and high-technology businesses because of potentially high profit margins and limited foreign competition. These moves place strong pressures on mega-organizations to change in similar ways and to adopt certain organizational forms. Much of this analysis does not apply to small corporations, especially those that are growing in single businesses or functioning in a protected niche.

Thus in a very large organization the process of change may be more complex, take longer, and require more active direction from the top. A corollary to these issues must certainly be that central control of the change process would become cumbersome in a very large organization, which makes it essential to establish centers of change throughout the organization. These differences are largely differences of degree. But there may also be differences in substance. Very large organizations may deal with different kinds of strategic changes than smaller organizations. The importance of this point must not be overstated, however, since there are many examples of small companies acquiring larger ones, small companies adopting service and high-technology postures to promote growth, and so forth. Likewise, subunits may be limited in the changes they make by the organizational context in which they exist. The hierarchy's ability to block action by a smaller unit may or may not be a different kind of constraint to the change process than other contextual limitations, such as the law, faced by both large and small organizations. Left unanswered is the question of whether large-scale change in a mega-organization involves different methodologies, different dynamics, and different actors.

Conclusion: Some Points of Disagreement

There is general agreement that large-scale organizational change deals with change that is both deep and pervasive, and a number of consequent points of agreement have been cited above. Nevertheless, a diversity of viewpoints are represented in this book. These are some of the controversial issues that stimulated discussion:

- Is there a logical sequence to a change process, or does it unfold through a series of opportunistic responses to organizational and environmental choice points?

- Can change be planned? Does it make sense to think in terms of lead and lag variables? Or does change unfold in unpredictable directions as the organization acts and learns? Is it best to address the systemic nature of the organization by initiating change in many variables simultaneously?
- Should consultants express their view of the change process so the client can make an informed choice? Or is it the consultant's role to lead the organization through a process that cannot be explained ahead of time?

There were differences among us on several points: who we considered to be our client; whether we espoused humanistic or productivity values for the change process; the extent to which we stressed the creative or the engineering aspect of design; whether we believed there is an organizational theory that can guide large-scale change. Although we found many points of commonality, the differences were always there. In trying to be a learning community, we ran into all the issues of communication between divergent worldviews and different character types that one encounters in a large-scale change effort. We viewed large-scale change from different vantage points and consequently had different interests in the status quo: Some of us are primarily consultants but also researchers; others are primarily researchers but also consultants. To a person outside the behavioral sciences or the world of organizational change, our professional and educational backgrounds would look quite similar; yet we viewed the same phenomenon through many sets of glasses.

In this complex process we have chosen to call large-scale organizational change, there is room for and indeed need for many kinds of change agents to deal with the many realities that exist in the organizational world. The forces for change are well beyond the control of any of us. None of us can offer the definitive response to the many challenges being faced by companies today. The best we can hope is that we have elucidated some of the principles that guide effective change agents as they deal in some small or large way with the transformation of organizations.

Index

A

Ackoff, R. B., 38, 45, 46, 186, 198

Action mode, and concepts of reality, 166, 167, 168, 170

Action plan, in open-system planning, 191

Adaptation, in organizational change, 102

Adizes, I., 192, 198

Adler, P., 280, 290

Aeronautical Staff of AERO Publishers, 231–232, 254

AFL-CIO, 130

Age, and organizational size, 19–20

Ahmedabad weaving shed experiment, 156

Aldrich, H. E., 6, 21, 28

Alger, H., 187

American Can Company, and level of analysis of change, 63

American Society for Quality Control, 232, 249

American Telephone and Telegraph (AT&T) Company: and environment for change, 41; and level of change, 64; and phenomenon of change, 1; and social character and organizational change, 123–124, 126–134, 136–139, 293, 299, 300

American Transtech, and social character, 136

Analytic mode of resolution, and meta-praxis, 174, 175, 176

Analytic process, and meta-praxis, 193, 195

Andrews, K., 94, 98

Anomalies and crises, in paradigm shift, 281–282

Argyris, C., 96, 98, 260, 269, 270

Arizona, Bell System in, 136

Assumptions, as barrier to success, 210, 216–217

Astley, W. G., 6, 28

Athos, A., 61

Automation, and development and recovery, 75, 85

Autonomy, of organization and sub-units, 25, 26

Axiotic mode of resolution, and meta-praxis, 174, 176, 177–178

B

Bahr, M., 138

Balzer, R., 131

Barnard, C., 55, 60

Barnes, L. B., 188, 198

Bass, B. M., 105, 118

Batista, J., 188, 198

Beckhard, R., 5, 28, 103, 118, 213, 227, 258, 262, 270

Beer, M., 214, 228

Bell, C. H., 5, 15, 29

Bell Labs, and social character, 120, 124, 125, 128, 135

Bell Operating Companies, and social character, 124, 134, 137, 138

Bell System: adaptations at, 137–139; bureaucracy transformation at, 123–137; and environment for change, 41; social character and organizational change at, 120–141, 295

L

M